ABORTION:

Pro and Con

ISSUES IN CONTEMPORARY ETHICS

A Schenkman Series, Peter A. French, Editor

INDIVIDUAL AND COLLECTIVE RESPONSIBILITY:
The Massacre at My Lai
    Edited by Peter A. French

THE MANSON MURDERS:
A Philosophical Inquiry
    Edited by David E. Cooper

CONSCIENTIOUS ACTIONS:
The Revelation of the Pentagon Papers
    Edited by Peter A. French

PUNISHMENT AND HUMAN RIGHTS
    Edited by Milton Goldinger

UTOPIA / DYSTOPIA ?
    Edited by Peyton Richter

ASSASSINATION
    Edited by Harold Zellner

ABORTION
    Edited by Robert L. Perkins

ABORTION:

Pro and Con

Edited by Robert L. Perkins

SCHENKMAN PUBLISHING COMPANY
Cambridge, Massachusetts

Schenkman books are distributed by
General Learning Press
250 James Street
Morristown, New Jersey

Copyright © 1974
Schenkman Publishing Company
Cambridge, Massachusetts

Library of Congress Catalog Card Number: 74-80367
Printed in the United States of America

All Rights reserved. This book, or parts thereof, may not be reproduced in any form without the written permission of the publishers.

ISBN 0-87073-501-2

DEDICATED
TO
TODD AND LESLIE

My adopted children and to their natural mothers who carried them to term in desperation, sorrow and loneliness

CONTENTS

Preface ix
ROBERT L. PERKINS
Introduction 1
WILLIAM E. MAY
Abortion and Man's Moral Being 13
HARMON L. SMITH
Abortion—The Theological Tradition 37
ROBERT E. GAHRINGER
Observations on the
Categorical Proscription of Abortion 53
BARUCH BRODY
On the Humanity of the Foetus 69
SISSELA BOK
Who shall Count as a Human Being?
A Treacherous Question in the
Abortion Discussion 91
ROGER WERTHEIMER
Philosophy on Humanity 107
LAURA PURDY and MICHAEL TOOLEY
Is Abortion Murder? 129
R. B. BRANDT
The Morality of Abortion 151

APPENDIX

Of The Production of Man
From the *Summa Theologica* by Thomas Aquinas,
Part I, Question 118, Articles 1-3 173

Abortion Law Reform:
The English Experience by Prof. H. L. A. Hart . . . 182

Roe v. Wade, Syllabus and Sections VII-XIII 211

House Joint Resolution 427 228

Senate Joint Resolution 119 229

BIBLIOGRAPHY 230

PREFACE

This volume adds a significant dimension to the distinguished series entitled, "Issues in Contemporary Ethics," editd by Peter French. Each volume features contributions written specifically for the volume by outstanding moral philosophers. The contributors did not have access to each other's new articles, though they did have access to each other's past writings. There is remarkably little repetition, which testifies to the breadth of the issues abortion raises as well as the wealth of philosophic and speculative viewpoints at the present time. Of course, some effort was expended to assure that the contributors represented divergent points of view. The variety of opinions expressed is as much a testimony to the pluralism of our society as to the fecundity of contemporary American philosophy.

First and foremost this is a philosophy series designed to help us to comprehend the overwhelming and serious issues of our day. The subject of this volume, abortion, is also to be thought of as the occasion for raising and investigating a number of moral, theological and legal questions whose pertinence goes far beyond this specific problem.

Perhaps no issue discussed in this series will touch as many persons directly as the subject of this volume, at least if estimates and statistics about the number of abortions obtained are any indication.

In this volume we are not attempting to pass judgment upon those who seek or avoid abortion for any reason whatsoever. The function of practical philosophy is to account for the reasons people give to justify their acts and to examine the justifications for and arguments against an action. Only for a small minority of people is abortion wrong in any instance. Many of these persons, though they might profit most from the study of this book, will probably not bother to disturb their prejudices. Another minority, including some of the authors of this book, think that abortion should be available on demand. The vast majority of us however, are not so sure about the issue of abortion. We are not sure that all the arguments are in, and we are not entirely convinced by the arguments we have heard. This book is an attempt to state the arguments, pro, con, and maybe, and to examine their logic. The authors reach no coercive conclusions, for conclusions about moral arguments do not occur between the covers of books but rather in the commitments people make and the actions that flow from them.

It has not been too many years since some moral philosophers, not at all like Socrates, the first moral philosopher, announced to their students in ethics courses, "Don't think for a moment that anything we will say in here has any relevance to anything you must do out there." Happily practical philosophy (or the philosophy of practice, i.e. action) has been rehabilitated from this dismal state of affairs, and philosophers now engage themselves with pragmatic and existential issues. To be sure, metaethics and the analysis of moral language are important in themselves, but they are justifiable in terms of the investment society makes in philosophy only if they lead back to the illumination of our common human experience. We, the editor and the authors, send forth this volume recognizing the claims of public accountability, asserting that "What we say and do in philosophy books, classrooms, symposia and bullsessions has immediate and direct relevance to what you do in the world. Others may inhabit the ivory towers and think important thoughts; we will try to understand the ordinary and everyday."

There are a number of people without whose cooperation this volume would not have come to light. Obviously, the several persons whose work comprises the body of this book are to be thanked for their confidence in the project from its inception. I am also indebted to Ms.'s Vi Harper and Anita Bayles of the Reference Department of the Library of the University of South Alabama for all kinds of extra labors on behalf of this volume; to Ms.'s Annie Lewis, Barbara Conner, and Ellie Worsham, student helpers and the secretary of the Philosophy Department; to Professor Peter French, the general editor of the series; to my wife, Clarise, and children, Todd and Leslie, who never recognized the necessity of certain off-limits hours for my office; and finally, to the skills of the numerous persons at the publisher's office.

Acknowledgment and appreciation are hereby expressed to *The Monist* for reprinting part of Professor Brandt's article of the same title published in that journal in 1972. Also the editor expresses appreciation to the *University of Melbourne (Australia) Law Review* for permission to reprint Professor Hart's article from their May, 1971 issue. Acknowledgment is also due to Burns, Oates and Washburn of London and Benzinger Brothers, New York, publishers, for permission to quote their edition of Thomas's *Summa Theologica*, translated by the Dominican Fathers.

ROBERT L. PERKINS

Introduction

Men attempt to extend their understanding of their existence and situation in a multitude of different ways. "Experience is the best teacher, but she keeps a dear school." In order not to pay the high tuition, face the examinations, and all the consequences our acts entail in that most highly populated academy, we have invented many ways of extending our experience vicariously. Two of these modes of vicarious experience are philosophy and the arts. Although many would agree that the arts generally, and the novel in particular, are forms of vicarious experience, the suggestion that philosophy is such may appear to be an embellishment. But to say that philosophy is a form of vicarious experience is not an effort to set forth a novel definition; it is only, more modestly, to focus on one facet of a multifaceted jewel.

The novelist is the rhetorician of practical philosophy. Observing the existentially vacuous course of much, if not most, twentieth century philosophy, the ordinary mortal can only rejoice that one philosopher chose to concretize his ideas in novels of exceptional quality and merit.

Of course, not every philosophy is sufficiently human or humane to allow novelization. Some philosophies no doubt have an importance in themselves far beyond any mere human, practical or ethical interests. Other philosophers find only ambiguity, contradictory values, confusion in practical philosophy and struggle through self-made and imposed meaninglessness.

In the tradition of Descartes, philosophy has despised the subject matter of human existence. This has resulted in the fate that many philosophers have uncritically accepted the terms of their times in moral matters much as Descartes did. They have left all the categories in which men actually exist unquestioned. This behavior causes philosophy to be quietistic and conventional. The similarity to the quietism and religious conventionalism of pietism is remarkable. These philosophers exist in categories they never hold up to philosophic scrutiny. Few are as forthright about the matter as Descartes was in his first discourse. On the other hand, those philosophers who analyze mundane, everyday existence find the vocabulary and methods of the Cartesian tradition not very useful. The search for an analytical method and communicative expression causes some to turn to literature, especially the novel.

The novel has been used as a means of philosophic analysis and expression by Jean-Paul Sartre, and few have used it better. He wrote a very suggestive novel about a proposed abortion in the last days before World War II in Paris. The theme of abortion is repeated time and again in different ways and in different contexts. This repetition of the theme of abortion indicates the way a novelist of philosophic bent or a philosopher of literary bent *shows* the philosophic points he wishes to make. The novel, *The Age of Reason,* is ostensibly about the effort of Mathieu, a rather lack-luster professor of philosophy, to secure the money to abort the pregnancy of his mistress, Marcelle. Yet, as one reads the novel, one finds abortion at several levels and in unexpected places. Abortion becomes a thematic instrument which characterizes a number of human relationships. Abortion is the paradigm of broken human relations, the lies one tells oneself and others, and most important, the means by which a person seeks to avoid the consequences of his acts. Not only is this effort to escape the consequences of one's acts personal; it is also national. The Munich agreement concluded by Chamberlain and Daladier is also an effort to escape the consequences of indecision and weakness by agreeing to the "abortion" of Czechoslovakia. So the figure of abortion is widened to include oppression. Let us look at the novel in some detail.

Mathieu has attempted all of his life to remain free at whatever cost. His effort, however, is in bad faith, i.e., dishonest, for he seeks a freedom which will protect him from the consequences of his freedom. He wishes to abort the pregnancy because it, if brought to term, will limit his freedom. One is reminded of Nietzsche's distinction between freedom from and freedom for when observing Mathieu's efforts, for these efforts are intended to free him from the consequences of his freedom in order that he may be willy-nilly free for no purpose save freedom itself. To be sure, freedom is an intrinsic good and an end-in-itself, but we still wonder, freedom for what? However, in this context the figure of abortion appears as the abortion of the consequences of our actions. Sartre is quite sure of the dishonesty of Mathieu's efforts because of the time honored unity of freedom and responsibility. There is, furthermore, another viewpoint from which Mathieu's obsession with freedom is a form of bondage. He has made one commitment to his freedom, but since he has no object for his freedom, it is subject to caprice and whim. His freedom is a miserable slavery to external circumstance and internal vacuity. Thus, because he has no content for his freedom, it too is aborted by happenstance and moral emptiness.

Mathieu's mistress, Marcelle, represents a claim against his freedom because of the pregnancy. Their relationship has lasted several years, and both, for different reasons, are tiring of it and silently desire to end it when the pregnancy occurs. Thus the abortion would be a symbol of their ending relationship as well as literally the end of the pregnancy. Figurally, they stand over against each other; each an object for the other. Theirs is not a whole human relationship which involves responsibility, openness, commitment, promises, etc. The end of the relationship itself is symbolized in the proposed abortion which crystalizes the issues ending it.

They were temporary conveniences to each other, never quite persons. As objects to each other they were bound in a conflict much as a master and slave are united in the non-personal stare they give each other as objects. In this relationship Marcelle is the victim, the slave, the passive partner, but as so often in the master-slave relation, the victim becomes the victor. Marcelle is the one who is needed, Mathieu depends upon her. He comes to her. By satisfying his sexual needs, she in a sense is superior. She is also the one with whom he is most revealing, most intimate. But the pregnancy destroys whatever intimacy there was previously, and Marcelle looks to Mathieu for a decision; he decides on an abortion. The fact that the decision is left up to Mathieu indicates another aborted aspect of their relationship and is a comment on the place of woman at that time in French society. Whereas Mathieu is indecent and despicable, Marcelle, who must look to others for decisions, is pitiable. Her full human development as a self-determining agent is aborted by the conventional agreement she and Mathieu made at the beginning of their relationship—that he should make the decisions about their relationship. So finally Mathieu must face one of the consequences of his free acts. This is quite distasteful to him; even the solution to the problem of the pregnancy through abortion will commit him at least financially, since the money must be borrowed.

The relationship between Marcelle and Mathieu, which had been so destructive for both, ends as a result of the pregnancy. However, Mathieu already had considered his next liaison. Ivich, a student, is almost by definition young, and youth has its attractions to all, but especially to a somewhat jaded intellectual like Mathieu. However, Mathieu is self-deceived, for Ivich is terrified by everything and everyone except possibly her brother. She is horrified by Mathieu's overtures, for she finds it almost impossible to respond to any situation which makes demands upon her. She is not able to respond to her studies and throughout the action of the novel lives under the impression she has failed an examination. She is desperately worried over this matter, but the examination as a demand upon her has "aborted" her desire to pass as well as her ability to do so. Several times in the book she expresses the horror of being touched. For Sartre, the touch is more demonstrative and demanding than the look, for the reach of the hand is an effort to possess. Ivich is also subject to her own bitterness, indecisiveness, and impulsiveness.

Mathieu falls in love with Ivich, largely because she is unobtainable. She attempts to escape any commitment, any involvement which would make her vulnerable, by achieving solitude within the highly populated world of Paris. She refuses the other person before she can be refused. Thus she aborts all possible human relationships in order to secure her solitude. What makes the university and the examination so horrible is that it demands risk and it places her at the mercy of the other. Yet, Mathieu desires her because of her very elusiveness. If he possessed her, she would lose the very quality that attracted him to her. Thus, the rejection of Mathieu by Ivich aborts their relation as would her acceptance of his interests.

What is significant in this relationship is the ambivalence persons have to themselves and to each other. Both Mathieu and Ivich recognize each other as 'an other who observes me.' Each, however, is a subject to himself as opposed to the other person's being an object. To the other person who considers himself a subject, the other is his

Introduction 5

object. What is lacking in this relationship is a sense of joint participation in a common venture. What is lacking is reciprocity, a common cause, intersubjectivity. As each subject observes the other as object, his aims and goals contradict those of the other. Only by self-imposed solitude from the other can he protect his vulnerability before the other. Mathieu lacks the strength of courage to pursue a common goal or aim with another except in one incident. The most bizarre incident in the book is when Ivich stabs her hand in a nightclub as a gesture of defiance and separateness from a couple seated at the next table. Mathieu, in spite of the fact that Ivich has just told him she despises imitation, stabs his hand also. This one inane common act brings them together, and honesty and happiness characterize the remainder of the evening. However, each reverts back to his or her isolation when the evening is over.

There is one other personage in the novel who merits attention here. Brunet is a communist organizer and the foil of Mathieu. Brunet is a man of thought, decision and action, whereas Mathieu is none of these. To be sure, Mathieu is a professor of philosophy, and that is evidence that he can think in some fashion. However, Sartre's point is that Mathieu is incapable of thinking a situation through to the end where action is produced. For Sartre, as for Brunet, thought leads to action, responsibility, involvement and commitment. Mathieu, incapable of them by his own designs makes excuses, keeps open escape routes from decisiveness and avoids action. Brunet has committed himself, has achieved a content for his freedom, has comrades who share his views and projects; he is someone. Compared to Brunet, Mathieu is a mere shadow of a man, an aborted man if you will.

In the eyes of all these people (and others) Mathieu is unmasked in his duplicity, dishonesty, hollowness and bad faith. He is the other to them and they to him. He cannot control them, he despises their gaze, but he cannot destroy them. At the age of sixteen in an act of revenge he had destroyed a vase because he knew what it was, and he did not know what he himself was. To abort and destroy this potential child will be an act of revenge against the world of the others who look at him in disapproval. Brunet urges him to choose what he is, his freedom. This he has done, but it has served no purpose for he has attempted to use his freedom as a freedom from the implications and consequences of freedom. To abort this child would be not only to avoid the gaze of one other (an offspring—a most intimate other) but would also cause him to have fewer responsibilities in the world.

It is in this context that the irony of the title of this volume, *The Age of Reason,* is apparent. A professor of philosophy should have attained the age of reason, but Sartre has shown us the shadow and outline of one who has and has not. As it turns out, the main victim of the decision to abort a pregnancy is the one who made the decision to do so—Mathieu himself.

Let us now turn to an explication of some of the problems of abortion in terms of freedom, consequence, responsibility, commitment and involvement—so dear to the heart of the existentialist.

There are many reasons to assert that considering abortion from the standpoint of personal moral freedom rather than from that of legality is in most respects an unquestioned gain. The first and perhaps most important consequence is that abortion is decriminalized. Only in recent centuries has abortion in western society been thought of as a punishable civil crime. The recent (January 22, 1973) Supreme Court decision has to a large measure returned to the terms of English common law. For many this was a step backward, but these persons must face two hard questions. First, it is evident that laws against abortion are not enforceable. Should such laws be on the books? Does the existence of unenforceable and unenforced laws contribute to respect for law and order or to disrespect for law and order? Is abortion a private moral issue or is it a matter of public concern? If the latter, what is the whole public's (not some of the public's) concern in the matter? How, specifically, is the common good attacked in the decision to abort a pregnancy? Second, with the presence of abortion laws and the consequent criminalizing of a segment of the society, an abortion racket emerges. What are the benefits to society from criminalizing a segment of the population? Does the society reap any benefit from the presence of a criminally organized and hygienically dangerous "health service"? Since abortions will occur, would it not be socially advantageous for them to be performed by the medical profession rather than by hacks? Besides the social advantages of decriminalizing an act, are there not also immense benefits for the person seeking an abortion? For instance, greater safety, better counseling, etc.?

It has occasionally been argued that abortion laws should be kept on the books so that all will know that the community has an interest in the unborn. Is it not rather the case that persons would, on the contrary, learn from such an unenforced and unenforceable law that there is a gap between the professions of a society expressed in the law and the actual values as expressed in the priorities by which public money is spent? Can it be argued that a society has an interest in the unborn when (1) there are few public clinics for pregnant women, (2) vitamins and other nutrients are not routinely furnished free to *all* pregnant women and (3) when excellent (the best) hospital care is not guaranteed every birth in this "solicitous" society? Would not the actual existence of the three above items *really* testify to the interest of the society in the unborn? Is it not rather the case that the society that makes the professions of interest in the unborn by having abortion laws, but does not perform also the three above items is as guilty of bad faith and doublemindedness as is Mathieu in his abstract and uncommitted freedom? Is not such a society as guilty of the use of arbitrary and irrational freedom as Mathieu's aimless whims?

It is sometimes argued that persons, in this instance pregnant women, should bear the consequences of their acts. Sartre argues this about Mathieu. However, is there not a difference between one such as Mathieu who almost pathologically seeks to avoid the consequences of his acts and the person who occasionally does? In a crunch, does not everyone put the best face possible on his participation in certain events? When caught driving through a stop sign, does not almost everyone have an extenuating reason? As an ordinary response all of us frequently attempt to avoid the disastrous consequences of our acts. Is not the demand that all pregnant women should bear the responsibility of their acts just a bit hypocritical?

Pregnancy, as we know, is a categorical condition, a matter of either/or. No woman was ever just a little bit pregnant. Is not the simple biological fact of pregnancy something that involves consequences? Is not undergoing an abortion bearing the consequences of a pregnancy as much as carrying the fetus to term? Is it not rather the case that those who argue that a pregnant woman should bear the responsibility of her acts arguing something which is all too obviously a matter of fact? Is not both abortion and carrying the fetus to term equally bearing the consequences? If one wishes to say that bearing a fetus to term is bearing the consequences of one's act, but that aborting is not, then one can only ask, "Please explain the distinction."

With all this talk about bearing responsibilities, another set of questions arises regarding the male. Except in cases of rape and incest these questions are never asked. Assuming a plain healthy sex act between two consenting parties (frequently one cannot say adults) and a resulting pregnancy, how is the male to assume the consequences of the act? Surely the responsibility for the act is mutual, but nature has so arranged it that the female bears most of the immediate physical consequences. What do those who argue for bearing the consequences of one's acts have in store of equal weightiness for the male? Or do they mean that only the female can or should bear the full consequences of their mutual act? Do the proponents of facing the consequences argue *in fact* for a double standard of morality, one for the male and one for the female? Is not equity the very heart of justice? Where is the justice in requiring the female to carry an unwanted child to term and not arranging something socially as difficult and hazardous for the male? Is "marrying her" all the consequence the male is expected to bear? What of the instances where marriage is not possible, i.e., adultery?

Is the phrase "abortion on demand" a philosophically clear slogan? Do slogans, generally, aid or stop the reflective processes? What would be the philosophic presuppositions of such a slogan and desire? Does a woman's desire to determine her own procreative history constitute the only moral issue in the decision to abort? If the "right to life" of the fetus is too narrow a conception upon which to determine the moral questions of abortion, is it not also possible that the slogan "the rights of women" is too narrow? Do not both slogans oversimplify? Are there not many rights and many interests to be considered?

Should a woman be compelled to bear a child she does not want? Should unwanted children be brought into the world? Were the abortion laws the result of masculine sadism? Does woman's freedom as a person depend on her complete control of her procreative life? Or should abortion be treated as a medical problem only? Should abortion be decided between the patient and the doctor like cutting out an ingrown toe nail? Is knowing how to do an abortion the same as knowing that one ought to be performed?

Would the certainty that the child would be born into an unsuitable environment be a sufficient reason to abort a fetus? Does it make any sense to say that in the interest of a fetus's future we will abort it today? Are all reasons why a child is unwanted of equal value? Poverty? Desire to pursue a career? Is an embryo a part of the mother's body like her left eye? How could the fetus be part of the mother's body since it has a different genetic structure?

This line of questioning leads to another important point. Why do some people argue that someone else should carry a fetus to term? What makes them think that it is any of their business? Suppose A's wife, B, is pregnant and they feel they cannot have a child or another child now for reasons that seem compelling to them. Enter C who asserts that B must carry the child to term as a consequence of the sex act. How did that become C's business? How could such a decision possibly be the concern of the whole society? It might be said that C has special authority in these matters. The question of moral authority over others is difficult indeed, as it has both political and religious overtones. Granted that a religion has some moral authority over its own adherents, can or should a religion attempt to enforce its views on non-adherents? At the political level, what interest does the state have in the private decision between husband and wife or in an unmarried woman's private decision not to bear a fetus to term? Is the stability of the state or any of its institutions attacked by such a decision? Is such a decision a threat to the continuance of the state? Could we not say that the interference of C is a manifestation of what Augustine called the "lust to dominate?" Are not abortion laws in general and religious legalisms in particular a manifestation of the same lust? This manifestation of the desire to oppress has the opposite result from Mathieu's. His desire to abort was a manifestation of his hatred of others, whereas in the present instances the desire to stop abortion could be understood as an effort to suppress the liberty and invade the privacy of the mother (and in marriage, the father also).

The above ambiguity suggests that the motives for abortion are complex, many-sided and subject to varied interpretations. Reflection on these may turn topsy-turvy some of our conventional ideas. Since we have been told authoritatively by no less than Jehovah's prophet Jeremiah that the heart is deceitful above all things, we had best look carefully at all who pass themselves off as virtuous moral authorities, be the subject "law and order," abortion, war, or what not. Does any external authority possess absolute right over conscience? What are the limits of authority in moral matters? Does the fact that one has carried a fetus to term mean she has done the right thing? Does the fact that one has aborted a fetus mean that she has done a wrong thing without qualification. Are moral distinctions simply yes and no without qualification by circumstance and situation?

Could not abortion be recommended as a birth control method if other methods have failed or not been practiced? Are there circumstances where abortion should be required by law? Suppose persons of low I.Q. (say 35) in an institution were to mate, should abortion be required by law? Is it conceivable that future studies in genetics and the adverse genetic load the race carries will increasingly require that certain people be declared genetically dead, if not first by sterilization, then later by abortion? Do the mentally and physically deficient (by genetic measurement) have the right to breed their deficiencies into the genetic pool of the race? If you answer "no," who will make such decisions and by what authority? If you answer "yes," are you willing in N generations to decree the genetic death of the race?

The dilemma has so many facets. Are those who argue that we can abort some now launching an attack on the future of the race? Many geneticists argue that some must be aborted now in order to save the race in the future. Is the dilemma somewhat qualified (or intensified) by the population explosion on the one hand, and the deteriorating resources of the genetic pool on the other? Future moral debates will bring together the issues of abortion, genetic load, and sterilization. Will science be dictating moral standards? More generally, what is the relation of science to ethics? In the present instance can a scientific fact (say, the measurement of brain waves) be a better indication than a court decision of whether the fetus should be declared a human being? If so, why? If not, why not?

Why has the legal history of abortion been so inconsistent? Why were abortion laws tightened in the nineteenth century? Was Lord Ellenborough's Act outlawing abortion based upon newly emerging moral sensitivities? Or was it to help increase the English population to man the new industrial machine and to defend the new Empire? Or was it a pre-Victorian repression of matters related to sex? What is the relation of cultural, social and economic factors to changing moral views? Does the present loosening of abortion laws indicate that we are less moral now than when the laws were imposed? Would anyone want to argue for the moral superiority of the present century over the last? Would that be an exercise in self-righteousness? Again, what is the relation of law, morality and ethics?

Is there a specifically religious base to current arguments against abortion? What arguments against abortion can be made without any appeal to religious authority? In the west, has the historical development of theological views been consistent? If there has beeen historical consistency in the development of the theological arguments, would that demonstrate their correctness? If one grants that there has been and is inconsistency and difference in theological views about abortion, does that mean that one or all are wrong? Granted inconsistency in the development of theological views and in the present status of theological positions on the subject, what does this inconsistency infer about the nature of religion and religious authority? In what ways does culture determine religion, and how does religion determine culture?

In the development of the theological views of abortion, what was the importance played by the concept of soul? To what extent was Christian theology generally influenced by the Platonic concepts of soul? Do the Hebrew words *n'shama* and *ruhi* perform the same function in Hebrew religion as *psyche* does in Plato's thought and *anima* in the Latin theologians? Is it not conceivable that Roman Catholic theology was influenced in its formation and present position more by Greek modes of thought than by classical Hebrew (i.e., Old Testament) thought? Did medieval Hebrew thought undergo the same Hellenizing that Christian thought underwent? Granted the confluence of these two currents to create the western moral tradition, has the confluence led to philosophical and theological clarity regarding abortion specifically? More generally, is the history of ideas philosophically pertinent to the solution of modern philosophic difficulties?

How do difficulties in philosophy reflect the difficulties people find themselves in? How do existential difficulties relate to philosophical problems? Does philosophy have anything to do with human practice? Does practice have anything to do with philosophy? Does philosophy have a subject matter separate from human practice? Is there something other than human practice, activity, or even belief which is more properly the subject of philosophy than these? What?

Finally, a few observations must be offered. First, as the reading of Sartre's novel suggests, abortion can be a figural representation to help us understand the nature of oppression, violence, bad faith and the gutlessness of our times. Perhaps Sartre intended that we should place the symbol of abortion alongside Hegel's figure of the master and slave as symbolic of the situation of man. This figural and phenomenological interpretation is herein only suggested with the hope that others will pursue the matter further. Second, as Sartre's novel and the preceding formidable set of questions show, men can do right and wrong in a thousand different ways. There are ambiguous corners of our experience. This should teach us a tolerance and forbearance for others and increase our suspicion of our own motives and desires "to do good." If this point sounds like the injunction of Jesus (Judge not . . .) and another oblique paraphrase of Jeremiah, be assured that I intended it. Injunctions such as Jesus' and observations such as Jeremiah's on the one hand, figural analyses such as Sartre's and Hegel's, philosophical analyses such as Marx on ideology, Socrates on the self and Sartre on bad faith meet at the crossroads of human activity and illumine each other. Third, the problem of abortion is an intensely personal one. To be sure there are all kinds of philosophical, theological, legal, social and medical aspects, but finally there is a lonely decision that can and may be shared with only a few. It is to the illumination of one of these lonely places that the authors dedicate this book. Fourth, neither the authors nor I know even an approximate answer to more than a few of the questions raised in this introduction. One could feel confidence and hope for some answers, if one were sure all the relevant questions had been listed. However, we do not know how many should be inserted in the above discussion, and there is no way of finding out. Some questions, indeed most, are probably not finally decidable. If we philosophers knew the answers we might go on and become doctors, businessmen or politicians, i.e., take up a profession that in the common mind is more "practical." Yet those of us for whom puzzlement and aggravation at ignorance is inescapable invite the reader to contribute to the dialogue and dialectic called philosophy. We send forth this book in the hope that its readers will become our teachers.[1]

[1]Though it is in bad taste to write footnotes for an introduction, two acknowledgements must be made. The interpretation of *The Age of Reason* was strengthened by Joseph H. McMahon's *Humans Being: The World of Jean-Paul Sartre* (Chicago: University of Chicago Press, 1971).
The more critical questions in this introduction about woman's liberation arguments were suggested by Daniel Callahan's book, *Abortion: Law, Choice, and Morality* (New York: Macmillan, 1970)

WILLIAM E. MAY

Abortion and Man's Moral Being

I have been asked to contribute an essay from the perspective of a Roman Catholic to this anthology. My intention in this paper is twofold: first, to state the official teaching of the Roman Catholic Church on the subject of abortion and to indicate the current status of the discussion taking place among Roman Catholic moralists with respect to this teaching; second, and this to me the more important objective, to show why I, as a philosopher, believe that the directly intended killing of human fetuses is an act that human beings ought not to do if they are to act intelligently and responsibly as human beings.

Stated briefly and accurately, the official teaching of the Roman Catholic Church is: direct abortion is always wrong.[1] This teaching is reflected in many official documents of the recent past. Three may be cited as illustrative. In an address on October 29, 1951, Pius XII stated:

> The baby in the mother's womb has the right to life immediately from God. Hence there is no man, no human authority, no science, no medical, eugenic, social, economic or moral "indication" which can establish or grant a valid judicial ground for a direct deliberate disposition of an innocent human life, that is, a disposition which looks to its destruction either as an end or as a means to another end perhaps in itself not illicit. The baby, still not born, is a man in the same degree and for the same reason as the mother.[2]

The bishops assembled at the Second Vatican Council maintained that:

> Whatever is opposed to life itself, such as any type of murder, genocide, abortion, euthanasia, or willful self-destruction . . . are infamies indeed. They poison human society, but they do more harm to those who practice them than those who suffer from the injury.[3]

> God, the Lord of life, has conferred on men the surpassing ministry of safeguarding life — a ministry which must be fulfilled in a manner which is worthy of man. Therefore from the moment of its conception life must be guarded with the greatest care, while abortion and infanticide are unspeakable crimes.[4]

Finally, Paul VI declared in his encyclical of July, 1968, on human life that

> the direct interruption of generation already begun, and especially direct abortion, except if done for therapeutic reasons, must be entirely repudiated.[5]

It should be noted that Pius XII and Paul VI both expressly stipulate that the morally proscribed act is that of *direct* abortion. The former explains in broad outline the difference between direct and indirect abortion as follows:

> We have on purpose always used the expression *"direct* attack on the life of the innocent," *"direct* killing." For if, for instance, the safety of the life of the mother-to-be, independently of her pregnant condition, should urgently require a surgical operation or other therapeutic treatment, which would have as a side effect, in no way willed or intended yet inevitable, the death of the fetus, then such an act could not any longer be called a *direct* attack on innocent life. With these conditions, the operation, like other similar medical interventions, can be allowable, always assuming that a good of great worth, such as life, is at stake, and that it is not possible to delay until after the baby is born or to make use of some other effective remedy.[6]

From the foregoing the official teaching of the Roman Catholic Church should be clear. It is morally wrong deliberately and of set purpose to destroy fetal life (= to commit an act of direct abortion), although under certain conditions therapeutic activities directly aimed at saving the life of the mother-to-be are permissible even if these activities do in fact result in the death of the unborn child. The basis of this teaching, as John T. Noonan, Jr.,[7] among others, has pointed out, is the dignity or sanctity of human life. The teaching is predicated upon the following beliefs: that fetal life is human life, that every human being is of equal worth, and that every human being is a subject of rights, such as the right to life, that are his because they are God-given (or, in humanistic terms, because he is a human being), and not because they have been conferred upon him by society or because he has achieved something through his own personal activity that gives him a claim to rights that others do not possess. Charles E. Curran has remarked that the official teaching of the Church "depends on two very important judgments: the judgment about when human life begins and the judgment about the solution of conflict situations involving the fetus and other values."[8] The first judgment of which Curran speaks is clear enough; by the second he has in mind the distinction between direct and indirect killing and the role that this distinction, as formulated in the principle of twofold effect,[9] has played in the development of Catholic moral thought, particularly with respect to the killing of one human being by another.

This official teaching of the Roman Catholic Church is being challenged today by many within the Catholic community, including prominent moralists. The challenge is focused on either or both of the two judgments to which Curran refers. Some Catholic writers, among them Joseph Donceel,[10] Thomas Wassmer,[11] Bruno Ribes,[12] and Louis Beirnaert,[13] argue that a fetus is not necessarily a human being, or at least not a human being in the sense that it is an entity that is the subject of rights. They propose either a theory of "mediate animation" or "delayed hominization" (Donceel, Wassmer), assigning to the fetus protectable humanity only after a certain stage of fetal development, or a "relationalistic" or "personalistic" theory (Ribes, Beirnaert), according to which fully protectable humanity is nonexistent until a definite relationship has been established between the child and his parents and society. Because of their view of the status of fetal life they hold that its deliberate destruction may be permitted for sufficient reasons either until a certain stage in its development has been attained or throughout the entire period of prenatal life.

Other Catholic writers question the validity of the distinction between direct and indirect abortion or killing or doing of evil in general. These authors, and among them the more important are Cornelius Van der Poél, William Van der Marck,[15] and Bruno Schüller,[16] believe that the principle of double effect is chiefly the result of casuistic quibbling and argue that the human act in its entirety and in its human significance may directly encompass evil, even the evil of killing, and still be a rightful human act. Their position has been formulated in different ways, but the major direction of their criticism has been well summarized by Richard A. McCormick. McCormick first notes that these writers distinguish between what we can call *premoral* or *nonmoral* evil and *moral* evil or *wickedness*. The former is any evil that we may bring about through our deeds, whereas the latter is evil that can rightly be attributed to us as moral agents. McCormick then sums up the position of these authors by saying:

> Would it not be clearer and more precise to say that it is legitimate to intend premoral evil *in ordine ad finem proportionatum* (in order to achieve a proportionate end)? I may choose and intend the pain of a child or a patient if it is the only way or the most reasonable way to secure his greater good. This "greater good" (i.e., proportionate reason) does not mean that the premoral disvalue is not intended; it means that it is not intended *propter se* (for itself). Therefore, would it not be better to say that it is legitimate to intend a disvalue *in se sed non propter se* (in itself but not for itself)? When there is no proportionate reason, the disvalue caused is chosen and intended *in se et propter se* (in itself and for itself), and it is this *propter se* (for itself) which makes the act immoral.[17]

On this view, consequently, not every act of direct abortion is to be judged morally wrong. The rightness or wrongness of the act depends upon the proportionate reason—or what Schüller calls "preference principle"[18]—involved. As one of the advocates of this position, Van der Poel, puts it, "In the killing of a human being, the issue is not whether the person who is going to be killed is guilty or innocent, nor whether the killing is direct or indirect; the question, rather, is what kind of human self-realization is taking place and what is the interpersonal impact of this action."[19] Accordingly these authors are ready to acknowledge the rightness of direct abortion in cases of rape and defective fetuses,[20] and, it can be assumed, in other instances as well when the proper kind of human self-realization and interpersonal relationships can be brought into being through an act of direct abortion.

Still other writers, and Daniel Callahan can be included here,[21] challenge both bases of the Roman Catholic prohibition of direct abortion. They maintain that fetal life is not, at least until a certain stage of development, protectable human life and that conflict situations can arise in which nuanced comparisons of one life with another may lead one to the judgment, however reluctant, that one human being's right to life justifies deliberately and directly killing (or, more euphemistically, "terminating the life of") another.[22]

This brief look at the nature of the discussion going on among Roman Catholic writers should suffice to show that the viewpoints set forth parallel, in large measure, viewpoints common to the general public. The official teaching of the Roman Catholic Church is clear; although this teaching is defended by the majority of Catholic authors, pre-eminently Germain G. Grisez,[23] John T. Noonan, Jr.,[24] Robert and Mary Rosera Joyce,[25] and others, it is seriously questioned by many.

Our purpose now is to examine the meaning of abortion as a human activity and to offer reasons why a sound moral philosophy should judge that abortion, understood as an activity that has as its direct intent the death of a fetus, as a wrongful act. In his important essay on abortion Noonan observed that "the teaching of a religious body may invoke revelation, claim authority, employ symbolism, which make the moral doctrine it teaches binding for believers in the religion but of academic concern to those outside its boundaries." Or it may, he continued, "embody insights, protect perceptions, exemplify values, which concern humanity."[26] My belief, as a human being and as a philosopher, is that the teaching of the Roman Catholic Church on abortion is of the latter variety. The question of abortion is *not* a "religious" issue in any narrow sense. It is a question that touches deeply the meaning of human existence and the character of human existence as a moral existence. If abortion is a wrongful human act, it is so not because it is judged to be so by a religious authority but because of what it means as a human deed. Consequently, before examining the important questions of the status of fetal life and the conditions under which the killing of one human being by another or others is morally permissible, I want to sketch briefly a general moral framework for evaluating human acts.

To be a human being is to be an animal; but it is, as René Dubos has so beautifully put it, to be so *human* an animal. It is to be an animal *with a difference*. The difference can be expressed in various ways, but one major and critically important way of putting this difference is to say that man, and man alone of all animals, is a *moral* being. That man, and man alone, is a moral being is illustrated in common speech. It is meaningful, for instance, to speak about making human life human. Yet to speak in this way is paradoxical. We would find it odd, indeed absurd, were someone to speak of making bovine life bovine or simian life simian. A cow, after all, is a cow and an ape is an ape. Yet it is not absurd or meaningless to speak about making human life human. Since it does make sense to speak in this fashion, it follows that man is indeed a unique kind of animal, and it also follows that the word *human* must be used in two quite distinct ways when we talk about making human life human. The second use of the term implies that a human being is not totally "human" when he comes into existence. Certainly no one who uses the term *human* in this second sense wants to deny that all men are equally human beings simply from the fact that they are all identifiably men, i.e., members of the same biological species. Yet he is affirming that "being human" is not something factually given but is rather a process, a growth. To use the term in this second sense is to imply that there is something or some set of things (what we can call the "human good" or *bonum humanum*) "perfective" of a human being precisely as a human being and that human beings are summoned, individually and as members of the human community, to struggle to achieve these goods that are perfective of them. In addition, to distinguish between two meanings of the term *human* is to affirm that not everything that men do and can do is really human. It is to distinguish between *is* and *ought*, between what men actually are and do and what men ought to be and ought to do.[27]

In common with many moralists in what can be termed the natural law tradition, I conceive the human good to be a totality composed of individual goods each of which corresponds to some basic human need, so that we can truthfully say that each is a good *of* man, not *for* man, that each is a good to be *prized*, not *priced*. Among such real goods may be included life itself, health, justice, friendship, peace, truth. These goods, which are constitutive of the *bonum humanum*, define aspects of our personal being. They are common insofar as they are not *my* goods or *your* goods but rather human personal goods capable of being communicated to and shared by every human being.[28] Because they are real goods corresponding to real needs existing in every human being just because he is human, they generate real rights: each human being has a right to them, a claim on them, precisely because he is a human being and because they are the realities that make a human being more human.[29]

Each of these goods, moreover, can serve as a purposeful goal of human activity. They are what the Scholastics termed "principles of practical reason" and what we can call "principles of intelligent activity." They shape our activity from within inasmuch as each can function as a choiceworthy purpose for doing anything. Each of these goods, moreover, is incommensurable with the others: how can one, for instance, compare a friend to his health, or his life to a just order among men? Because of this, none of these goods is the absolute good in the sense of the *summum bonum;* none is the be-all and end-all of human existence to which the others must be subordinated. Although none of these goods is the absolute human good, "none is so relative," Grisez observes, "that it does not resist submergence."[30] That is, each of the particular goods comprising the *bonum humanum* is a real human good and demands to be recognized as such and respected as such. To repudiate one of these goods by declaring it to be evil and to be willing to destroy it in oneself and in others is to repudiate a meaningful dimension of human existence, to reject one's humanity, to act irrationally.

Man's supreme or absolute good, at least from the perspective of moral philosophy, consists in his goodness precisely as a human being, that is, as the moral being capable of distinguishing between *is* and *ought* and of acting responsibly in accordance with his judgments of what he ought to do if he is to become more fully human. Man makes his moral being in and through his deeds, because it is in and through them that he both discloses his moral identity to himself and to others and achieves this moral identity. In and through his deeds he reveals his attitudes toward the goods constitutive of the *bonum humanum,* whether he respects them for what they are, real goods intended for and perfective of all human beings, just because they are human beings; or whether he pursues them for himself and his friends alone, ready to destroy them in others, or irrationally erects one into an absolute to which he is ready to sacrifice all others and for which he is ready to repudiate all others.

As a moral being, moreover, man is the animal who is not only capable of distinguishing between *is* and *ought* and of acting responsibly in the light of his judgments of what he ought and ought not to do, he is also the animal of moral worth or value. Because he is this kind of being, he surpasses or transcends the world about him. Each of us is, as an *individual* human being, a part of a larger whole, of the society of which we are members; but each of us is, as an individual *human* or *moral* being, related to this society not simply as a part to a whole but as a whole to a whole. By this I mean that every human being, because he is a moral entity and a being of moral worth, has moral rights that are his because of what he is. It is for this reason that we abhor totalitarianism, which would subordinate individual human beings completely to the good of the state (i.e., of those in power) and crush their rights in order to achieve goals worthwhile in themselves. Because men are moral beings the common good of human societies, as noted previously, must flow back to and be sharable by all the members of those societies.[31]

In acting to pursue the real goods constitutive of the *bonum humanum* each of us, as a moral being, is obliged to respect these goods for what they are, that is, goods meriting our love because they are the goods that are indeed perfective of ourselves and of all other human beings, that is, of all those who have, with us, *equal* claims on or titles toward these goods. Although we may at times, because of the situations in which we are placed, be compelled to do something that results in the destruction of one of these goods either in ourselves or in others, this does not mean that we can repudiate or deny their goodness or the value of the human beings in whom they are destroyed. For instance, we may be called upon to forego our health in order to care for the sick; in doing this we do not repudiate health as a human good. We willingly, although reluctantly, allow our health to be destroyed while we are engaged in activities that *of themselves* are directly aimed at serving some other human good (e.g., friendship or justice). We may, in order to protect a person being viciously assaulted, deliver a mortal blow to his assailant. In doing this we do not necessarily repudiate or reject the life of the assailant as a human good, but rather willingly perform a deed of itself directed to saving his victim and properly describable as an act of defense that we foresee will have as one of its consequences the death of the assailant. To make the destruction of one of these goods, however, the precise point of our deed, even if this deed is itself ordered to serving some other human good, is to act immorally. It is to declare ourselves ready to accept, as part of our moral identity, the identity of a destroyer of some basic human good. We shall return later to this point, for it requires fuller exposition, but for the present the basic thrust of the position I am developing should be clear.

We are now ready to reflect on the important questions of the status of fetal life and the conditions under which the killing of one human being by another is morally permissible. The status of fetal life (and I use this term in an inclusive manner to refer to the unborn organism from conception until birth[32]) is central to the abortion debate, a factor recognized by the Supreme Court in its decisions of Roe v. Wade and Doe v. Bolton. The Court, it may be noted, expressly declared that it had no intent to "resolve the difficult question of when life begins."[33] Yet it may likewise be noted that the Court did, in fact, pronounce judgment on this difficult question, inasmuch as it found that the fetus is not, prior to viability, a being to be protected and that the fetus, even after viability, is only the "potentiality of human life," or "potential life."[34] Obviously if the fetus is only "potential life" or the "potentiality of human life" it is *not* itself life. If a being is only potentially something, then it is not now that something which it *can* become. My oldest boy is a potential father, but he is not now a father, nor could he be a *potential* father if, in fact, he actually were a father. Thus one must conclude that the Supreme Court did, in truth, resolve the question of when life begins: it begins when one is born.[35]

There are many different attitudes toward the status of fetal life. They range from the view, expressed by Philip Wylie, that the fetus is "protoplasmic rubbish" or a "gobbet of meat,"[36] through the views that it is simply "gametic materials" (Joseph Fletcher),[37] a "blueprint" (Garret Hardin),[38] a "part of the mother" (Havelock Ellis),[39] to the views that it is alive and human although not the subject of protectable rights (Daniel Callahan, Michael Tooley),[40] that it is indeed an individual human being and the subject of protectable rights (Germain Grisez).[41] I submit that the views regarding the fetus as non-human are indefensible in view of *reality-making* factors disclosed by contemporary biomedical research. As C. G. Goodhart of the zoology department at Cambridge University remarked in an exchange with Malcolm Potts:

> Dr. Potts has argued that human development is a continuous process . . . and that it is in principle impossible to define when a new human individual comes into existence. May I with great respect suggest that this

is a view which is contradicted by biological knowledge? For there is a real discontinuity at fertilization, or to be pedantic, at the "activation" of the ovum which is not necessarily always the same thing. This is the point after, but not before, it becomes capable of completing its development without any further stimulus from outside. Once activated, the organism will carry on its development until it dies. That is what most of us would have called the moment of conception, however else the British Council of Churches may now have decided to define the word. But whatever we call it, it occurs at a specific point in time, after, but not before which, development can proceed; and that is a real *discontinuity* marking the coming into existence of a new biological organism.[42]

Calling a human fetus "protoplasmic rubbish," "gametic materials," a "blueprint," or a "part of the mother" is to engage in rhetoric and to evade the issues raised by abortion. The fetus, and we are here concerned with the human fetus, is obviously an entity that is living, that is individuated at least with respect to its parents if not (prior to segmentation) with respect to any possible twins it might have, and that is human. There is an identity *in being* between the zygote, the fetus, the neonate, the child, the adolescent, the adult, the senior citizen. The central issue in the abortion debate, as Paul Ramsey forcefully notes, is not when does human life begin, but "When does equally protectable life begin?"[43] My life, as yours, began "as a minute informational speck, drawn at random from many other minute informational specks [my] parents possessed out of the common human gene pool. This took place at the moment of impregnation,"[44] or, to use Goodhart's terminology, at the moment of "activation." But was I then—and were *you* then—a being possessed of rights that ought to be acknowledged by other men?

If, in order to be a being possessing moral rights, it is necessary to pass the criteria set forth by Joseph Fletcher in his list of "indicators of humanhood" (an I.Q. of at least 20 and probably 40, self-awareness, self-control, a sense of time, the capability to relate to others, etc.)[45] or the criterion stipulated by Michael Tooley that one possess "the concept of a self as a continuing subject of experiences and other mental states" and believe "that it is itself such a continuing entity,"[46] it is obvious that neither I nor you nor any other human being was the subject of moral rights during the fetal stage of our development. But on these criteria we possessed no rights for a considerable period after birth either, and according to these criteria we might rightfully dismiss significant numbers of individuals readily numbered among the human race as of no moral significance or worth. Common to the thought of Fletcher, Tooley and those who would agree with them is the belief that "membership in a species is of no moral significance."[47] This belief is warranted *only* if one is capable of showing that man's significance as a *moral* being (for this is one crucial way in which he differs from other animals) is ultimately explicable fully and adequately in terms of a difference in the degree of development of man (or some men) over the development that has taken place in other animals and is *not* rooted in man's being a different *kind* of animal from all other animals. My position is that our belief that a human being is a moral being and thus the subject of moral rights is based on a belief that human beings differ radically in kind from other animals: men are moral beings not because of something that they achieve or do but because of what they are. My point may be made clearer, perhaps, if we cite a passage from Mortimer Adler. According to Adler, if men differ from other animals only in degree, that is, by doing something that other animals do not do but do not do only because they have not attained the stage of development that men have attained, then:

> those who now oppose injurious discrimination on the moral ground that all human beings, being equal in their humanity, should be treated equally in all those respects that concern their common humanity, would have no solid basis in fact to support their normative principle. A social and political ideal that has operated with revolutionary force in human history could be validly dismissed as a hollow illusion that should become defunct . . . We can now imagine a future state of affairs in which a new global division of mankind replaces all the old parochial divisions based upon race, nationality, or ethnic group . . . a division that separates the human elite at the top of the scale from the human scum at the bottom, a division based on accurate scientific measurement of human ability and achievement and one, therefore, that is factually incontrovertible . . . .[48]

Put another way, I believe that the major area of disagreement between those who defend abortion and those who oppose abortion over the status of fetal life comes down to the question: Is humanity, in the sense of being an entity that is the subject of rights, an endowment or an achievement? Those who accept abortion accept, with Ashley Montagu,[49] Joseph Fletcher,[50] Gerald Leach,[51] and Michael Tooley,[52] and others, the assumption that humanity or being human in a significant moral sense, is an achievement. In order to be a human being for whom society should be concerned, one must *do* something or actually be capable of doing something that will enhance or promote human welfare (e.g., be capable of actually entering into meaningful human relations). There are, in other words, some kinds of tests, variously described by various authors, that one must pass before he is entitled to be called a human being in a meaningful sense. For those, on the contrary, who oppose what could be called an ethic of abortion, being human is not primarily a matter of achievement; rather it is a gift, an endowment that one has not because he has already done something worthwhile or is actually capable of doing something worthwhile but simply because he is and is present (even if hidden in the womb) to his fellow men. On this latter view I am— and you are—a being of moral worth not because of anything that I have done or actually can do but simply because I am. On this latter view each of us holds our humanity as a gift, a gift (for those who are religiously motivated) from God, a gift (for those motivated by a humanistic spirit) from our fellow men. On this latter view the words of Ralph Potter—if not those of Jeremiah who wrote: "Before I formed thee in the belly I knew thee" (1:5)—carry weight: "the fetus symbolizes you and me and our tenuous hold upon a future here at the mercy of our fellow men."[53]

I realize that in the foregoing I have not offered any kind of irrefutable scientific or philosophical "proof" for the humanity (i.e. moral worth) of the fetus, although the consideration of man's difference as a moral animal from other animals as being a difference *in kind* and not *in degree* gives a general indication of the type of argument that could be developed.[54] Nonetheless those who oppose the humanity of fetal life must either explain away considerable scientific evidence that human fetuses are alive and humanly alive (in the sense of being specifiably biologically human in their life rather than non-human) or evolve arguments that go counter to the democratic and humane tendency to extend the protection of human society to secure the basic human rights of those human beings who are defenseless and incapable of claiming and asserting the rights that are theirs by reason of their humanness, and not by reason of some accomplishments that they have made by reason of their own efforts.

What of the morally permissible taking of the life of one human being by another? This, I believe in company with Paul Ramsey[55] and Germain Grisez,[56] is *the* issue at stake in the abortion controversy. What are the conditions under which the doing of the deadly deed is permissible? One way of answering this question is adopted by those who endorse a situational, consequentialistic, or utilitarian approach to solving conflict situations. The ethical position defended is what can be called an *ethics of intended consequences* or an *ethics of intent*. Those who espouse this approach, and I would include here those Catholic moralists mentioned previously who reject the principle of double effect as a matter of casuistic quibbling, are primarily interested in what our deeds as human beings *do*, that is, in their results. They urge that the ultimate criterion in evaluating human acts is the net balance of good over evil, or what some, like Van der Poel, call "its impact upon the well-being of the individual and the human society,"[57] or what others, like Van der Marck, describe as its ability to "build up community."[58] This way of evaluating human deeds can make the claim of being a compassionate ethic; one concerned to help suffering human beings, to provide support and dignity to women who become pregnant when they really do not want to and when the birth of a child will cause serious hardships and threaten the attainment of real human goods. This is a claim sincerely advanced by many who adopt this ethical approach, and it ought to be recognized that many who defend abortion as a human act and social practice do so because of a burning sense of justice, of compassion, of human concern. Their intention or what they have in view in their activity, is to do good and to promote human welfare.

Yet it must be pointed out that this way of justifying the deadly deed *is* a consequentialistic ethics or an ethics of intent as related to consequences and not what can be called an *ethics of intent + content*. The ethics of intent justifies the destruction of fetal life because of the beneficial consequences that will result from this destruction. It justifies this act precisely because, in the judgment of those who defend it, it will bring about a net balance of good over evil; it will contribute to the building up the community and will lead to the well-being of the pregnant woman and to society at large by preventing the birth of a child who is not wanted for one reason or another. This type of ethics, it should be clear, is an ethics primarily concerned with ends, not means; it is an ethics that sees the significance of human acts in what they *do* and not in what they *say*.

The ethics that I have termed an ethics of intent + content, on the other hand, is concerned with means as well as ends; it is interested in the results of our acts, to be sure, but in addition to being interested in what our acts *do* it is also immensely interested in what they *say,* in what they disclose or reveal about us as human beings and about the meaning of human existence.[59] In this type of ethics, consequences are, of course, important in judging the morality of our deeds, but there are reality-making factors *other than consequences* or results that simply must be taken into account. The activity in question is one of these factors, and it is one precisely because it is a *human* activity and is thus a revelation or disclosure of human identity. In addition, one's intentions or what one "has in view" and seeks to effect through his activity include not only the larger goals or ends one wishes to achieve but also the activity that one chooses to use as a way toward their attainment.[60]

If we now look at the activity (and practice) that we call abortion we realize that for an ethics of intent + content (and this is the ethics that is behind the thinking that gave rise to the principle of double effect) it is necessary to take into account not only the real goods that can be realized if an abortion is performed but also the character of the abortion itself as an expression of human identity. And direct abortion as a human activity inescapably, inevitably, requires as *one* of its purposes, as one of the elements unavoidably and necessarily within the scope of one's intentions, the death of the fetus, the destruction, within the fetus, of the life that it has. This death is an ineluctable part both of the intent and the content of the act. It is so in *direct* abortion because, in acts properly describable as directly abortive, the death of the fetus is itself the *means* to attaining the desired results *and* is the *terminus or end of the action* itself; that is, the destruction of the fetus is what an older, Scholastic terminology called the *finis operis* (end of the act) in contradistinction to the *finis operantis* (end of the agent) or *subjective motives* of the agent, or it is what a contemporary writer, Paul Ramsey, calls the "primary thrust" of the activity itself.[61] In direct abortion, and this is the kind of activity involved when abortion is undertaken to prevent the birth of babies unwanted either because of fetal defects, socioeconomic factors, or other reasons, the purpose of the activity (its "primary thrust" or direction, the *finis operis,* the "intention" of the action) is necessarily directed to the death of the human fetus.

It may be suggested (and indeed *is* argued by some) that many women who have abortions and that many people who may be disposed to accept abortion as an acceptable human solution to some agonizing human problems, do not really *want* to destroy fetal life. They see the activity in question as being something other than the destruction of a fetus; they see it in terms of the good that is sought through the abortion itself. By this I mean that these persons are not really ready to accept, as part of their own personal identity, the identity of persons responsible for feticide. They are not willing, deep in their own consciousness, to endorse and ratify the wrong that their act is causing to the developing human existent that is the fetus. This, I believe, is why abortion is so frequently described in euphemistic terms as the removal of the products of conception or as the elimination from the womb of genetic materials or tissue or protoplasm. There is, in other words, an attempt to conceal the nature of the activity. There is operative, as Eric D'Arcy has noted, a human propensity to *redescribe* the act in question in terms of its intended consequences.[62] But, as D'Arcy also noted, it is simply not truthful to reality to redescribe acts in this manner when doing so "conceal(s), or even fail(s) to reveal, the nature of the act itself."[63] And, in cases properly describable as acts of direct abortion, the nature of the *act itself* is such that its primary thrust, direction, or whatever one may wish to term it, is to destroy the life of the fetus. This is precisely what is meant by the expression *direct abortion*.

What are instances when an abortive act, that is an act resulting in the death of the fetus, can be described properly as an act of *indirect abortion?* The principle of double effect was developed by moralists who wanted both to be truthful in their way of describing moral reality and to provide a philosophically intelligent justification of doing deeds that inevitably and unavoidably caused injury or evil as well as good. They recognized that frequently in life we are put in situations when no matter what we do some evil is going to result. Their purpose was not, as Callahan suggests,[64] to devise a clever way for insuring "clean" consciences, but was rather, as Ramsey observes,[65] a desire to explicate the requirements for judging the objective conditions under which actions can rightfully be done. An accurate statement of the principle involves four points, and these are well stated by Grisez as follows:

> One may perform an act having two effects, one good and the other bad,

if four conditions are fulfilled simultaneously.

1. The act must not be wrong in itself, even apart from consideration of the bad effects . . .

2. The agent's intention must be right . . .

3. The evil effect must not be the means to the good effect, for then evil would fall within the scope of one's intention, and evil may not be intended even for the sake of an ulterior good purpose . . .

4. There must be a proportionately grave reason for doing such an act, since there is a general obligation to avoid evil so far as possible . . .[66]

The principle was meant to clarify in specific ways the critically important distinction between the "indirectly voluntary" and the "directly voluntary." This key distinction and its relevance to the principle of double effect have been accurately stated by Philippa Foot:

> The doctrine of the double effect is based on a distinction between what a man foresees as a result of his voluntary action and what, in the strict sense, he intends. He intends in the strictest sense both those things that he aims at as ends [e.g., in abortion, the avoidance of the socioeconomic and personal costs entailed in caring for a mongoloid child] and those that he aims at as means to his ends [e.g., the abortion of a child discovered through amniocentesis to be mongoloid]. The latter may be regretted in themselves but nevertheless desired for the sake of the end. . . . By contrast a man is said not strictly, or directly, to intend the foreseen consequences of his voluntary actions where these are neither the end at which he is aiming nor the means to this end.[67]

Controversy over the principle has focused primarily on the third requirement in Grisez's list, and it can surely be admitted that the principle, as developed and employed by Roman Catholic manuals of moral theology in the past, did frequently give rise to disputatious "quibbling" and that the principle, as interpreted, at times unnecessarily restricted the evil that one could rightfully do in pursuit of good. Classic examples center on cases when the life of the mother-to-be is in danger and an abortive act could save her. One such case is that cited by Jonathan Bennett and involves the situation of a woman who will surely die unless an operation is performed in which the head of her unborn child is crushed or dissected, whereas if the act is not undertaken the child may be safely delivered alive by post-mortem Caesarian section.[68] Most Roman Catholic moralists of the past, seeking to apply the principle of double effect to situations of this kind, held that it was wrong to abort the child in this way because this would be to violate the third condition of the principle of double effect and would constitute doing evil in order that good might result.

Although this type of situation (and others can be and have been brought forward of similar character) raises serious difficulties for those who believe that the principle of double effect embodies a significant effort to be faithful to reality-making factors in determining objectively what men may rightfully do, the response required is *not* to abandon the principle and, even more importantly, the critical distinction between the directly voluntary and the indirectly voluntary upon which it is based, but rather to think more deeply about what the directly voluntary and indirectly voluntary *mean*. I believe that a proper moral analysis of the type of situation described above will lead one to the conclusion that in instances of this nature the activity in question does not constitute "direct" killing; it is not a matter of the "directly voluntary" destruction of fetal life but rather an "indirectly voluntary" deed so far as the death of the fetus is concerned. Here Germain Grisez and Paul Ramsey, despite real differences between them,[69] help us to understand the moral realities at stake. Although Ramsey, in one essay (even as revised),[70] believes that some of the acts resulting in the death of the fetus in situations of this kind can properly be called "direct abortion," he agrees ultimately with Grisez "that any killing of man by man must be 'indirect.' "[71] His point is that, in acts that do kill the fetus but are undertaken *only* because the abortion in question is necessary to save the life of the mother-to-be (a condition that satisfies the fourth requirement of the principle of double effect), "the intention of the action, and in this sense its direction, is not upon the *death* of the fetus." He continues by stating:

> The intention of the action is directed toward the *incapacitation* of the fetus from doing what it is doing to the life of the mother, and is not directed toward the death of the fetus, as such, even in the killing of it. The child, of course, is only doing what comes naturally, i.e., growing and attempting to be born. But he is, objectively and materially, aggressing upon the life of the mother. Her life, which alone can be saved, can be saved only if this is stopped; and to incapacitate the fetus from doing this can be done only . . . by a direct [?] act of killing nascent life. Still, in this situation, it is correct to say that the intention of the action is not the killing, not the death of the fetus, but the incapacitation of it from carry-

ing out the material aggression that it is effecting upon the life of the mother.[72]

In sum, in instances when an act that results in the death of the fetus and is foreseen to issue in this consequence, the abortion is "indirectly voluntary" and not directly so if, and *only* if, the trust of the action—*its* "intention" or direction or what used to be called the *finis operis*—is itself targeted, not upon the life of the fetus, but upon countering the injurious effect that the fetus, simply by its presence, is causing its mother. The case here is parallel to the taking of the life of one human being by another in an act properly describable as an act of self-defense.[73] The justification of the deadly deed is not based upon consequentialistic factors as such. The good consequences do enter in as providing a "proportionate reason" for undertaking the activity in question, but they do not, just by themselves, sufficiently ground the rightness of the deed. In order for the act to be justified as one in which human beings may rightfully engage, it is also necessary that the *activity itself,* considered from the perspective of its content or meaningful intelligibility, be truthfully describable as primarily an act of what Aquinas called a "measured force" countering a force directed against the life that is being imperiled. The act of abortion, in such instances when the death of the fetus is "indirectly voluntary" and is only *one* aspect of an act that in its totality can properly be said to be directed to saving the life of the mother-to-be, is justifiable. But it is critically significant, I believe, to the meaning of human existence as a moral existence, to show that it is justifiable not because of factors extrinsic to the activity itself (e.g., the good that will come about as a result of the deed) but because of the inherent intelligibility of the deed itself as an expression of man's moral being, because of factors intelligently discernible within the activity itself.

In concluding this paper, in which I hope I have articulated the reasons why I believe it wrong directly to destroy fetal life and under what conditions this destruction may rightfully be permitted to happen as a result of one's activities, I want to affirm my conviction that a truly human ethics, one opposed to what can be called an ethic of abortion, must be just as concerned with alleviating the terrible human problems for which abortion is proposed as is the consequentialist ethics that defends abortion—only more so. Too frequently those who decry abortion as inhuman ignore the agonizing personal and social suffering for which it is intended as a remedy. Abortion is not the right way to meet these real human needs, but neither is the refusal to see them and to do something about them.

NOTES

In thinking through the issue of abortion I have found the writings of Paul Ramsey and Germain Grisez particularly helpful. I wish here to express my gratitude to them for the insights that they have given me.

[1] Competent presentations of the official teaching of the Roman Catholic Church on abortion may be found in Germain G. Grisez, *Abortion: The Myths, the Realities and the Arguments* (New York: Corpus, 1970), pp. 165-184 and in Richard A. McCormick, "Past Church Teaching on Abortion," *Proceedings of the Twenty-Third Annual Convention* (Yonkers, N. Y.: Catholic Theological Society of America, 1969), pp. 131-151.

[2] *Acta Apostolicae Sedis* 43 (1951) 838-839.

[3] "The Pastoral Constitution on the Church in the Modern World" *(Gaudium et Spes)*, in *Documents of Vatican II*, edited by Walter A. Abbott (New York: Guild, 1966), par. 27, pp. 226-227.

[4] *Ibid.*, par. 51, pp. 255-256.

[5] *Humanae Vitae*, par. 14; *Ada Apostolicae Sedis* 60 (1968) 490.

[6] *Discorsi e Radio messaoi di sua Santita Pio XII*, 6 (12 November, 1944), 191-192, cited in Grisez, *op. cit.*, pp. 182-183.

[7] John T. Noonan, Jr., "An Almost Absolute Value in History," in *The Morality of Abortion*, edited by John T. Noonan, Jr., (Cambridge, Mass: Harvard University Press, 1970), pp. 1-59.

[8] Charles E. Curran, "Abortion: Law and Morality in Recent Catholic Thought," to appear in *The Jurist* (1973). I am grateful to Professor Curran for allowing me to read his manuscript prior to publication.

[9] Several recent articles have been devoted to a discussion of this principle. Among the more important are the following: Peter Knauer, "The Hermeneutic Function of the Principle of Double Effect," *Natural Law Forum* 12 (1967) 132-162; Cornelius Van der Poel, "The Principle of Double Effect," in *Absolutes in Moral Theology?*, edited by Charles E. Curran (Washington: Corpus, 1968), pp. 186-210; and Germain Grisez, "Toward a Consistent Natural-Law Ethics of Killing," *American Journal of Jurisprudence* (—Natural Law Forum) 15 (1970) 64-96.

[10] Joseph F. Donceel, "Immediate Animation and Delayed Hominization," *Theological Studies* 31.1 (March, 1970) 76-105.

[11] Thomas Wassmer, *Christian Ethics for Today* (Milwaukee: The Bruce Publishing Company, 1969), "The Moral Problem of Abortion," pp. 193-202.

[12] Bruno Ribes, "Recherche philosophique et théologique," in *Avortement et respect de la vie humaine: Colloque du Centre catholique des medecins français* (Paris: Editions du Seuil, 1972), pp. 194-206.

[13] Louis Beirnaert, "L'avortement est-il infanticide?" *Etudes* 337 (1970) 552; cited by Curran in *art. cit.*

[14] Cornelius Van der Poel, *art. cit.*, note 9 and *The Search for Human Values* (New York: Newman, 1971), pp. 39-71.

[15] William Vander Marck, *Toward a Christian Ethic* (New York: Newman, 1967), pp. 48-70.

[16] Bruno Schüller, "Typen ethischer Argumentation in der katholischen Moraltheologie," *Theologie und Philosophie* 45 (1970) 526-550, and "Direkte Tötung — indirekte Tötung," *Theologie und Philosophie* 47 (1972).

[17] Richard A. McCormick, "Notes on Moral Theology," *Theological Studies* 33 (1972), pp. 74-75. It should be noted that in this article McCormick is expressly concerned with summarizing the thought of Bruno Schüller. His summary, however, applies with equal validity to the thought of Van der Poel and Van der Marck.

[18] Bruno Schüller, "What Ethical Principles Are Universally Valid?" *Theology Digest* 19 (1971) 23-28.

[19] Van der Poel, *The Search for Human Values*, p. 57.

[20] See, for instance, Van der Poel, *The Search for Human Values*, pp. 52-53.

[21] Daniel Callahan, *Abortion: Law, Choice and Morality* (New York: Macmillan, 1970). See in particular pp. 388-89, where Callahan seeks to develop "a way of choosing which would allow us to weigh the different values of different human lives in a nonarbitrary way; we would, to be exact, compare these lives on the scale of 'personhood,' a scale more nuanced than that provided by a totally genetic form of humanity."

[22] For an excellent critique of Callahan's book, justly attributing to him uses to which his approach has been put that Callahan did not seemingly want to endorse personally, see Paul Ramsey, "Abortion: A Review Article," *The Thomist* 37 (Jaunary, 1973) 174-210.

[23] Germain G. Grisez, *op. cit.*, note 1, in particular pp. 267-345.

[24] John T. Noonan, Jr., *art. cit.*, note 7.

[25] Robert Joyce and Mary Rosera Joyce, *Let Me Be Born* (Chicago: Franciscan Herald Press, 1971).

[26] Noonan, *art. cit.*, p. 3.

[27] On this matter it is useful to note a passage from Roger L. Shinn in his book *Man: The New Humanism* (Philadelphia: Westminster, 1968). Shinn distinguishes between the *empirical* human and the *normative* human, and writes: "the word 'human' has both an empirical and a normative sense, and the gap between the two is immense. In the empirical sense any thing that men do is human. Human behavior is a mixed bag, containing all that the newspapers report or suppress, all that priests and psychiatrists hear in clerical or secular confessionals, all that people think or do. In this sense humanization is unnecessary. Men are already humanized. . . . In the normative sense, the human is assumed to be good."

[28] In developing the ideas set forth in the preceding two paragraphs I have been immeasurably aided by reflecting on the way in which this ethical tradition has been articulated by Germain G. Grisez. See in particular his *Contraception and the Natural Law* (Milwaukee: The Bruce Publishing Company, 1964), pp. 60-72, his book on abortion (n. 1), pp. 307-321, and his article on

killing (n. 9).

[29] On the question of real goods generating real rights see Mortimer Adler, *The Time of Our Lives* (New York: Holt, Rinehart, and Winston, 1970), pp. 137-156.

[30] Grisez, *Contraception and the Natural Law,* p. 69.

[31] On this whole issue of man as a being of moral or personal worth and as being related to human society not simply as a part but as a whole, see Jacques Maritain, *The Person and the Common Good* (New York: Charles Scribners, 1947), chapter 3.

[32] Here a word about terminology may be useful. *Zygote* refers to the unicellular organism resulting from the fertilization of an egg by a sperm; *embryo* in the strict sense refers to the developing organism from implantation until the end of the sixth or eighth week; *fetus* in the narrow sense refers to the developing organism from the sixth or eighth week of development until the end of the seventh month. In ordinary language both fetus and embryo are used synonymously and are used to refer to the developing being from the time of conception until birth.

[33] Roe V. Wade, X, *The United States Law Week* 41 LW (1-23-73) 4227.

[34] *Ibid.,* X and XI, 4228, 4229.

[35] On this point the perceptive comments of John T. Noonan, Jr., in *The National Catholic Reporter* of February 3, 1973 are pertinent.

[36] Philip Wylie, *The Magic Animal* (New York: Doubleday, 1968), p. 272, a particularly virulent passage filled with invective against the notion of the "sanctity" of human life.

[37] Joseph Fletcher, "New Beginnings of Life," in William Hamilton, editor, *The New Genetics and the Future of Man* (Grand Rapids, Mich.: Eerdmans, 1972), pp. 76-91.

[38] Garrett Hardin, "Abortion — or Compulsory Pregancy?" *Journal of Marriage and the Family* 30 (May, 1968), 250.

[39] Havelock Ellis, *Studies in the Psychology of Sex* (New York, 1924) 6, 607.

[40] Callahan, *op. cit.,* note 21, pp. 378-409. Michael Tooley, "Abortion and Infanticide," *Philosophy and Public Affairs* (Fall, 1972) 37-65.

[41] Grisez, *op. cit.,* note 1, pp. 273-286, 410-423.

[42] C. B. Goodhart, "Reply to Dr. Potts," in *Biology and Ethics,* edited by F. C. Ebling (New York/London: Academic Press, 1969), pp. 101-103. Potts' position is developed in *ibid.,* pp. 74-75.

[43] Ramsey, "Abortion: A Review Article," *loc. cit.,* 182.

[44] Ramsey, "The Morality of Abortion," in *Moral Problems,* edited by James Rachel (New York: Harper & Row, 1971), pp. 4-5. This essay is a revised version of a paper that first appeared in *The Dublin Review* (Spring, 1967) 1-27 and then in *Life or Death: Ethics and Options,* edited by Daniel H. Labby (Seattle, Wash.: University of Washington Press, 1968).

[45] See Joseph Fletcher, "Indicators of Humanhood: A Tentative Profile of Man," in *The Hastings Center Report* 2.5 (November, 1972) 1-4.

[46] Michael Tooley, *art. cit.* (note 40) 44.

[47] See Tooley, *ibid.,* 48, 55.

[48] Mortimer Adler, *The Difference of Man and the Difference It Makes* (New York: Meridan, 1968), pp. 264-265.

[49] Ashley Montagu, in a letter to *The New York Times*, March 3, 1967, in which he rejected the use that some who oppose abortion had put to a statement in his *Life Before Birth* (New York: Signet, 1965) in which he had stated that life began at conception.

[50] See the way Fletcher develops his position in his "Indicators of Humanhood," *loc. cit.*, note 45.

[51] Gerald Leach, *The Biocrats* (Baltimore: Penguin, 1972), p. 104 f.

[52] Tooley, *loc. cit.*, note 40.

[53] Ralph Potter, "The Abortion Debate," in *The Religious Situation 1968*, edited by Donald Culter (Boston: Beacon, 1968), p. 157.

[54] My basic point is that *being* a human being *does* make a significant moral difference because the difference between man and other animals demands, for its sufficient explanation, the presence within man's makeup, that is, within his being, of an element not found at all in other animals, namely spirit. I believe that the most coherent and logically structured argument in defense of this position is that developed by Adler in his *The Difference of Man and the Difference It Makes.*

[55] Ramsey, "Abortion: A Review Article," *loc. cit.*, p. 211.

[56] Grisez, *Abortion: The Myths, the Realities and the Arguments*, p. 321 ff.

[57] Van der Poel, *The Search for Human Values*, p. 56.

[58] *Van der Marck, Toward a Christian Ethic*, pp. 60-69.

[59] On this see the perceptive work by Herbert McCabe, *What Is Ethics All About?* (Washington: Corpus, 1969), in particular pp. 90-94.

[60] On willing the means as well as the needs see, among other sources, Thomas Aquinas, *Summa Theologica*, I-II, 6-10.

[61] Ramsey, "The Morality of Abortion," in Rachels, *op. cit.*, pp. 16-17.

[62] Eric D'Arcy, *Human Acts: An Essay on Their Moral Evaluation* (Oxford: Oxford University Press, 1963), p. 25. See Ramsey's expansion of D'Arcy's ideas in his Deeds and Rules in Christian Ethics (New York: Charles Scribner's, 1967), pp. 192-200.

[63] D'Arcy, *op. cit.*, p. 18.

[64] Callahan, *op. cit.*, p. 429.

[65] Ramsey, "Abortion: A Review Article," *loc. cit.*, 208.

[66] Grisez, *Abortion: The Myths, The Realities, and The Arguments*, p. 329.

[67] Philippa Foot, "Abortion and the Doctrine of the Double Effect," in Rachels, ed. *Moral Problems*, p. 29.

[68] Jonathan Bennett, "Whatever the Consequences," in Rachels, *op. cit.*, p. 43.

[69] Grisez, in reinterpreting the principle of double effect, insists that the evil caused through our actions must be *one* aspect of an act that itself brings about good. One of his tests for determining whether an act *is* in fact of this kind is whether any other human act, one's own or another, need intervene or could intervene to bring about the good effect (see his *Abortion* ..., p. 333). Ramsey (in "Abortion: A Review Article," 215 f) believes that this is too stringent a

requirement and offers cases that he thinks justifiable but that he believes could not be justified if this requirement is demanded. For Ramsey the "crucial test" is not . . . whether the death-dealing act may precede the life-saving component of the same human action . . . but whether in (justifiably) doing the deadly deed, the target is upon that life or upon what it is doing to another life" (221). I would like to note here that I think Ramsey, in his article (224-226) erroneously concludes that Grisez's position on abortion, because of Grisez's way of describing the nature of "indirect intent", is, quite paradoxically, similar to that of Judith Thompson in her "Defense of Abortion" in *Philosophy and Public Policy* (Fall, 1971) 47-66. My reasons for saying this is that I think Ramsey fails to pay serious enough attention to Grisez's insistence that an abortion properly described as "indirect" might nevertheless be an immoral act.

[70]"The Morality of Abortion," in Rachels, op. cit., pp. 3-27. As noted in note 44 this article originally appeared in *The Dublin Review* in 1967, was revised for Labby's 1968 anthology, and revised again for Rachels' 1971 anthology. Ramsey himself notes, in this "Abortion: A Review Article" (219) that Richard A. McCormick in the article cited in our note 1, had argued that Ramsey's analysis of what he had termed *direct* abortion "could, if correct, be readily brought under the meaning of the indirectly voluntary." MrCormick, I believe, is correct in his appraisal and the justic of his appraisal is effectively acknowledged by Ramsey in his most recent essay on the subject ("Abortion: A Review Article") particularly by his agreement with Grisez that any taking of the life of one human being by another must, if it is to be justifiable, be indirect (220).

[72]Ramsey, "The Morality of Abortion," in Rachels, *op. cit.*, pp. 20-21.

[73]On this see Thomas Aquinas, *Summa Theologica,* II-II, 164, 7, and the comment on this by Grisez in his "Toward a Consistent Natural-Law Ethics of Killing," *loc. cit.,* note 9. It should be noted that both Grisez and Ramsey appeal to this article in developing their positions.

HARMON L. SMITH

Abortion —
The Theological Tradition

It is probably the case that more people know better what is meant by "abortion" than what is signified by "the theological tradition"— a commentary in itself on our life and times! So an introductory comment about the title of this essay may be appropriate.

At one time in the history of the West it would have been self-evident that "the theological tradition" meant "the Christian tradition"; more recently, when ecumenism and inter-religious charity were flowering and emphasis was upon commonality rather than difference, "the theological tradition" meant "the Judaeo-Christian tradition." Now, amid the current cultural confusion about religion in general and theology in particular, "the theological tradition" might mean virtually anything from trendy theologies of leisure or liberation to religious traditions which antedate both Judaism and Christianity.

The theological tradition with which we are concerned here is embraced by the term "Judaeo-Christian" principally because, within the cultural matrix of the United States, we are *de facto* Judaeo-Christian. To say this is not to suggest, of course, that all of us affirm the same doctrines or assent to the same creeds or practice the same morals; the point is rather that, whatever our professed religious and theological commitments and however we formulate and express them privately, the cultural condition within which we elaborate and act on moral issues posits a common core of values and a particular view of man and the world which can be called Judaeo-Christian.

Rabbi Irwin Blank is formally correct in asserting that since the third century "Christianity is not a special case of Judaism," that where "specific (Jewish and Christian) ethical responses coincide, they are coincidental," and that the conceptual frameworks of Judaism and Christianity are no longer as contiguous as they once were.[1] Nevertheless, Will Herberg convincingly demonstrated[2] that good Americans understand themselves as Protestant, Catholic, or Jew; and even the prominence attributed to mystical sects among American youth in recent years has not (yet!) invalidated Herberg's fundamental thesis. Most Americans still consider Protestantism, Catholicism, and Judaism to be the acceptable varieties of what President Eisenhower once called the "basic expressions of Americanism." The 1973 inaugural of President Nixon only confirmed as current this long-standing function of religion in American life when prayers by a Baptist pastor, a Jewish rabbi, an Orthodox archbishop, and a Roman Catholic cardinal punctuated the beginning, middle, and conclusion of the inauguration.

Thus, there is a sense in which what is the case with us already commits us to a discussion of what ought to be with us; and our decisions and choices are ineluctably colored by that fact of our cultural and intellectual (as well as religious) history. Our task here is therefore to try to speak intelligently about a theological tradition which is deeply embedded in Judaism and Christianity and yet so thoroughly acculturated as "the American way of life" that it often bears little resemblance to either. A brief look at where we have come from will help us to see where we are and where we appear to be going.

The notion of "soul" is present in both Judaism (*n'shamah* or *ruhi*) and Christianity (*anima*), and from early periods of their formation; but the meaning of the word varies in both concept and application. Rabbi David Feldman has examined the question of the time of ensoulment and cited the Talmud record of a conversation between the Roman Emperor Antoninus and the compiler of the Mishnah, who is called simply "Rabbi":

> Antoninus said to Rabbi: "From when is the soul *(n'shamah)* endowed in man, from the time of conception or from the time of [the embryo's] formation?" Rabbi replied: "From the time of formation." The emperor demurred: "Can meat remain three days without salt and not putrefy? You must concede that the soul enters at conception." Rabbi [later]

said, "Antoninus taught me this, and Scripture supports him, as it is said (Job 10:12): 'and Thy visitation hath preserved my spirit *(ruhi).*' "[3]

In a parallel Midrashic version of this dialogue, Rabbi had earlier placed ensoulment at the time of birth; but this apparent contradiction of opinion is not unique in the history of theology, and particularly when there is no specific revelation which directly addresses the issue in question. As we will see when the evolution of Roman Catholic teaching is described, both the time of ensoulment and the nature of that soul are highly speculative and, as the rabbinic tradition puts it, among the "secrets of God." These questions, nevertheless, are not irrelevant or inconsequential because they are speculative. Indeed, the converse is more often the case: the absence of a divinely given categorical answer tends to emphasize the seriousness of the question.

Agnosticism regarding the status of fetal life, and the protections and prohibitions which would derive to it from ensoulment, thus evolved in the Jewish tradition to locate the question of abortion in earthly courts which are concerned with human problems. The laws which govern abortion hold that the fetus has no "juridical personality" of its own because it is deemed to be a "part of its mother" and not an independent human entity.[4] But the function of these laws appears to be less directed toward abortion *per se* than toward defining ownership for torts.[5] Thus Exodus 21:22 provides that a pregnant woman is entitled to monetary compensation if she is assaulted and miscarries, and that her assailants be fined for this damage. Then, continuing the logic of not attributing "juridical personality" to the fetus, Exodus 21:23-25 provides the well-known *lex talionis* for any harm that should be done the woman!

The sum of the matter (though there are many more subtleties and nuances than there is space here to investigate) is, as Rabbi Immanuel Jakobovits shows, that according to both the Talmud and subsequent rabbinic interpretation,

> The point at which human life commences to be inviolable and of equal value to that of any adult person is . . . distinctly fixed at the moment when the greater part of the body — or, according to some versions, the head — has emerged from the birth canal.[6]

Thus, the fetus in the womb is not a person and it only becomes a person when it enters the world at birth. Feticide is therefore neither homicide nor infanticide.

It would be a serious mistake, however, as it would grossly misrepresent Jewish sensibilities toward nascent life, to suppose that fetal life is thus liable to assault without any restraint or that Jewish women might lawfully claim abortion "on demand." Indeed, since Maimonides (12th c.), Responsa have tended to affirm that feticide, while not forbidden, is limited in its permissibility to life-threatening situations, i.e., situations which threaten maternal life up to the moment of birth or situations which threaten both maternal and fetal life up to and even after the moment of birth. These situations were chiefly applicable to the terminal stages of pregnancy and ordinarily embryotomy or craniotomy were employed for relief; and abortion at earlier stages was probably not contemplated in either Mishnaic law or Maimonides' Code, since rabbinic attitudes toward abortion at prior times in the gestating process remained to be formulated. The sum of the matter varies somewhat among Conservative and Reform and Orthodox groups. R. Feldman, speaking for the former, states that abortion is not permitted without reason and that reasons are assessed in accordance with the gravity of the situation:

> Abortion . . . for ephemeral pain or for capricious reasons is clearly not intended here; in such cases the legal "warrants" and the extra-legal attitudes of reverence for life play their part. They may even save a woman from herself, so to speak, from sacrificing ultimate blessing to the apprehensions of the moment . . . Abortion for less than a serious reason can be a serious mistake, and even the permissive Responsa are weighted with a solemn awareness of the potential life involved. Yet "the judge can rule only on the evidence before his eyes" — the situation of the woman before him.[7]

The Orthodox position, as stated by R. Jakobovits, is rather more rigorous in its insistence that abortion is to be sanctioned only to save the life and/or health, both psychic and somatic, of the woman. But excluded from permissible cases, in order to deter sin and guarantee the right to birth, are pregnancies which result from incest or adultery or rape.[8]

Initial Christian objection to abortion was grounded in speculation about the soul—its origin, existence in time, and ultimate destiny; and the roots of Christian reflection are therefore better to be found in

Pythagorean Greek conjecture than in either Roman or Hebrew law.[9] Despite developed notions about the soul as an eternal and indestructible part of human being, both Plato and Aristotle sanctioned (and, on occasion, encouraged) abortion; so perhaps it was the Christian doctrine of divine sovereignty, which embraced the beginning and continuation and ending of creation as God's work, that eventually swung the balance in the Christian West. Tracing the development of Christian teaching may, certainly in its earlier stages, appear to be more grope than grasp; but at least three different theories emerge historically to account for the classical Roman Catholic distinction between *foetus animatus* and *foetus inanimatus*.

The third-century Church Father, Tertullian, represents the view called Traducianism or Generationism which holds that the soul (*anima*) comes into existence with the body in and through generation by parents, as a biological transmission from the seed of Adam.[10] A second view, called Creationism, was held by Tertullian's contemporary, Clement of Alexandria. The creationist theory was that the soul was immediately and directly created by God at the moment of each new conception.[11] In the fifth century, Augustine of Hippo introduced the distinction (based on the Septuagint expansion of Ex. 21:22-23) or "formed" (*animatus*) and "unformed" (*inanimatus*) fetal life, and taught that no soul was present in the fetus until the moment of "quickening" (or the moment the mother-to-be initially detects the stirrings of life in her womb). The reasons for this were twofold: (1) the Traducianist and Creationist arguments are to be avoided as theological traps because the Scriptures offer no conclusive proof that the soul is directly created by God and, moreover, the stain of original sin upon the soul should make one cautious about attributing immediate and direct creation of the soul (including that blot upon it!) to God; (2) on the other side, Augustine's controversy with the Pelagians (who taught an early version of the "Yankee ethic" or what is sometimes called "bootstrap theology") made him wary of supposing that the soul comes by only natural generation.[12]

Because of the uncertainties surrounding ensoulment, there was no definitive position generally accepted by Christians until the late Middle Ages; but a series of important teachings were being propounded, the cumulative weight of which would settle the question (at least for Roman Catholics). In the thirteenth century St. Thomas, probably influenced by interpretive clues from the Mediterranean world as well as Christian speculators, concluded that the soul is not generated with or at conception but that it is created at the same time that it is "infused" into the body. He reckoned further that this "infusion" occurred at about the fortieth day post-conception in the male embryo and at about the eightieth day post-conception in the female embryo.[13]

At the direction of the Council of Trent (1545-63), the Roman Catechism (1566) was prepared in order to address the purposes of marriage. Among its teachings (2.7.13) was an emphatic denunciation of abortion:

> ... it is a most grave crime for those joined in matrimony to use medicines to impede the conceptus or to abort birth: this impious conspiracy in murders must be extirpated.

Only twenty-two years later, Sixtus V issued his bull *Effraenatam*, which invoked all the penalties of both canon and secular law against persons producing an abortion. Within a year of Sixtus' death (1590), his successor, Gregory XIV, repealed all the penalties of *Effraenatam except* those which applied to the abortion of an ensouled, forty-day-old embryo. And so it went. The terminus of this long and sometimes bitter debate began to appear in the 1679 decree, *Errores doctrinae moralix laxioris,* of Innocent XI. The substance of that decree, for our purposes, was three-fold: it held (1) that it is illicit to induce abortion before animation in order to spare a pregnant girl death or shame, (2) that it is erroneous doctrine that every fetus lacks a rational soul so long as it is confined to the womb and only begins to have a soul at the time it is born, and (3) that it is prohibited to hold any longer "that no homicide is committed in any abortion."[14] The function of Innocent's decree was to abate the ensoulment controversy by mooting the question of the time of animation and, further, to declare that abortion at any point in the gestating process is equated with homicide.

This necessarily brief and highly selective excursus demonstrates that Christians possess no divine revelation on this subject. Still, Roman Catholicism has come to a developed position on abortion which, as we have seen, resolves theoretical uncertainty on so important a matter into practical certainty: practically we should act *as if* we knew that soul is present from the moment of conception.[15] The evolution of this view eventually terminated in Pius XI's encyclical *Casti Connubii* (1930), which maintained the inviolability of fetal life on the ground that it is "equally sacred" with maternal life and which further described so-called medical and therapeutic indications for abortion as excusing "the direct murder of the innocent."

It is, of course, in view of these assumptions that the official teachings of the Roman Catholic Church have developed. Thus, Fr. Charles McFadden puts the Roman Catholic position succinctly: "Direct and voluntary abortion is a moral offence of the gravest nature. . . . Such an action is essentially murder."[16] Nevertheless there are moral theologians who question the rigidity of the Church's formal position and criticize particularly the conventional distinctions between "direct" and "indirect" actions.[17] Under this rubric a hysterectomy may be performed for malignant ovarian tumor even when a pregnant uterus is involved, but an abortion may not be performed when the best available medical information indicates that a woman cannot bring her pregnancy to term in a live birth.

Among those who challenge this way of resolving a conflict situation is Fr. Charles Curran, who argues that neither the physical structure of an action nor the physical effect of an action (nor, for that matter, both of these together) adequately takes account of the complex circumstances which sometimes surround the option to abort. There is no suggestion in Curran's argument that embryonic or fetal life is to be shown less respect or treated with less value than it enjoys in the more traditional view. He does maintain, however, that an "assisted abortion" (as e.g., in the second situation above) illustrates "the impossibility of establishing an absolute moral norm based on the physical description of the action considered only in itself. . . ."[18]

The point of this brief excursus is only to point out that Roman Catholic moral teaching is not the monolithic structure many think it to be, that not only is there religious pluralism but even intra-religious pluralism! Nowhere is that assessment of the religious situation truer than in Protestantism; and we turn now to a very brief (and hence unavoidably superficial) summary of Protestant views.

Among Protestant denominational statements there is a rather wide diversity of opinion, which we will simply report here without interpretation or comment. The 182nd General Assembly of the United Presbyterian Church, USA, received and directed the church to study a statement which affirms that:

... abortion should be taken out of the realm of law altogether and be made a matter of careful ethical decision of a woman, her physician and her pastor or other counselor ... we do not think that abortion should be relied upon as a means of limiting family size. Contraceptive procedures are more desirable ... but when ... contraception fails and an unwanted pregnancy is established, we do not think it either compassionate or just to insist that available help be withheld.[19]

The Lutheran Church in America policy statement asserts that:

Since the fetus is the organic beginning of human life, the termination of its development is always a serious matter. Nevertheless, a qualitative distinction must be made between its claims and the rights of a responsible person made in God's image who is in living relationship with God and with other human beings ... On the basis of the evangelical ethic, a woman or couple may decide responsibly to seek an abortion.[20]

The United Church of Christ adopted a statement in 1971 which declares that:

A responsible position concerning abortion should be based on a consideration of the rights of the individual woman, her potential child, her family and society, as well as the rights of the fetus. ... The General Synod calls upon the churches ... and their members to involve themselves extensively in programs which would support the repeal of overly restrictive abortion legislation and to expand their ministries of counsel and concern to all women who have problems related to unwanted pregnancies.[21]

The United Methodist Church, at its General Conference in 1972, adopted the position that:

When an unaccepted pregancy occurs, a family, and most of all the pregnant woman, is confronted with the need to make a difficult decision. We believe that continuation of a pregnancy endangering the life of the mother *(sic!)* is not a moral necessity. In such case, we believe the path of mature Christian judgment may indicate the advisability of abortion. Good social policy, it seems to us, calls for the removal of abortion from the criminal codes, so that women in counsel with husbands, doctors, and pastors, are free to make their own responsible decisions concerning the personal and moral questions surrounding the issue of abortion.[22]

This is, I think, a fairly representative though certainly not exhaustive sampling of official Protestant denominational pronouncements. The churches tend generally to be permissive toward abortion while varying somewhat with respect to both the predicates and limits of that permissiveness.

Protestant theologians, on the other hand, exhibit a somewhat wider and more substantial diversity of opinion than do church pronouncements. Some hold a view of nascent human species life which closely approximates the classical Roman Catholic position; others describe an embryo as "mere tissue" or, in a rather extreme formulation, as "a wart on the womb"; and still others try to wed both modern biology and Biblical theism by holding in tension simultaneous awareness of life-against-life conflict and God's value for all human species life. Protestant views on abortion therefore range from "never" to "whenever pregnancy is unwanted" to "sometimes."[23]

Having surveyed (much too cursorily!) several centuries of moral opinion-making, we will conclude with a look at where we are and where it appears that we are headed. In 1959 the American Law Institute put forward suggestions for uniform state abortion statutes in its Model Penal Code and, for over a decade, state legislatures undertook to revise their abortion laws. Prior to this time, most states provided that abortion was lawful if necessary to save the life (and sometimes "health") of a pregnant woman. During the 1960's, many states revised their statutes to provide for the ALI proposals; that is, that abortion may be lawful when indicated by (1) substantial risk that continuation of the pregnancy would gravely impair the physical or mental health of the woman, (2) substantial risk that the pregnancy would issue in a child who was born with grave physical or mental defects, or (3) pregnancy which was the result of legally established rape or incest.[24] Three states (Alaska, Hawaii, and New York) and the District of Columbia adopted statutes which permitted abortion "on request," leaving the question of the decision to the pregnant woman and a physician *without* any statutory restraints such as the ones specified in the ALI proposal.

In January, 1973, the United States Supreme Court, in response to cases from Georgia and Texas, overruled all state laws which prohibit or restrict a woman's right to obtain an abortion during the first trimester of pregnancy. That decision also provided that "from and after this point (i.e., the end of the first trimester), a state may regulate the abortion procedure to the extent that the regulation reasonably relates to the preservation and protection of maternal health." The Court held, moreover, that "if the state is interested in protecting fetal life after viability (which the Court defined as the last 10 weeks of pregnancy), it may go so far as to proscribe abortion during that period except when it is necessary to preserve the life or health of the mother." That appears to be, just now, where we are as a society.

The Court's decision is not, of course, without broad social and ethical implications, and certain private and public costs will almost certainly be entailed in gaining the benefits it alleges to provide. One important question before us is whether these benefits are proportional to the costs. Some of my lawyer-friends tell me, for example, that the majority opinion that "the unborn have never been recognized in the law as persons in the whole sense" is contradictory of a distinct trend in recent years in property, criminal, and tort law, a trend which regards the fetus as a human being from the time of conception and accords the fetus rights consistent with this recognition.[25]

Some of us wonder, in addition, what it means for the Court to guarantee a "right" without guaranteeing also the securing of that "right." In this case, a woman's "right" to obtain an abortion is not to be prohibited or restricted prior to the last ten weeks of pregnancy; but is this only a formal (and therefore possibly hollow) "right" if the woman is dependent upon physicians who reserve their own "right" either conscientiously to refuse or to arbitrate the *woman's* right on *medical* grounds? Is the present situation with women somewhat analogous with the circumstance of black people after the time of the Emancipation Proclamation but before civil rights legislation?

It deserves asking, moreover, whether there are also other important social and ethical implications in this decision—for marriage relationships (when one partner is the single possessor of unilateral power in a situation in which both partners presumably have a serious interest), or for respect for life (when abortion functions in the popular mind to retard contraceptive information and distribution), or for the socialization of citizens (when the pedagogy of the law leads many to suppose that because an action is legal it must also be right)? These are not merely rhetorical questions since, if they are answered affirmatively, they bid well to alter a significant aspect of American life, and one that far exceeds (certainly on the face of it) the limits of the abortion controversy alone.

Now this is not the whole story, of course; but it does indicate in

Abortion—The Theological Tradition

some ways where we *are* just now as a society. Where we are *headed* appears to be an extension of where we are; at the very least, it does not seem likely at present that we will return, in the foreseeable future, to a time of stringent prohibition against abortion.

Indeed, the promise of prostaglandins[26] together with the safer development of so-called "morning-after" pills,[27] suggests that we may soon have available abortifacient devices which will recast, in subtle and tedious ways, the moral aspects of abortion. Prostaglandins, for example, function as an abortifacient; but, owing to the manner of administration and effect, women who receive prostaglandins will never *know* whether they aborted during the effective period of this medication or whether they only failed to achieve fertilization. The post-coital abortifacients, like DES, function in much the same way. Will moral awareness, which is requisite to any meaningful responsibility, be possible under circumstances like this, when one does not know whether an action has been accomplished but only that it was intended? Will these medications blunt further our already sluggish moral sensibilities about abortion?

The moral problem with abortion, as with any other conflict of life-against-life, is chiefly the question of how to balance rights—in this case, the rights of the unborn against the rights of a woman. That conflict has long been recognized in the theological tradition, but in ways which do not appear to speak compellingly to the present situation. Indeed the tendency, in our recent past, has been to deny that there is any genuine conflict—by describing abortion as a "procedure" (which suggests that it is only a technical matter) or as "therapeutic" (which suggests that the fetus is a disease and acknowledges benefit to a woman without admitting that the minimal good cure is a very dead fetus) or as "a woman's right to control her body" (which nullifies in principle all talk about the sanctity of the life of the unborn). To point out these ways in which rhetoric shields behavior is only to remind us that we seem to want somehow to deny what happens in every abortion—and that is that a fetus is killed when a valuing choice is acted on in the face of apparently irreconcilable conflict.

Acknowledging that primary fact does not (to my mind!) overcome all the reasons for this action which are put forward by advocates of abortion on request. On the other hand, acknowledging that primary fact should invest all the other reasons with a gravity and solemnity that they otherwise appear to want. We need not brutalize our moral sensibilities in order to act responsibly in the face of conflict. So, one way to frame the tradition in language appropriate to the contemporary situation might be this: abortion, like all killing of our species life, is wrong because it presumes a dominion over our species life which we have not been given; but sometimes, within the limits of finite choice and apparently irreconcilable conflict between lives, abortion is preferable to the conditions which would prevail in the absence of abortion. On such an understanding, abortion is not murder but it is killing. And to understand that, with all the tragedy and pain and relief and benefit that attends it, may yet enable us to make hard moral choices like this without sacrificing our own essential humanity. Only at the most serious risk to the noblest sentiments which inform our life together could killing ever be uncritically argued as a licit means to any good end.

The companion acknowledgment to "a fetus is killed" is that this action results from a valuing choice in the fact of apparently irreconcilable conflict. This is the awareness that one's moral vision has been challenged—by whatever it is that prompts one to call this pregnancy a "problem pregnancy"—and that the option for *abortion* is expressive of an affective choice.

There is nothing fundamentally new about this awareness, especially for those of us in the Christian tradition, since from St. Augustine onwards we have known that choices—for all their cognitive and discursive supports—are pre-eminently a function of will or affection. Our desiring, feeling, wanting, and loving may be largely inarticulate —and to the extent that this is so, a way of knowing that is very different from perception of objective data which everyone can (more or less) affirm. But they are no less real for all that; and to be satisfied about a choice entails not only—and maybe not even most importantly—reasons based on information, but also beliefs and sentiments which reside deeply within us. It is, in other words, tacit or personal rather than propositional knowledge.

And since none of us is free, however much we try to be, from the tendency to place reason in the service of value, we would probably do well simply to acknowledge that this is how it is with us. It is proper to ask people to give reasons for doing what they do—and that is what the elaborate talk about "indications" for abortion is all about—but it is also proper to appreciate and affirm the noncognitive valuing which underlies (and sometimes gives articulate expression to) choice-making.

There is, then, a very real and profound sense in which—when we are honest with ourselves—we do what we love; and it is the fundamental honesty which that awareness requires that the theological tradition has long affirmed. *Conscientia est consequentia;* conscience is always to be obeyed.

The present situation is full of both peril and promise. The peril is that the advocacy of limited options for problem pregnancy, and the rhetoric which shields us from the full range of human reason and sentiment, may further erode our best moral sensibilities. The promise is that men and women—but in this case, pre-eminently women— may assume more fully the humane accountabilities, both to themselves and the larger society, for discrete choices which prohibitory legislation did not allow. That circumstance, it seems to me, allows the moral struggle to be a real struggle and not merely a charade.

NOTES

[1] Irwin M. Blank, "Is There a Common Judaeo-Christian Ethical Tradition?" *Judaism and Ethics,* ed. Daniel J. Silver (Cleveland: KTAV Publishing House, Inc., 1970), p. 108.

[2] Will Herberg, *Protestant-Catholic-Jew* (Garden City: Doubleday, 1955).

[3] David M. Feldman, *Birth Control in Jewish Law* (New York: New York University Press, 1968), p. 271. Cf. *Tal. Bab. Sanhedrin* 9 1b.

[4] *Ibid.,* p. 253. The phrase from the Talmud is *ubar yerekh imo* ("the fetus is the thigh of its mother"), *Tal. Bab. Hulin* 58a. Its Latin counterpart, *pars viscerum matris,* reflects a similar principle in Roman jurisprudence.

[5] At law, torts covers a wrongful act of injury or damage for which a civil action can be brought.

[6] Immanuel Jakobovits, *Jewish Medical Ethics* (New York: Bloch Publishing Company, 1962), p. 184.

[7] Feldman, *op. cit.,* p. 294. Cf., for Reform Judaism, Fred Rosner, *Modern Medicine and Jewish Law* (New York: Yeshiva University Press, 1972).

[8] Immanuel Jakobovits, "Jewish Views on Abortion," *Abortion and the Law,* ed., David T. Smith (Cleveland: Western Reserve University, 1967), ch. 6.

[9] For a more detailed description and analysis of the evolution of Christian teaching, see my *Ethics and the New Medicine* (Nashville: Abington, 1970), ch. 1.

[10] Tertullian, "De Anima," 27, in J.-P. Migne, ed., *Patrologiae Cursus Completus,* Series Latina (Parisii: Apud Garnier Fratres, 1879), II, 694.

[11] Clement of Alexandria, "Stromata," IV, 6. Alexander Roberts and James Donaldson (eds.), *The Ante-Nicene Fathers* (Grand Rapids: Wm. B. Eerdmans, 1951), II, 413-16.

[12] Augustine, *Questiones in Exodum*, 80 (re. *embryo formatus* and *embryo informatus*); *"De Anima et ejus Origine,"* in Philip Schaff, ed., *A Select Library of the Nicene and Post-Nicene Fathers of the Christian Church* (Grand Rapids: Wm. B. Eerdmans, 1956), V, 315-71; and *"Ad. Optat."* 190, al. 157, in Migne, *Patrologiae Cursus Completus*, Series Latina, XXXIII, 861.

[13] Thomas Aquinas, *Summa Theologica*, trans. Fathers of the English Dominican Province (New York: Benziger Brothers, 1947), Part 1, q. 118, arts. 1-3. See also *De animalibus historiae*, 7, 3, or *De generatione animalium*.

[14] Henricus Denzinger, *Enchiridion Symbolorum: Definitionum et Declarationum de Rebus Fidei et Morum* (32nd ed. rev.; Freiburg im Breisgau: Verlag Herder KG, 1963), p. 461.

[15] I have not treated Orthodox teaching here because of the limits imposed upon this essay. Moreover, although Orthodox theologians have been less preoccupied with this question than their Roman Catholic counterparts, both share the same conclusion. This is not inconsequential when the number of adherents to these respective communions is considered: in North America there are 52 million Roman Catholics and 3.2 million Eastern and Orthodox Christians (together with 77 million Protestants, including Anglicans); in the world there are 494 million Roman Catholics and 97 million Eastern and Orthodox Christians (together with 264 million Protestants, including Anglicans).

[16] Charles J. McFadden, *Medical Ethics* (5th ed. rev.; Philadelphia: F. A. Davis Co., 1961), p. 132. Cf. Fr. Eberhard Welty, *A Handbook of Christian Social Ethics* (Freiburg: Herder & Herder, 1953), II, p. 123: "At the moment when conception occurs in the mother's womb, God infuses the soul and human life begins. . . . To kill this helpless creature with full knowledge and free consent is to commit murder. This argument admits of no exception."

[17] "Direct abortion is the performance of an act, the primary and natural effect of which is to expel a nonviable fetus from its mother's womb." (John McCarthy, *Problems in Theology II: The Commandments* [Westminster, Md.: Newman Press, 1960], p. 160). Indirect abortion, on the other hand, is permitted under the rule (or principle) of double-effect: an action which has two results, one of which is good and intended and the other of which is evil and unintended but unavoidable, is licit if (a) the action by itself and independently of its effects is not morally evil, (b) the evil effect is not the means of producing the good effect, (c) the evil effect is genuinely *un*intended and merely tolerated, and (d) there is a proportionate reason for the action despite its evil consequences.

[18] Charles E. Curran, *Contemporary Problems in Moral Theology* (Notre Dame, Ind.: Fides Publishers, Inc., 1970), pp. 143-5. See also Curran's *A New Look at Christian Morality* (Notre Dame, Ind.: Fides, 1968), esp. pp. 237-42, and his *Catholic Moral Theology in Dialogue* (Notre Dame, Ind.: Fides, 1972), pp. 256-9.

[19] Richard Unsworth, *Sexuality and the Human Community*, available from 510 Witherspoon Bldg., Philadelphia, Pa., 191-7. 1970.

[20] Cedric W. Tilberg, ed., *Sex, Marriage, and Family: A Contemporary*

Christian Perspective, available from the Board of Social Ministry, Lutheran Church in America, 231 Madison Avenue, New York, N. Y., 10016. 1970.

[21]"A Proposal for Action: Toward Freedom of Choice in the Area of Abortion," available from the Council for Christian Social Action, 289 Park Avenue South, New York, N. Y., 10010. 1971.

[22]"Responsible Parenthood," available from the Service Department, Board of Church and Society, 100 Maryland Ave., N. E., Washington, D. C. 20002.

[23] The limits of this essay do not permit more extensive treatment of the varieties of reflection by Protestant theologians and ethicists, but a documented review of the principal literature may be found in my *Ethics and the New Medicine, op. cit.,* ch. 1.

[24]*Model Penal Code,* Section 230.3 (2), (3). Proposed Official Draft, 1962.

[25]C.f. W. Prosser, *Handbook of the Law of Torts,* (3rd ed.; St. Paul: West Publishing Co., 1964), Section 56; and D. A. Louisell, "Abortion, the Practice of Medicine and the Due Process of Law," *UCLA Law Review* (1969), 16:223; and North Carolina General Statutes 41-5.

[26]A family of 20-carbon carboxylic acids which stimulates uterine contraction and induces regression of the corpus luteum of the ovary, both of which tend to inhibit or prevent implantation of a fertilized ovum in the endometrium.

[27]The most prominent of these currently is diethylstilbestrol (DES), a synthetic estrogen, which apparently prevents pregnancy by blocking implantation.

ROBERT E. GAHRINGER

Observations on the Categorical Proscription of Abortion

When the late Pope John was dying of cancer, medical treatment was used to prolong his life beyond what would have been its natural end. If we can judge from news accounts, he suffered intensely during that time.[1] This apparently unnecessary suffering was inflicted on him as a moral duty and by the application of a principle that one ought not to take by either commission or omission the life of an innocent human being.

It should be obvious that in Pope John's case moral respect and human compassion were ill served by ethical scrupulousness. One does not respect a man when one compels him to suffer virtually unendurable pain needlessly. But still we cannot deny the validity of the principle prohibiting the taking of innocent human life. The fault must lie in its interpretation and application.

At the extreme other end of life we find that the same principle can yield an equally inhumane result when used to prohibit abortion unconditionally. This is the position summarized in the basic slogan of anti-abortion literature: *abortion is murder*. Undoubtedly Pope John's doctors also regarded any refusal to prolong life to the limits of one's capacity as murder.

That there are inhumane consequences of the unconditional application of the principle proscribing abortion is usually concealed by the type of case discussed—predicaments where the mother will not survive childbirth, unwed mothers, oversized families, etc. and by hopeful anticipations of new institutions to care for unwanted and deformed children. Mention is sometimes made of the spiritual values associated with the care of these unfortunates: many of the saints achieved their holiness in caring for the homeless and destitute. But the suffering and depravity remain, and the indisputable spiritual advantage of caring for those in need can hardly compensate for the misery of those who need care and cannot find it.

One can observe the facts about the insufficiency of institutions for the care of normal unadopted children. Where these institutions are most needed in the deprived countries of the world, they often do not exist. And in the most affluent countries, where they do exist they are often far less in quality than they ought to be, a failing that may not be merely a matter of resources, but may be traceable to an essential function of the family[2] which the institutions cannot serve.

The situation is far worse with respect to the abnormal unadoptable child. Very few deaf and blind children can have the advantages of a devoted nurse such as Helen Keller had. There are not many with that talent, and of these, few can give themselves as completely as she did. Moreover, institutions for the physically and emotionally impaired are expensive to maintain and thus bound to be in short supply. It is, of course, possible that such professional people and institutions could exist, but it is at the very best no more than a merely "logical" possibility, amounting to a virtual impossibility where the standard of living is minimal and population increasing rapidly.

There is, however, another kind of case, seldom mentioned, where remedial institutions cannot be provided, regardless of talent and resources. This is the case where a child is born to an unwanting mother who will often seek an abortion when she first discovers her pregnancy but whose deep emotional problem prevents her from admitting that she does not want her child once it is born and who will not give it up for adoption, even imagining herself to be an ideal mother while in effect destroying her hated child psychologically. The damage done in these cases can be extraordinary and the suffering intense. It can be transmitted to future generations, for such mothers were often themselves unwanted and mistreated as children. Lee Harvey Oswald[3] was an unwanted child, as were Charles Manson, James Earl Ray and Jack Ruby. And so also are countless psychotic cripples who daily injure themselves and everyone else with whom they are intimately associated. Yet in a free society there can be no institution sufficient to take these children from their mothers, unless all children be taken. For it is impossible to identify by any simple test the unwanting parent who will damage her (or his) child psychologically. Indeed, it is often impossible to take a child from a parent who physically mutilates or tortures it, before irremediable damage has been done. Many of these suffering unfortunates might never have come into the world had an option been allowed the mother to abort her child in the early stages of pregnancy. The categorical proscription of abortion would prevent such an option.

Plainly, fewer cases of these various types would occur were people universally restrained by constant attention to the significance and possibility of procreation, or were they in possession of a reliable contraceptive technique and willing to use it, or were science able to prevent and cure physical and psychological abnormalities. But human nature and science both fall far short of the ideal, and situations do in fact occur where early abortions alone could prevent debilitating and unrelievable suffering. The indifference of those who would proscribe abortion categorically to the occasions of pointless and unrelievable suffering suggests an indifference to the quality of life maintained that poorly comports with their claims to a moral or spiritual foundation for their position.[4] It is accordingly imperative that we inquire concerning the foundation of the principle to which they appeal, and that we consider whether their interpretation and application of that principle is not possibly other than it ought to be.

I

The primary popular[5] argument for the principle prohibiting abortion categorically is the simple identification of abortion in any case with murder. This identification of abortion with murder is often taken as virtually an analytic truth following from definitions alone. Thus the Archbishop of Boston, Humberto S. Medeiros, moves immediately from his definition of murder as "the intentional taking of an innocent human life" to the conclusion that abortion is murder. It is not noticed that the human life taken in abortion is not innocent, but only non-guilty. Nor is it noticed that the movement depends on the equivocal meaning of "human life." In speaking of abortion, "human life" is the life of a living entity belonging to the human species; while in speaking of murder, "human life" refers to what we commonly mean by "human being." Thus "taking human life" (in abortion) slides unnoticed into "taking the life of a human being" (in murder) —just as "non-guilty" slides into "innocent." It should be noted, incidentally, that "innocent" does not play an innocent role here: "innocent" urges us to interpret "human life" as "the life of a human being," since mere human protoplasm is neither innocent nor guilty. It may be argued in reply that there is no distinction between a human life and the life of a human being. But such a position is possible only if it is assumed that an embryo or fetus is a human being from the moment of conception. And that is not an intuition, but the conclusion of an argument, unless it be allowed as a simple assertion of faith. In any case, the equivocal nature of "human life" conceals this assumption.

More carefully expressed and analyzed, the argument for a categorical prohibition of abortion on the ground that it constitutes murder has three parts or assumptions, two of which require demonstration or defense. The first is that *abortion is in every case homicide* (i.e., it takes the life of a human being); the second is that *this homicide is in no case justified,* i.e., other than murder. It also assumes that the homicide in question is intentional, a point that we simply grant.

That the second assumption needs to be argued is apparent from two observations. One is that in common belief some homicides are justified—e.g., killing in self-defense. The other is that even where it is held that an embryo or fetus is a human being it is always acknowledged that a significant question can be asked as to whether abortion is justified in cases of the incipient insanity or death of the mother and in cases of rape-induced pregnancies.

But the first assumption is plainly the basic one. It in effect denies that we can draw any line between the fertilized egg at conception and the grown man with respect to status as a human being, as having a right to life.

Defenses of this assumption tend to trade on the ambiguity of "human" that we encountered in the Archbishop's argument. Thus it is sometimes argued ingenuously that "if the human fetus (or embryo) is not human, then it must be something else, which it obviously is not." This, of course, can be applied as well to an unfertilized egg or a tooth and proves no more than that they are parts of the biological processes of human rather than non-human life, not that they are human beings. If the supposed conclusion is not a fallacy of equivocation, the argument is itself an *ignoratio elenchi* or proof of the wrong point.

A more sophisticated defense attempts to establish the ground for holding that abortion is not concerned with mere human protoplasm, by introducing biological material into its argument, as if it were concerned with an empirical matter. It is observed that at conception an embryo is formed that has a full complement of chromosomes, and that these function from the moment that egg and sperm unite, to direct the generative processes that eventuate in a mature adult, without any direction whatever from the mother's body, which only supplies nourishment and a suitable environment. The fact that the generative process begins at conception and remains continuous and of unimpaired integrity through gestation suggests a single organic entity. It would seem an analytic inference that this human entity is a human being.

Unfortunately, if "human being" means any more than "human organism," as it must to contribute to any point against abortion, the inference is not analytic. The linguistic identity of "entity" and "being" only covers a confusion of two very different concepts. Talk about the functions of chromosomes is appropriate to all organisms and cannot define a being that differs from all other organisms in such a way that it has "by its nature" the rights we hold appropriate to human beings. The movement from "human organism" or "entity" to "human being" plainly presupposes something that is not expressed in terms of chromosomes, and that something extra is what used to be—but in discussions of abortion now seldom is—expressed by "soul."

That soul should appear at this point is not surprising for those in the Aristotelian tradition. Chromosomes suggest very strongly what Aristotle referred to as the "animal soul," the "form of the body," which he took to be of the essence of the being realized. It is but a step then to the belief that the human soul appears when the chromosomes begin to direct generation in the fertilized human egg. But a step it is nonetheless, and wanting support that biology cannot provide. Aristotle's animal soul directs development in all organisms, and the human animal soul is merely another of these, providing no ground for inferences to obligations expressable as rights. Plainly, the human soul, as commonly understood, is a soul of a special kind, by its nature divine, or an image of the Divine or of special interest to the Divine, and just for that reason inviolable. (This is essential to the Catholic position.) This is an extra-biological consideration, which slips in easily through the equivocal meaning of "soul" (animal soul and eternal, immortal or human soul). Since its ground is in religious *faith* and not biology, biology obviously cannot locate the point at which the human soul, as commonly understood, appears in generation.

We may thus conclude that as the first ingenuous effort to prove that embryo or fetus is a human being attempted to move from "human" to "human being" by an equivocation on "human," here the effort at proof, although more sophisticated, turns on a similar equivocation, this time on "human being," which is taken in the argument as meaning "human organism or entity" and in the conclusion as meaning "bearer of rights, person, etc." The inference from "human organism or entity" ("human being" in an unusual, lean sense) to "human being" ("human being" in the ordinary, rich sense of "bearer of rights, persons, etc.") is not analytic, but trades on the not normally equivocal meaning of "human being." The effort to relieve the difficulty by introducing "soul" into the argument only introduces an equivocation on "soul."

The argument is thus more persuasive when it is put without reference to chromosomes or soul, as it were, linguistically: the fetus (or embryo) is a stage in the human life-process, which is a self-directing unity from conception; at no point does it *become* a human being, for a human being is the whole self-directing process throughout a lifetime.

By this argument we seem to be able to conclude that a human being is realized (or occurs) at conception. But the price may be a serious confusion in language. To say that a human being is realized at conception would seem to be like saying that an oak tree is realized at the moment an acorn begins to germinate, when all that anyone would want to say, using the language of potentiality and actuality, is that at the moment that an acorn begins to germinate what was once potentially a germinating acorn is now actually a germinating acorn and potentially (i.e., in the process of becoming) whatever the next major phase in the generation of an oak tree is. Similarly, we would seem to want to say that what was once a human zygote will at conception become an actual human zygote and potentially an embryo, and that this in turn will become an actual embryo and a potential fetus, etc.; and that at some point in this sequence there will appear the potentiality for becoming a human being, which will be realized, as development continues, as an actual human being.

We may thus confuse language in applying "human being" to the whole sequence. But obviously something is also confused in introducing "human being" into the biological sequence. This becomes evident when we state the matter more exactly. The unfertilized egg and sperm prior to conception are potentially a zygote, and the actualized zygote is potentially an embryo, and the actualized embryo is potentially a fetus, and the actualized fetus is potentially in *infant*—not "a human being." Thus we must ask at what point we should introduce the real potentiality for being a human being and the actualization of that potentiality, and we find ourselves beset by a certain vagueness and confusion. The question involves a mixed vocabulary: the concept "human being" does not belong in the list of biological concepts along with "human organism" and "infant."

It is thus not surprising that when we ask at what point in generation a human being is realized, biology provides no answer, and that those who suppose that it does seem more to be dictating to the biologist what he should say than to be listening to him. The intrusion is understandable, for when the biologist is pressed to make a decision within the limits of his discipline concerning the appearance of a human being, he is as likely to draw the line at the point that the fetus is viable outside the womb as at the midpoint in gestation or at the appearance of certain organs; and he is more likely to draw the line at one of these places than at "the moment of conception." He would have no such difficulty were he asked at what moment a human organism appears, viz., at conception or at what moment a human infant appears, viz., at birth. Were it not for the noted ambiguity of "human being," biologists would refuse to answer, just as they refuse to answer questions about the human soul.

II

The disqualification of biology for the determination of the existence of a human being has led some to suppose that since the line cannot be drawn biologically it cannot be drawn at all. It has led others to resort to the practical device of including too much rather than too little in the comprehension of "human being" so as to be sure to err on the safe side. Thus the embryo is accorded the same respect as a newborn infant. This not only confuses the vocabulary, as noted earlier, but conflicts with our natural intuitions in special cases.

A third effort to save a failing position asserts that no decision concerning the point at which a human being appears in the generative process need be made to determine our obligation. The fact that a potential human being exists is sufficient to allow inferences to rights. Thus it is argued that as one respects the right of an unconscious man to life on the ground that he has the potentiality for recovering consciousness, so one should respect the right of the fetus to life on the ground that it has the potentiality for becoming a fully realized human being. But this argument fails to recognize that the right of the unconscious man rests on a right existing prior to the loss of consciousness. One is not bound by a mere potentiality for future consciousness, but by the potentiality of an extension of a prior consciousness, with which we have, as it were, a tacit agreement by virtue of a social relationship. Plainly, the analogy is insufficient. Still, as we shall see, the position has hold of an important truth for which we will have to find a place.

There remains one more critical question: if "human being" does not belong in the biological vocabulary (save in a very lean, unusual sense), does it belong in the vocabulary that contains "potential" and "actual?" I.e., can "potential" and "actual" be predicated of "human being?" Admittedly, "potential human being" seems as odd as does "human being" when used in a biological context. But the fault may also be a matter of what a vocabulary is used to express: "potential human being" does not seem right because we do not want to allow that "human being" admits of degrees of realization. Such would in any case account for the preference for the concept of "the moment of conception," which suggests an instantaneous introduction of an underived element (cp. the creation of the world *ex nihilo* or the first occurrence of life as an act of God), over a belief in stages in the generative process. The ground of this unwillingness to allow that "human being" admits of degrees is another matter.

One good explanation of this ground is that "human being" is really an *imputation,* a way of saying that something is to be regarded as having rights (or that we have obligations toward it), as being an end in itself or sacred by its nature, as being necessarily a subject of moral concern, etc. (cp. "responsible for" in punishing[6]). (This would explain why "potential human being" feels odd while "potentially a person of character," said of a child, does not.) If so, the question that we have been considering in terms of potentiality and actuality will then be: at what point in the development of the human organism must we regard it in this special way? The answer to that question will not be *solely* in terms of properties in the entity itself. For such a view, the spiritual interest would not be merely an interest in the factual existence of "spirits" or souls, but an interest in the realization and perfection of a spiritual nature in all parties to every act. Imputations of responsibility and the status of being a human being would be devices to this end. And faith would be not merely a belief about things, but a way of regarding certain things.

III

When we cut loose from the spurious appeals to biology and simply consider the ways in which the line between the human being and the mere human organism has been drawn, we find that it has historically been drawn in many places. In the *Old Testament,* Onan is condemned for "spilling his seed upon the ground," i.e., for wasting or destroying spermatazoa. At the other extreme, the Greeks were willing to expose to death deformed or weak new-born infants as if they were not yet really human beings, and some pre-Civil War slave holders (and ancient Greeks too) held that mature Negroes were not in the fullest sense human beings. Some of the Greeks held such a view of women generally. It was not entirely a lack of biological information that caused the line to be drawn in different places: the matter plainly belonged to another area of thought.

Although the analogy is imperfect, the problem of distinguishing a mature tree from a sapling suggests an important point about drawing such lines. As the line between the mature tree and the sapling is drawn according to the interest which the distinction serves—lumbering, nursery propagation, landscaping, etc.—might it not also be that we distinguish the human being from the mere human organism according to the interest served by the making of the distinction?

That the distinction serves different interests should not need demonstration. Plainly, the interests of those who advocate unrestricted abortion appear to be *practical* or *utilitarian,* at least in the United States. Although the Women's Liberation Movement expresses its extreme position in moral and even political terms, e.g., a woman's right to control her own body—the fundamental consideration is almost always the women's convenience. Elsewhere the argument is often *economic or sociological*—e.g., in discussing abortion as a means of managing India's starving masses. But the extreme opponents of abortion rest their case on a *religious* ground: their interest is always their religious duty toward God and God's creation. And the interest of the present inquiry is essentially *moral,* insisting that considerations of convenience and religion must not contravene morality, while holding that morality cannot be reduced to prudence or faith. Small wonder it is that in each case the line is drawn in a different place.[7]

As our concern here is with the critique of the extreme negative position, it is with the religious view that we must deal. So far we have exposed its efforts to cover by biological references what is essentially the old theological question of the point in development when the soul enters the body.[8] The introduction of soul—really implicit in "human being," religiously viewed—could not avoid an element of faith. But faith is not something to be rejected out of hand: to strip it of that in which it is concealed is not to render it unworthy of respect. It must, however, be held to the spirituality from which it claims to be derived and which it claims to serve. We thus must go on to determine how that which is offered on faith must be interpreted when held to that spiritual commitment.

When we examine this spiritual foundation of the religious position, we usually find an assumed *theological realism:* spirit or soul is simply created, and religious morality consists in obeying God's will with respect to it. Thus "God creates; we must not interfere."[9] The position need not be elaborated. Its deficiency is, however, plain if one seriously considers the cases of the radically deformed child with no access to adequate institutions and of the brutalized child that abortion would have prevented. These are not discussed by the religious realist. The only human answer that he can provide in such cases comes from an unquestioning religious faith: do nothing; God will provide; such is God's way. But this is *quietism,* which if applicable here is applicable everywhere. And this we cannot accept. No duty will stand if we can entertain the possibility that God will take care of all, no matter what we do. Why act if all is going to come out for the best anyway? Or worse, if whatever we do by our own judgment will only hinder God's special purposes? As long as we entertain the possibility of any imperative to act we must rule out quietism *a priori* as an option, and with that whatever positions press it on us. Otherwise the foundation of all practical reason is undercut.

It would thus seem that the theological position ends in a callousness to suffering and degradation that is inconsistent with its professed spirituality and compassion, or in a quietism that undercuts the condition of all action.[10] The prospect remains, however, that the fault lies in the manner in which the spiritual ground of the theological position is interpreted. The fault may lie in its assumed realism.

An alternative appears in what may be called *theological idealism:* the position that spirit or soul is given only potentially or immanently and must in some sense realize itself. Thus St. Paul speaks of being saved by a faith transcending the Old Law, and faith is said to make one whole. Spirit is seen here as a project, and the principle of *the absolute respect for human life*—i.e., the respect for human beings and, by implication, the lives of human beings—is seen as a principle *a priori* and essential for a spiritual realization. Such a principle is not merely received from God; it is God's law because without it the spiritual nature of the human would not be. As common sense recognizes, men become beasts when they fail to have respect for human life. And as Kantians say it is *a priori* for any realization of spirit (freedom), just as the rejection of quietism is *a priori* for the practical life: one can be human only as one respects rational human nature unconditionally as end in itself in every instance. To this we may add, using a common and inexact form of expression, that to *respect the human is to respect the potentially human,* or expressed more exactly, that to respect whatever has the potentiality for becoming a human being or which we have reason to believe we will on some future occasion regard as a human being. This, at last, is the authentic ground for the proscription of abortion. In it the theological view finds its moral foundation.

But such a principle cannot be implemented as it stands. One must still ask and answer the secondary question: *what are the modes of respect in different circumstances?* Plainly, Pope John's humanity was not respected when he was forced to suffer needlessly. Similarly, we must allow, humanity is not respected when we force children to be born who will be tortured and brutalized in situations that cannot be corrected or prevented and in which their suffering cannot be relieved, and where they in turn will transmit their faults to their progeny. In the absence of the institutions for removing the unwanted child from its hateful mother or restoring the emotionally damaged, it would seem that there are occasions where abortion can fulfill a spiritual demand.

Thus it would seem that on a spiritual ground we draw a line between what is and what is not a human being where we *must* in order to do what a humane concern requires us to do. To do this, we draw the line where it is in fact usually drawn: where identifiable human features appear, *where the fetus begins to look human*. This is merely a matter of appearance: biology is relevant here in merely a commonsense way. The reason that we draw the line there is that such a dividing point has symbolic value; the more developed fetus suggests an actual human being. A line drawn later than that would too obviously conflict with our basic principle of unconditional respect for the human as end in itself and its correlative principle of respect for the "potentially human."[12]

This position has the support of our common moral intuition, which puts great weight on the circumstances under which a human life is taken. Murder is not countenanced; but killing in war, self-defense and punishment may be justified, even though such acts are regretted and an effort is made to eliminate the occasions where we are compelled to do them. That there is a similar attitude toward abortion should be apparent from two observations: (a) if someone were to produce a fetus by artificial insemination in an artificial womb as a laboratory experiment, most people would be inclined to insist that the life produced by such an unnatural procedure be terminated and the experiment closed down. A greater disapproval would be placed on the intrusion of technology into what we deeply believe an inviolable area of human life than on the destruction of its unnatural product. (b) When a woman willfully terminates her pregnancy, it is upon her, the mother, more than upon the physician who performs the abortion—assuming that he is not merely an "abortionist" exploiting her weaknesses—that moral disapproval is focused. It is felt that there is something depraved about a woman who cannot discipline herself by the life that she has brought into being, treating it as if it were merely something that she could put off at her convenience, repudiating her natural role as mother and subverting her natural instincts to protect and nurture. (Significantly, it appears that the strongest supporters of unrestricted abortion are those members of the Women's Liberation Movement who are most contemptuous of motherhood as a role in life.) That moral disapproval is founded on the depravity of the mother rather than on the act of the physician, is supported by the fact that where there is evidence that the mother is not merely concerned with her convenience, but yields, as it were to an impossibility—physiological, psychological or social—of carrying

Observations on the Categorical Proscription of Abortion

the pregnancy to term, disapproval softens. In the case of rape-induced pregnancies, it may disappear altogether, to be replaced by sympathy, pity and regret. In the case where the life of the mother will have to be sacrificed if the pregnancy is not terminated, it may be converted to virtually an acknowledgment of a duty to abort.

It should not be supposed that abortion is herewith defended unconditionally. Quite the contrary. The Kantian principle of the absolute and unconditional respect for the human remains untouched, as does the principle that the respect for the human is the respect for the "potentially human." It has only been noted that we live in a finite world in which the pure ideal is not entirely practicable. In order to respect human nature in this finite world, where human beings do not infrequently look upon human life as merely something one might or might not desire, where human beings often do not seem to act under a spiirtual ideal, and where institutions to remedy the defects or to compensate for them do not and often could not exist, we have to do as we must to prevent depraved and inhumane situations. We are able to do this because of a fundamental vagueness in the definition of a human being. If we have to, we can draw a line in such a way as to permit us to do what is clearly our humane though distasteful duty.[13]

There are, of course, radical alternatives. Universally practiced birth control might be one. But even that might not be enough. More than likely, forced sterilization, state regulated conception, and confiscation of children at birth would be required. But the evils associated with these could hardly be less than the evils associated with abortion. We cannot avoid the choice. We simply cannot persist in our apparently irreversibly sexually over-stimulated society, with its cheapened view of life and of human qualities, which is the product of our sensate culture, without some concession in the name of humanity to prevent its cruelest consequences.

Yet the *ideal* of a universal proscription of abortion remains valid. To respect the human is to respect the "potentially human" unconditionally. The matter is not unlike capital punishment and war, and the practical fallacy associated with it is the same. One tends to suppose that we can eliminate these evils by simply refusing to participate in them. Thus some ingenuously suppose that we can stop war by refusing to fight. Plainly it is not that simple. We cannot eliminate the evils of this world by pretending that the compromises that are necessary to prevent them are not necessary. To refuse to acknowledge these necessities is often to arrest or even reverse progress toward that state of affairs in which they are no longer necessary. Surely the refusal to fight the Nazis would only have made future wars and the dehumanization of man more certain. And the present elimination of capital punishment is now corroding the consciousness of the supremacy of the rule of law and the principle of the inviolability of human life upon which non-violent relations depend.[14] It is the same with abortion: the only hope that we have to lessen the hideous chain of pathological cruelty is the prevention of the progeny who are fated to become part of it. The least that can be said about abortion is that we move farther away from its elimination every time we compel an unwillingly pregnant woman to bear the burden of a hated child.

NOTES

[1]"He was said to be in great pain despite massive sedation. He received injections to sustain the heart". (UPI in *The New York Times* June 3, 1963, p. 22). This was well after Pope John's illness was known to be terminal.

[2]The characteristics of the children of the Israeli Kibbutzim, which are among the most refined of institutions for the total care of children apart from their parents, suggest a deficiency that may not be remediable without the family. Bruno Bettelheim observes: "the kibbutz-born generation is committed to an entirely different Sachlichkeit, a literalness, a matter-of-fact objectivity which has no place for emotions . . ." (p. 277); "an emotional flatness" (p. 288); "intimacy is essentially not available to many kibbutz-born" (p. 317); etc. *The Children of the Dream* [New York: Macmillan, 1969]. See also Melford E. Spiro, The Children of the Kibbutz (New York: Schocken, 1965).

[3]Jean Stafford gives an excellent account of this case in *A Mother in History* (New York: Farrar, Straus and Giroux, 1966).

[4]This *ad hominem* is of the legitimate sort presupposed in all dialectical philosophy: it simply holds the advocates of a position to their own most basic commitment.

[5]Since the Supreme Court threw the abortion issue to the conscience of every man, consideration of the matter now proceeds by arguments as often popular as of systematic origin. I have accordingly attempted to make my way through conversations, popular publications, lectures and sermons, etc. This is, of course, no novelty in philosophy: Socrates and Hegel did not disdain the arguments of the marketplace. Nor does it need an apology: any philosopher who would discharge his social obligation must deal with the thought that is actually at work in the world, often in preference to the inefficacious abstractions of the classroom and the learned journal.

[6] See the author's "Punishment and Responsibility" in *The Journal of Philosophy*, May 22, 1969, especially pp. 296;.

[7] One might say that the basis in every case is psychological and that references to non-psychological interests only serve rationalization. Thus psychological interests provide the rational foundations.

[8] When the argument was treated by theology alone, the line was drawn in several places, even distinguishing between male and female. There is a discussion of the various positions on "ensoulment" in John T. Noonan Jr.'s "An Almost Absolute Value in History' in his *The Morality of Abortion* (Cambridge: Harvard University Press, 1970) pp. 18-39.

[9] One might hold analogously that "God takes; we must not interfere," were it not that an unwillingness to draw the line between natural death and artifically maintained life converts this to "God gives; we must preserve," as in the case of Pope John.

[10] Let the reader who doubts this ask himself how in his own heart, and not in accordance with some rule or theory, he would treat the rape-induced pregnancy, where the rapist is known to be mentally defective.

[11] See note six above.

[12] Unlike the Principle of Double Effect, which is a device for reconciling dogma and natural intuition, this taking advantage of the lack of an exact criterion of "human being" is an expression of a natural principle that we all commonly employ. It is not entirely as a persuasive device that anti-abortionist literature exhibits pictures of the most human appearing fetuses.

[13] See note 10.

[14] That this is not a contradiction, see "Punishment and Responsibility".

BARUCH BRODY

On the Humanity of the Foetus

In earlier essays,[1] I have argued that if there is some point in the development of the foetus from which time on it is a living human being with all the rights of such an entity, then it would be wrong (except in one special case) to abort the foetus even to save the life of the mother, and then there should be strong laws prohibiting such abortions. In neither of those essays did I consider the question as to whether there is such a point, so I should like, in this essay, to outline an approach to finding the answer to that question.

I

Moral philosophers are in definite disagreement about this issue. Among positions as to when the foetus becomes a living human being with all the rights of such an entity are the claims that it does so at the moment of conception, at the time (around the seventh or eighth day) at which segmentation, if it is to take place, takes place, at the time (around the end of the sixth week) at which foetal brain activity commences, at the moment (sometime between the thirteenth and twentieth week) of quickening when the mother begins to feel the movements of the foetus, at the time (around the twenty-fourth week) at which the foetus becomes viable, i.e., has a reasonable chance of survival if born, and at the moment of birth.

It is difficult to see how one is to decide between these conflicting claims. The trouble is not merely that there are conflicting claims; the trouble is that the proponents of each of these claims seem to have somewhat persuasive arguments for their claims. Let us begin, therefore, by trying to understand each of these positions by looking at the arguments offered for them by their adherents. The following seem to be the major reasons for supposing that the foetus becomes a living human being with all the rights that such an entity normally has at the moment of conception:

(1) At the moment of conception, the foetus is biologically determined by its genetic code. It is, from that point on, an individual unique creature, and everything that happens to it after that point is merely an unfolding of its unique selfhood. As Paul Ramsey[2] put it:

> Thus it might be said that in all essential respects the individual is whoever he is going to become from the moment of impregnation. He already is this while not knowing this or anything else. Therefore, his subsequent development cannot be described as becoming something he is not now. It can only be described as a process of achieving, a process of becoming the one he already is. Genetics teaches us that we were from the beginning what we essentially still are in every cell and in every generally human attribute and in every individual attribute.

(2) Until the moment of conception, the likelihood of whatever is present (the spermatozoa, the ova) developing into a clear-cut living human being is very small. But once conception has taken place, the resulting fertilized cell has a very high probability of developing into a clear-cut living human being. Indeed, 4 out of 5 of these entities do survive to birth. So these new entities, as opposed to the spermatozoa and ova, do have a human right to life. John Noonan, the leading advocate of this argument, put it[3] as follows:

> ... part of the business of a moralist is drawing lines. One evidence of the nonarbitrary character of the line drawn is the difference of probabilities on either side of it. If a spermatozoon is destroyed, one destroys a being which had a chance of far less than 1 in 200 million of developing into a reasoned being, possessed of the genetic code, a heart and other organs, and capable of pain. If a fetus is destroyed, one destroys a being already possessed of the genetic code, organs, and sensitivity to pain, and one which had an 80 percent chance of developing further into a baby outside the womb, who, in time, would reason.

(3) There is a continuity of development from the moment of conception on. There are constant changes in the foetal condition; the foetus is constantly acquiring new structures and characteristics, but there is no one stage which is radically different from any other. Since

that is so, there is no one stage in the process of foetal development, after the moment of conception, which could plausibly be picked out as the moment at which the foetus becomes a living human being. The moment of conception is, however, different in this respect. It marks the beginning of this continuous process of development and introduces something new which is radically discontinuous with what has come before it. Therefore, the moment of conception, and only it, is a plausible candidate for being that moment at which the foetus becomes a living human being. Roger Wertheimer (who is not, himself, an advocate of this position) summarized this argument[4] very well as follows:

> ... going back stage by stage from the infant to the zygote, one will not find any differences between successive stages significant enough to bear the enormous moral burden of allowing wholesale slaughter at the earlier stage while categorically denying that permission at the next state.

In order to understand the second position, the position that the foetus becomes a living human being at that moment at which, if it is to take place, segmentation takes place, it is necessary to remind ourselves of one or two key points about early foetal development. In a case in which there are identical twins, a primitive streak across the blastocyst signals the separation of the two twins. This occurs about the seventh day after fertilization. Although it occurs around the same time as implantation, it is an entirely separate process. And, of course, it is only a process that occurs when there are identical twins.

Now the argument for treating the foetus as a living human being only from this point on is really very simple. The individual in question only comes into existence, as a unique individual, at this point. Until then, for all we know, there may be two entities in the blastocyst. Paul Ramsey, the first one to raise this argument (which we shall label argument [4]), put it as follows:[5]

> It might be asserted that it is at the time of segmentation, not earlier, that life comes to be the individual human being it is thereafter to be ... If there is a moment in the development of these nascent lives of ours subsequent to fertilization and prior to birth (or graduation from college) at which it would be reasonable to believe that a human life begins and therefore begins to be inviolate, that moment is arguably at the stage

when segmentation may or may not take place.

The next three positions to be considered (the moment at which foetal brain activity begins, the moment of quickening, and the moment of viability), all share in common two basic ideas, the idea that the foetus does not become human until some point at which it has far more of the abilities and structures of a developed human being than it has at the moment of conception, and the idea that there is some point between conception and birth at which the foetus has acquired enough of these significant characteristics so that it becomes plausible to think of the foetus as a living human being. These three positions differ only over the question as to when this point is.

The proponents of the claim that the foetus becomes a living human being at about six weeks are primarily impressed with the fact that it is about that time that electroencephalographic waves have been noted,[6] and that, therefore, the foetal brain must clearly be functioning after this date. There are two main reasons for taking this development to be the one that marks the time at which the foetus becomes a living human being:

(5) It is just this indicator which is used in determining the moment of death, the moment at which the entity in question is no longer a living human being. So, on grounds of symmetry, it would seem appropriate to treat it as the moment at which the entity in question becomes a living human being.[7] Callahan (who is not entirely convinced by this argument) puts it as follows:[8]

> ... it is very rare, for instance, to find a discussion of when life begins (pertinent to abortion) related to a discussion of when life ends (pertinent to euthanasia and the artificial prolongation of life). Yet both problems turn on what is meant by human life, and the illumination we gain in dealing with one of the problems will be useful when we deal with the other. Similarly, there is much to be said for trying to work out some consistent standards regarding the use of empirical data.

(6) One of the characteristics that are certainly essential to being a living human being is that the entity in question is capable of conscious experience, at least of a primitive level. Before the sixth week, it is not. Thereafter, it is. Consequently, that is the time at which the foetus becomes a living human being.

Those who claim that the foetus becomes a living human being at the moment of quickening seem to be impressed with its significance for the following two reasons:

(7) Quickening is an indication of foetal movement. We would certainly want to think of the ability to move as one of those characteristics that are essential to living human beings (not, of course, only to living human beings). So it is only at quickening, when there is a definite indication of foetal movement, that we are justified in thinking of the foetus as a living human being.

(8) There is an important sense in which it is true that quickening is that occasion from which the foetus can be perceived by other human beings. From that point on, the foetus can at least be felt by the mother. And anything which is not perceivable by other human beings cannot be thought of as a living human being. So the foetus becomes a living human being only at the moment of quickening, only at the moment at which it enters into the realm of the perceivable.

The following seems to be the main argument for supposing that the foetus becomes a living human being at the moment of viability:

(9) There is no doubt that the foetus is human from the moment of conception; it is certainly a human foetus. The question that we have to consider, however, is about when it becomes a living human being, and that is an entirely different matter. How can anything be a living human being if it is incapable of existing on its own? The foetus cannot do so until it becomes viable, so it cannot be a living human being until then. But when it does become viable, then it has that degree of independence that is required for its being a living human being.

We come finally to the position that the foetus becomes a living human being only at its birth. It is clear that there is no special structure or capacity that it develops at that point. Indeed, this is so, in the last few months of pregnancy. So those who argue for birth as the moment at which the foetus becomes a living human being cannot be doing so on the grounds that it is then that they develop that which makes them a living human being. It is this that sets this position off from the last three that we have considered. What then are the main arguments for supposing that the foetus becomes a living human being at the moment of birth? These seem to be the main points:

(10) As long as the foetus is in the mother, it is more appropriate to think of it as a part of the mother, rather than as an individual separate living human being. That status can accrue to the foetus,

therefore, only when it emerges from the mother at the moment of birth.

(11) While it is true that the foetus has the capacity for independent existence from the time of viability, it does not actually have that independent existence until birth. Until then, its intake of oxygen and food, and its expelling of wastes (among other things) is parasitic on that of the mother's. So it is only at the moment of birth at which the foetus acquires that independence that is essential for its being a living human being.

(12) It is only after that birth that the foetus can interact with other humans, and vice versa. But certainly it is this interaction, and no the mere abstract possibility of it, that is essential for being a living human being. So the foetus can be considered as a living human being only after its birth.

II

In light of the existence of these arguments, one can easily understand how many would conclude that something has gone wrong and that a fundamentally different approach is required. There is one such fundamental alternative that we should consider. It claims that there is a common but questionable presupposition of all the positions and arguments that we have been considering, viz., that there is an answer to the question as to when the foetus becomes a living human being with all the associated rights, an answer whose truth is independent of what we think or feel. It is just this presupposition that is rejected by the adherents of this fundamental alternative. According to them, the humanity of the foetus depends upon certain decisions involving it made by, and/or certain reactions to it of, other human beings.

One such version of this thesis is held by Professor John O'Connor.[9] While agreeing that once the criterion for humanity (for having the rights of a living human being) are settled, the question of the humanity of a foetus is a purely scientific one, O'Connor claims that it is we who have to decide upon the criterion of humanity, and, therefore, in an indirect way, it is we who ultimately have to make the decisions that will determine whether the foetus has the rights that a living human being has:[10]

> I suggest that the fundamental defect in Noonan's account is his assumption that the criterion of humanity needs to be discovered. Rather I suggest that we must *decide* what the criterion is to be.

In another passage, O'Connor puts his point as follows:[11]

> It is possible to agree with Noonan that, in a sense, it is certainly an objective matter whether or not a being is human, but point out that it becomes objective only when human beings have decided what the criterion of humanity is.

There are a variety of objections that might be raised against this view. But the most important one is that this seems to place the matter of human rights open to too many objectionable decisions. After all, there are all types of people with all types of prejudices about what is or is not required for being a living human being. And would we want to say that members of some minority group are really not living human beings just because they fail to meet the criterion of humanity established by some prejudiced majority, where the criterion in question reflects the prejudices of that majority group? If there were a vast majority prejudiced against redheads, and if that prejudice were reflected in some decision to include non-redheadedness as one of the necessary conditions for being a living human being, should we feel, as O'Connor's position seems to entail, that redheads then have no rights as living human beings? I think not. So O'Connor's position seems wrong.

O'Connor is, of course, aware of this possible objection, and he attempts to state the basis for his rejection of it in the following passage:[12]

> This is not, of course, to say that it is a subjective matter. Rather, there are good and bad reasons for deciding in the way we do.

There are two questions that naturally arise in response to such a remark: (1) what is the basis for distinguishing between good and bad reasons for such a decision (2) is that basis such that it does not also serve as a basis for distinguishing between correct and incorrect answers to the question as to what is the criterion for being a living human being? It is extremely important that O'Connor should be able to say 'no' in response to this second question, for if he cannot, then he will have avoided the subjectivism he recognizes as dangerous only at the cost of giving up his idea that the criteria of humanity are a matter to be decided upon and at the cost of adopting our position that there is an objectively true answer to the moral question 'when is something a living human being?' It can, of course, be done. One way would be to provide a basis that picked out the reasons for several conflicting, but not all, proposed decisions as good reasons.

Let us now look at exactly what O'Connor does set out as his theory of good reasons and bad reasons. He puts it as follows:[13]

> The reason that humanity is of interest to a person concerned with the moral status of abortion is that he wants a way to decide the scope of the moral principle to the effect that the taking of human life is wrong. Hence humanity should be characterized in terms of those features which are in fact related to the moral sensibility of human beings ... It would do little good to couch the criterion of humanity in such a way that the moral judgments we now make concerning human beings would be felt to have no moral force when applied to the 'newly qualified' humans, whose humanity was first recognized only by the new criterion of humanity.

There is something obscure about this passage in this context, because it looks like a statement of a basis for distinguishing good decisions from bad ones (although not, of course, correct answers from incorrect ones) rather than good reasons for adopting one decision from bad reasons for adopting one. So there seems to be a shift here in O'Connor's strategy. But it is close enough to what we want anyway, since having a criterion for good decisions is, for O'Conor's purpose, as satisfactory as having a criterion for good reasons for decisions.

But there is a great deal of trouble with O'Connor's answer. After all, it fails to meet the original objection. In a highly prejudiced society that has incorporated its prejudices into its criterion of humanity, it will be the case, according to O'Connor, that the only good criteria of humanity will be those that retain these prejudicial features. If we try to drop them out, so as to extend human rights to the minority in question, our new criterion of humanity will be a bad one, according to O'Connor's criterion, since it is not related to the moral sensibility of the human beings in that society. Going back once more to the case of redheads who, in their society, are not viewed as living human beings entitled to human rights, one would have to say that, according to O'Connor, it would be a bad decision to leave nonredheadedness out of the criterion for humanity.

Moreover, the reasons that O'Connor gives for adopting his criterion for good and bad decisions are not very convincing. To be sure,

On the Humanity of the Foetus 77

if one's decision extends the rules about human rights to entities not generally recognized as living human beings by most people, there is a very good chance that those rules will be broken in connection with these entities. In that sense, then, such a decision "would do little good." It might, however, do a great deal of good in other ways; it might serve an educational role (by making people think again about whether this minority is human), it might serve as an important protest of principle, etc. So it is not at all clear that such a decision would be a bad one. Moreover, the mere fact that a correct decision will not have the desired consequences should not, by itself, take away from its correctness.

In short, then, O'Connor's way of distinguishing good from bad decisions will not do, partially because it does not solve the problem raised by prejudiced societies and partially because the reasons for it are unconvincing. So we are left with our original objection to his whole approach, viz., that it seems to allow for the loss of human rights by some minority merely because some society has adopted a criterion of humanity that excludes that minority.

A very similar difficulty is faced by Professor Wertheimer, who offers another version of the thesis we are considering now. Professor Wertheimer is sympathetic to the suggestion[14] that

> ... what our natural response is to a thing, how we naturally react, cognitively, affectively, and behaviorally, is partly definitive of how we ought to respond to that thing. Often only an actual confrontation will tell us what we need to know, and sometimes we may each respond differently, and thus have different understandings.

It is just this suggestion that we want to consider now.

Wertheimer himself is pessimistic of using his approach in the near future to resolve the problem of the status of the foetus. He feels that there would have to be serious modifications in the foetal condition before we could have enough interactions with, and responses to, the foetus so that we could see what we feel about it. Moreover, what we would feel about this new type of creature is not clearly relevant to the status of foetuses as they now exist.

It is not clear that Wertheimer's pessimism here is justified. Paul Ramsey[15] has called our attention to one possibility of studying human reactions to foetuses, even given their current condition, by letting the response to viewing these pictures. Such an experiment has never been carried out, but there is at least some data that suggests that its people see pictures of foetuses and of foetal behavior and studying results might be quite significant. When Lennart Nilsson's photographs of foetuses were published in *Life* in 1965, many readers wrote in reporting their reactions, which generally tended to be that they could no longer view the foetus, at least in the later stages, as a disposable thing. Naturally, no conclusions should be drawn from this small sample, but it does at least suggest that, were we to adopt Wertheimer's approach to the question of when something is a living human being, some progress could be made on the question of foetal humanity.

Of course the question that we must consider first is whether we want to adopt Wertheimer's approach. The question is, once more, whether his approach can meet the problem raised by the responses of a prejudiced society. He puts the problem as follows:[16]

> We surely want to say that Negroes are and always have been full-fledged human beings, no matter what certain segments of mankind may have thought, and no matter how numerous or unanimous those segments were.

His problem is how to reconcile this with the view that humanity is determined by how people respond to the entity in question.

It is obvious that Wertheimer can meet this problem only by ruling out certain responses, only by showing that certain responses are not relevant to the determination of the status of the creature in question. He offers us no full account of how he would do this, but we get some idea of what he has in mind when we see how he rules out as irrelevant to the status of the Negro slave the response to him of the slaveholders:[17]

> We argue that his form of life is, so to speak, an accident of history, explicable by reference to special sociopsychological circumstances, that are inessential to the nature of blacks and whites. The fact that Negroes can, and, special circumstances aside, naturally would be regarded and treated no differently than a Caucasion is at once a necessary and a sufficient condition for its being right to so regard and treat them.

Looking at this remark from our perspective, we see the following theory suggested here. A decision to count an entity as a human being is a good one only if it is in accord with the natural responses of clear-cut human beings to the entity in question. This criterion is thought reasonable because it reflects our privileged natural response and it solves the problem of the responses of the prejudiced society on the grounds that their responses are conditioned rather than natural.

Does this suggestion work? I think not. To begin with, can the distinction between the natural response and the socio-psychologically determined response do the work that Wertheimer needs it to do? I do not now want to raise the standard challenges to this distinction; rather, I would like to point out just how unclear the notion of the natural response is in this context. In one important sense, the slaveholder's response to the Negro is perfectly natural. Wertheimer himself points this out (without, I think, recognizing its full significance) in a footnote to his discussion of the slaveholder's response:[18]

> We develop our concept of a human through our relations with those near us and like us, and thus, at least initially, an isolated culture will generally perceive and describe foreigners as alien, strange, and not four-square human.

On the other hand, there is an important sense in which the response of the integrationist is the natural one. As Huck Finn learnt, it is very natural, when put into situations in which one lives with Negroes, to respond to them as living human beings. So, the viability of Wertheimer's solution to the problem raised by the reactions of the prejudiced society is very unclear, because, in this context, appeals to what is a natural response seem to lead to hopelessly conflicting results.

Secondly, it is not clear that this criterion is reasonable. Why should we ascribe to the natural response the special status implicit in Wertheimer's proposal? Why should we suppose that the natural response gives us any deeper insight into the status of the entity in question than some historically and/or socio-psychologically determined response? I think that we have lurking here a new, and far more dangerous, naturalistic fallacy, the fallacy of supposing that what is natural is necessarily insightful.

Given, then, that neither Wertheimer nor O'Connor have been able to meet the problem of the prejudiced society, we cannot help but feel that this problem is going to destroy any version of this fundamental alternative approach that we are considering. This leads us then to the conclusion that we should return to the positions and arguments discussed in section I, that we should return to attempting to answer the question as to when the foetus really does become a living human being with all the rights that such an entity normally has.

III

As one looks over the various arguments, one is struck by the fact that they divide into two groups. The arguments in one group (consisting of arguments (3), (5), (6), (7), (8), (9), (11), and (12)) are based upon the consideration of the nature of foetal development, and whether there are some essential properties of being human that the foetus acquires at some point in its development that makes that point sharply discontinuous from what has come before it and which is therefore the time at which the foetus becomes a living human being. All of the arguments except (3) assert that there are such properties. We will be concerned with these arguments, and the theoretical issues that they raise, in the final sections of this article. But before doing so, we must first see why the remaining group of arguments ((1), (2), (4) and (10)), each of which is based upon some special feature, can be disregarded.

Argument (1), the genetic argument, begins from the biological fact that, at the moment of conception, the fertilized cell has the unique chromosomal structure that will be found in all of the cells of the living human being that will develop from this cell. But it goes on to conclude from that that the entity in question is, from the moment of conception, whatever it is going to become, and that therefore it is a living human being. But how are these conclusions supposed to follow from the premise in question?

As we reflect upon the argument, it seems to come to the following: For any living human being there is a set of properties which can properly be considered the basic attributes of that human being. Some of these are shared with others, while others of these attributes are unique to the particular living human being in question. Now, that human being has these characteristics because of the chromosomal makeup of his cells; it is that that gives him these characteristics. But the foetus has already got that chromosomal makeup from the moment of conception; so it is also a living human being identical with the adult living human being.

The first thing that one should note about this argument is its somewhat dubious assumption that all of the basic characteristics of a human being (including those which he alone possesses) are genetically determined. That is to say, this argument presupposes that none of them is environmentally determined. It is, of course, difficult to decide whether or not this is so without an account of which characteristics are basic to that individual living human being, but the justification for assuming that they are all genetically determined is very unclear.

There is, moreover, a fallacy in the logic of this argument. Even if it is true that anything that possesses the basic properties of some living human being a is identical with a and is like a, a living human being, and even if it is true that these characteristics are determined by the chromosomal structure that the foetus already has, it doesn't follow, and it is clearly not true, that the foetus already has all of these characteristics; therefore, it certainly does not follow that the foetus out of which a will develop is identical with a and is like a, a living human being.

We turn now to argument (2), the argument from probabilities. This argument certainly does call attention to an important difference between foetuses (even from the moment of conception) on the one hand, and spermatazoa and ova, on the other hand. But it is not immediately clear why this difference is supposed to show that the foetus (from the moment of conception) is a living human being.

There is one passage in which Noonan[19] explains the rationale for his argument:

> I had supposed that the appeal to probabilities was the most commonsensical of arguments, that to a greater or smaller degree all of us based our actions on probabilities, and that in morals, as in law, prudence and negligence were often measured by the account one had taken of the probabilities. If the chance were 300,000,000 to 1 that the movement in the bushes into which you shot was a man's, I doubt if many persons would hold you careless in shooting; but if the chances were 4 out of 5 that the movement was a human being's few would acquit you of blame in shooting.

It is difficult to know what to make of this argument. To begin with, Noonan switches, at the key point where he provides us with his example, from the question of the morality of the action to the very different question of whether you are to blame for something you did, and the considerations that are relevant to one type of question are not necessarily relevant to the other type. But more importantly, the analogy is very unapt. In the case of the movement in the bushes, the probability of 4/5 is the probability of the entity in question already being a living human being. In the case of the foetus, the probability of 4/5 is the probability of the entity in question developing into a clear-cut living human being. And I cannot see how it follows from the fact that one ought to suppose that the entity in question is a living human being when the probability of its already being one is 4/5 that one therefore ought to suppose that the entity in question is a living human being when the probability of its developing into a clearcut living human being is 4/5.

There is, however, a different suggestion that might be advanced as to the relevance of this probability data. The following argument is often advanced for the claim that the foetus, from the moment of conception, is a living human being: from the moment of conception, the foetus has the potentiality for engaging in all of those activities that are typically human. Now, it is the potentiality for doing that that makes one a living human being. So the foetus is a living human being from the moment of conception. In connection with this argument, the question naturally arises as to whether the foetus does indeed already have these potentialities at the moment of conception. It might be felt that he does so just because of this difference in probabilities. An entity, like the foetus even from the moment of conception, who has a 4/5 probability of developing into a being that actually engages in these activities is an entity that has the potentiality of engaging in them.

Two additional points should be noted about this argument: (a) the claim that the foetus has these potentialities can be reinforced by an appeal to the facts about the genetic code. After all, there is, because of the presence of the genetic code in the foetal cells, a biological basis for these potentialities; (b) the argument we are considering now is not claiming that the foetus is a living human being because it is a potential human being. Such a claim is, of course, incoherent, for to be at a given time a potential P is precisely not to be, at that time, a P. Rather, it is arguing that the foetus is a living human being from the moment of conception because it has, from that moment, the potentiality of engaging in typically human activities, and it has that potentiality because of the probability consideration raised by Noonan (together, perhaps, with the facts about the genetic code).

There are several very difficult issues raised by this argument. The first has to do with what it is to possess the potentiality of engaging in human activities. It might be argued that, contra the argument we are considering, something more is required if the foetus is to be said to possess those potentialities. After all, consider as an example of a typical human activity, the activity of thinking. We have good reason to suppose that thinking can only take place in a living human being when certain physiological structures (in this case, neural structures) are present and operating. Would it not then be reasonable to say that an entity has the potentiality of engaging in these activities only when those structures are present? And if so, we certainly cannot say of the foetus, at the moment of conception, that it has the potentiality of engaging in thought. And, of course, a similar argument could be raised in connection with other typically human activities.

There is, moreover, a second objection to the whole argument that the foetus is a living human being because of its potentialities. Perhaps some actual human activity, in addition to the potentiality (in any sense) of human activity, is required if the entity in question is to be a living human being? There is, after all, a certain intuitive plausibility to this claim. If we suppose that a sufficient condition for being a living human being is the engagement in typically human activities, then isn't it plausible to suppose (admittedly, it does not follow) that the potentiality of engaging in these activities is sufficient only for being a potential human being? So even if we grant the foetus's potentialities on the basis of Noonan's statistical considerations, it hardly seems to follow that the foetus is a living human being.

We come now to argument (4), the argument for the time of segmentation as the time at which the foetus becomes a living human being. If we were to formalize this argument, it would run as follows:

(a) Until the time of segmentation, but not thereafter, it is physically possible that more than one living human being develop out of that which resulted from the fertilization of the ovum by the sperm.

(b) Therefore, that which results from the fertilization of the ovum by the sperm (i) cannot be a living human being until the time of segmentation and (ii) is a living human being after that time.

The trouble here is, of course, that it is totally unclear as to how either part of (b) follows from (a). Why should (i) be true just because (a) is true? The following suggests itself: if the foetus were a living human being at some time before segmentation, and then it were to split into two living human beings, then we would have one living human being becoming two, and that is not possible. Unfortunately, although initially persuasive, this argument must be rejected. One amoeba can become two,[20] so why can't one living human being become two?

It is equally unclear as to why it should be thought that (ii) should follow from (a). Even if we suppose that (i) follows, this only means that the foetus, by the time of segmentation, has passed one hurdle in its path towards becoming a living human being. It is now a unique individual that will not split into two others. But it certainly does not follow that it has passed all the hurdles; it certainly does not follow that it is now a living human being.

We come finally to the very weak argument (10), the argument that claims that the foetus is not a living human being until the moment of birth because, until then, it is only a part of the mother since it is in the mother. The inference here seems to be from the foetus's (a) being in the mother (b) to its being a part of the mother and not an independent entity. But one certainly cannot infer merely from the fact that a is in b that a is a part of b (and certainly not that a is not an independent entity). I am in this room, but I am certainly not a part of this room. Jonah in the whale was not a part of the whale. To be sure, the foetus is in the mother in the stronger sense that it is dependent upon the mother, etc. That is, of course, a very different matter, and argument (11) which raises it is a serious argument which cannot be dismissed so easily and which we will consider below. For the moment, we need only note that the mere fact that the foetus is in the mother says nothing about its status as a living human being.

IV

We turn finally to a consideration of the remaining arguments. With the exception of (3), the argument from the continuity of foetal development, they all seem to be of the following form:

(a) there is a property P which is such that every living human being must have it; it is essential for its being a living human being.

(b) when the foetus acquires P, it becomes a living human being. And even argument (3) is best viewed as denying that, at any point after conception, the foetus acquires any property that satisfies premise (a).

In this final section, I would like to consider some of the difficulties that might be involved in trying to defend an argument of this type and briefly sketch a possible way of dealing with them. The first point to be noted is that none of the arguments, as currently formulated, is valid. After all, if there are two such properties P and Q, the mere possession of one cannot make the foetus a living human being so long as it does not possess the other. So (b) cannot follow from (a). In order to meet this point, one would have to modify our arguments so that they would be of the following structure:

(c) there is a property P which is such that every living human being must have it; it is essential for its being a living human being.

(d) by the time an entity acquires P, it has every other property Q which is essential for its being a living human being.

(e) when the foetus acquires P, it becomes a living human being.

Even with this reformulation, however, none of these arguments would be valid. As they stand, all that the premises guarantee is that, by the time the foetus has acquired P, it will have also acquired all those other properties that living human beings must have, i.e., it will have satisfied all of the necessary conditions for being a living human being. But they do not guarantee that the foetus will have satisfied any condition that is sufficient for its being a living human being, i.e., they do not guarantee that (e) is true.

So the first major problem that any proponents of our arguments will have to consider is the following: is it possible to develop a theory of what properties are essential for being a human being according to which it will be true that

(d) when an entity acquires every property which is essential for its being a living human being, it becomes a living human being? It is only if such a premise is true that any of the arguments that we are considering will be valid.

There is, of course, a second problem that the proponents of any of our arguments will have to face: how are we to determine whether or not the possession of a given property is or is not essential for being a living human being? It should be kept in mind that this is an extremely difficult problem given our reformulation of the arguments. It is not enough that we know whether or not the given property P is essential for being a living human being. It would seem that we have to have a complete list of all of the properties that are essential for being a living human being. Otherwise, how would we know that the premise of type (d) is true? And how are we going to ascertain what is the full list of these properties essential to being human?

So much for the problems. Now for a brief sketch of a possible way of dealing with them.[21] Let us begin with the following account[22] of when it is that an object has a property essentially. An object a has a property P essentially just in the case that a cannot lose it without going out of existence, while a has P accidentally just in the case that a can change and lose the property without going out of existence. Thus, it is an accidental property of my tree that it has 832 leaves on it since it could grow an additional leaf and still continue to exist. But it is an essential property of it that it is a tree, for if it were chopped down and cut into lumber (so that it were no longer a tree), it would no longer exist. Now, we shall say that any property had essentially by some object and accidentally by none (whether actual or potential) determines a natural kind, and that the set of objects having that property is a natural kind. In short, a natural kind is a set of objects each of which has a certain property essentially, and nothing else has that property. Now, the set of white objects is not a natural kind, since the only property that all white objects, but nothing else, has is the property of being white, and not all white objects have that property essentially. After all, my desk, which is white, could be painted blue and still exist. On the other hand, the set of living human beings seems to be a natural kind, since there seems to be a property which only its members have (the property of being a living human being) and they all seem to have it essentially. After all, when we die, when we stop being a living human being, we (but not our body and perhaps not our soul) cease to exist. Surely that is why we treat death so differently than anything else that might happen to us. As Wittgenstein[23] put it, "Death is not an event in life: we do not live to experience death."

With these preliminaries out of the way, I should now like to introduce several claims about what properties are essential for membership in a natural kind:

(1) only the possession of properties had essentially by every member of a natural kind is essential for membership in that natural kind.

(2) only the possession of all properties had essentially by every member of a natural kind is sufficient for membership in that natural

kind.

Claim (1) tells us what properties are such that their possession is essential (necessary) for membership in natural kinds while claim (2) tells us what properties are such that their joint possession is sufficient for membership in the class in question.

Both of these claims are false if we are dealing with classes in general, and not just with natural kinds. Consider once more the class of white objects which is, as we have seen, not a natural kind. Certainly, being white is essential for membership in that class but being white is not, as we have seen, an essential property of every member of that class. So claim (1) would be false for this non-natural kind. Similarly, the only properties had essentially by every member of this class are those had essentially by all colored objects (i.e., those had essentially by all objects and the property of being colored), but the possession of those properties is not sufficient for membership in the class of white objects (a blue object would, after all, also have them). What is sufficient is being white. So claim (2) would also be false for this non-natural kind.

Intuitively, what is happening here is the following: assume that, for every class, there are some properties[24] which are such that the possession of each of them is necessary and their joint possession is sufficient for membership in the class in question. Now (1) claims that the only necessary properties are those had essentially by all members of that class and (2) claims that their joint possession is the only sufficient condition. This must be false in the case of non-natural kinds for precisely what they lack are some properties that their members, and only their members, have essentially and the possession of which could therefore be the necessary and sufficient conditions for membership in the class in question. But in the case of natural kind, where all members have some properties essentially, and nothing else has them at all, it is plausible to conjecture that it is the possession of these properties, and only them, which is necessary and sufficient for membership in the natural kind. This is, of course, precisely what is claimed in (1) and (2).

I have no proof that (1) and (2) are true. But they are intuitively plausible and no counter-examples seem to be immediately forthcoming. So I will tentatively adopt them in this sketch. Given, then, (1) and (2), and our previous claim that humanity is a natural kind, we are now in a position to properly evaluate our remaining argu-

ments. Their common structure was the following:
(c) there is a property P which is such that its possession is essential for being a living human being.
(d) by the time an entity acquires P, it has every other property Q which is essential for being a living human being.
(e) when the foetus acquires P, it becomes a living human being.
And there were two major problems with each of these arguments, viz., how to tell whether their essentialist claims are true and how to fix up their logic so that (e) will follow from the appropriate (c) and (d). We can now see how to solve these problems. Since humanity is a natural kind, given assumption (1), the only properties essential for being a human being are those had essentially by every human being, i.e., those which are such that their loss would mean that the entity in question has gone out of existence. We can therefore use the going-out-of-existence test to determine the truth of claims (c) and (d) in any given argument. And given assumption (2), (e) does follow straightforwardly from (c) and (d).

In short, then, our technical excursus has put us into a position for dealing with the problem of the essence of humanity. And it suggests to us that the soundest argument is (5), the brain-function argument. After all, it and only it seems to rest upon the claim that the foetus becomes a living human being when it acquires that characteristic which is such that its loss entails that a living human being no longer exists. But this, like all other points in this sketch, needs further investigation.

V

Where, then, do we stand on this vexing issue of foetal humanity? We have seen pretty clearly that it is not a matter to be resolved upon the basis of human decisions and reactions; it is, in that sense, a more objective mater. We have seen, moreover, that the crucial objective factors are ones having to do with the essence of humanity and not ones having to do with genetic codes and with probabilities of development. Finally, we have sketched (although certainly not proved the truth of) an approach to the essence of humanity according to which the foetus would be a living human being from about six weeks, the time at which we begin to note foetal brain activity.

NOTES

[1]"Abortion and the Law," *Journal of Philosophy* (1971) and "Abortion and the Sanctity of Human Life," *American Philosophical Quarterly* (1973).

[2]In "Points in Deciding about Abortion" in Noonan's *The Morality of Abortion* (Harvard, 1970) pp. 66-67. In that essay, Ramsey seems to alternate between that position and the time-of-segmentation position.

[3]In "An Almost Absolute Value in History" in his *The Morality of Abortion* (Harvard, 1970) pp. 56-57.

[4]In his "Understanding the Abortion Argument," *Philosophy and Public Affairs* (1971), p. 83.

[5]*Op. cit.*, p. 66.

[6]It is interesting to note that Glanville-Williams, in his *The Sanctity of Life and the Criminal Law* (Stevens, 1961) thinks of the presence of foetal brain activity as a good compromise date for the beginning of foetal humanity, but only because he mistakenly thought that foetal brain activity is first detectable in the seventh month.

[7]This argument is sometimes turned around in very strange ways. Thus, writing in a letter to the *New York Times* (dated March 6, 1972), Cyril C. Means, Professor of Constitutional Law at New York Law School, argued as follows:

> An adult heart donor, suffering from irreversible brain damage, is also a living human "being," but he is no longer a human "person." That is why his life may be ended by the excision of his heart for the benefit of another, the donee, who is still a human person. If there can be human "beings" who are non persons at one end of the life span, why not also at the other end?

Professor Means seems to be missing the point. If we took the analogy he, and the argument we are considering both suggest, then, in his termiology, the foetus will be a person, as well as a human being, from the sixth week on and will, from that point on, be entitled to the full rights of such an entity.

[8]In his *Abortion: Law, Choice, and Morality* (Macmillan, 1970), p. 334.

[9]In his "On Humanity and Abortion," *Natural Law Forum* (1968).

[10]*Ibid.*, p. 13.

[11]*Ibid.*

[12]*Ibid.*

[13]*Ibid.*, p. 130.

[14]*Op. cit.*, p. 92.

[15]*Op. cit.*, 74. It should be noted that Ramsey himself is dubious about the value and importance of these results: "Medical science knows the babies to be present in all essential respects earlier in foetal development than the women who wrote into *Life* magazine perceived them in the pictures. It is the rational account of the nature of foetal development that matters most."

[16]*Op. cit.*, p. 86.

[17]*Ibid.*, p. 87.

[18]*Ibid.*

[19]"Deciding Who Is Human," *Natural Law Forum* (1968), p. 136.

[20] A whole literature has arisen about this so-called splitting problem and the difficulties that arise for the theory of personal identity. See, for example, D. Parfit's "Personal Identity," *Philosophical Review* (1971). But the example of the amoeba shows that, one way or another, we can live with it.

[21] I hope to be able to present in the not-too-far future a fuller version of this sketched approach.

[22] For a full defense of this account, see my "De Re and De Dicto Interpretations of Modal Logic," *Philosophia* (1972) and "Why Settle for Anything Less than Good Old-Fashioned Aristotelean Essentialism?" *Nous* (1973).

[23] *Tractatus Logico-Philosophicus* (Routledge and Kegan Paul, 1961), 6.4311.

[24] To make this assumption plausible, we have to keep in mind disjunctive and degree-of-resemblance properties. Even with that complication, there may be further difficulties, but we shall ignore them for now.

SISSELA BOK

Who Shall Count as a Human Being? A Treacherous Question in the Abortion Discussion

"The temptation to introduce premature ultimates — Beauty in Aesthetics, the Mind and its faculties in Psychology, Life in Physiology, are representative examples — is especially great for believers in Abstract Entities. The objection to such Ultimates is that they bring an investigation to a dead end too suddenly."
I.A. Richards, *Principles of Literary Criticism*, p. 40.

In discussions of abortion policy, the premature ultimate is 'humanity.' Does the fetus possess 'humanity'? How does one go about deciding whether a living being possesses it? And what rights go with such possession? These and similar questions have arisen beginning with the earliest speculations about human origins and characteristics. They are still thought central to the abortion debate. I propose to show in this paper that they cannot help us come to grips with the problem of abortion; indeed that they obfuscate all discussion in this domain and lend themselves to dangerous interpretations precisely because of their obscurity.

The concept of 'humanity' is indispensable to two main arguments against abortion. The first defines the fetus as a human being and then concludes that abortion must be murder since it is generally considered murder to take the life of a human being. The second argument is designed to speak to those who do not believe that fetuses are human and cannot share, therefore, the conclusion that abortion is murder. It stresses, not the inherent wrong in individual acts of abortion, but rather the fearful consequences flowing from a *social acceptance* of abortion. According to this argument, it is impossible to draw a line in the period of prenatal development when humanity can be said to begin. There will therefore be no way to stop at early abortions, since they cannot be distinguished from later and yet later abortions; eventually society may even come to permit infanticide and the taking of lives generally. We are all at risk, according to such an argument, once we allow abortions to take place.

An analysis of these two arguments will show the ways in which the concept of 'humanity' operates as a premature ultimate.[1] I propose to substitute for this vague concept an inquiry into the commonly shared principles concerning the protection of life. These principles help to define workable rules for abortions and make it possible to draw a clear line between abortion, on the one hand, and the taking of life in infanticide, euthanasia, and genocide, on the other.

A. Humanity. A long tradition of religious and philosophical and legal thought has approached the problem of abortion by trying to determine whether there is human life before birth, and, if so, when it *becomes* human. If human life is present from conception on, according to this tradition, it must be protected as such from that moment. And if the embryo becomes human at some point during the pregnancy, then that is the point at which the protection should set in.

John Noonan[2] generalizes the predominant Catholic view as follows:

> "Once conceived, the being was recognized as a man because he had man's potential. The criterion for humanity, then, was simple and all-embracing: If you are conceived by human parents, you are human."

Similarly, no less than ten resolutions had been introduced in Congress in the three months following the U.S. Supreme Court's decisions on abortion.[3] These resolutions call for a constitutional amendment providing that

> "neither the United States, nor any state shall deprive any human being, *from the moment of conception,* of life without the due process of law..."

Others have held that the moment when *implantation* of the fertilized egg occurs, 6-7 days after conception, is more significant from

Who Shall Count as a Human Being? 93

the point of view of individual humanity than conception itself. This view permits them to allow the intrauterine device and the 'morning after pill' as not taking human life, merely interfering with implantation. Whether or not one considers such distinctions to be theoretically possible, however, modern contraceptive developments are making them increasingly difficult to draw in practice.

Another widely shared approach to establishing humanity is that of stressing the time when the embryo first begins to *look human*. A photo of the first cell having divided in half clearly does not depict what most people mean when they use the expression 'human being.' Even the four-week embryo does not look human in this sense, whereas the six-week-old one begins to do so. Recent techniques of depicting the embryo and the fetus have remarkably increased our awareness of this early stage; this new 'seeing' of life before birth may come to increase the psychological recoil from aborting those who already look human—thus adding a psychological factor to the medical and other factors already influencing the trend to earlier and earlier abortions.

Another dividing line, once more having to do with perceiving the the fetus, is held to occur when the mother can feel the fetus moving. *Quickening*—when these moments are first felt—has traditionally represented an important distinction; in some legal traditions, such as that of the common law, abortion was permitted before quickening, but considered a misdemeanor afterwards, until the more restrictive 19th century legislation was established. It is certain that the first-felt movements of the fetus represent an awe-inspiring change for the mother, comparable perhaps, in some primitive sense, to a 'coming to life' or the being she carries.

Yet another distinction occurs when the fetus is considered *viable*. According to this view, once the fetus is capable of living independently of its mother, it must be regarded as a human being and protected as such. The U.S. Supreme Court decisions on abortion established viability as the "compelling" point for the state's "important and legitimate interest in potential life," while eschewing the question of when 'life' or 'human life' begins.[4]

A set of later distinctions cluster around the process of birth itself. This is the moment when life begins, according to certain religious traditions, and the point at which 'persons' are fully recognized in the law, according to the Supreme Court.[5] The first breaths taken by newborn babies have been invested with symbolic meaning since the earliest gropings toward understanding what it means to be alive and human. And the rituals of acceptance of babies or children have often defined humanity to the point where the baby could be killed if it were not named or declared accepted by the elders of the community or by the head of the household.

In the positions here examined, and in the abortion debate generally, a number of concepts are at times used as if they were interchangeable. 'Humanity,' 'human life,' 'life,' are such concepts, as are 'man,' 'person,' 'human being,' or 'human individual.' In particular, those who hold that humanity begins at conception or at implantation often have the tendency to say that at that time a human being or a person or a man exists as well, whereas others find it impossible to equate them.

Each of these terms can, in addition, be used in different senses which overlap but are not interchangeable. For instance, humanity and human life, in one sense, are possessed by every cell in our bodies. Many cells have the full genetic makeup required for asexual reproduction—so called cloning—of a human being. Yet clearly this is not the sense of those words intended when the protection of humanity or human life is advocated. Such protection would press the reverence for human life to the mad extreme of ruling out haircuts and considering mosquito bites murder.

It may be argued, however, that for most cells which have the potential of cloning to form a human being, extraordinarily complex measures would be required which are not as yet perfected beyond the animal stage. Is there, then, a difference, from the point of view of human potential, between these cells and egg cells or sperm cells? And is there still another difference in potential between the egg cell before and after conception? While there is a statistical difference in the *likelihood* of their developing into a human being, it does not seem possible to draw a clear line where humanity definitely begins.

The different views as to when humanity begins are little dependent upon factual information. Rather, these views are representative of different world-views, often of a religious nature involving deeply held commitments with moral consequences. There is no disagreement as to what we now know about life and its development before and after conception; differences arise only about the names and moral consequences we attach to the changes in this development and the distinctions we consider important. Just as there is no point at which Achilles can be pinpointed as catching up with the tortoise, though everyone knows he does, so everyone is aware of the distance traveled, in terms of humanity, from before conception to birth, though there is no one point at which humanity can be agreed upon as setting in. Our efforts to pinpoint and to define reflect the urgency with which we reach for abstract labels and absolute certainty in facts and in nature; and the resulting confusion and puzzlement are close to what Wittgenstein described, in *Philosophical Investigations,* as the "bewitchment of our intelligence by means of language."

Even if some see the fertilized egg as possessing humanity and as being "a man" in the words used by Noonan, however, it would be quite unthinkable to act upon all the consequences of such a view. It would be necessary to undertake a monumental struggle against all spontaneous abortions—known as miscarriages—often of severely malformed embryos expelled by the mother's body. This struggle would appear increasingly misguided as we learn more about how to preserve early prenatal life. Those who could not be saved would have to be buried in the same way as dead infants. Those who engaged in abortion would have to be prosecuted for murder. Extraordinary practical complexities would arise with respect to detection of early abortion, and to the question of whether the use of abortifacients in the first few days after conception should also count as murder. In view of these inconsistencies, it seems likely that this view of humanity, like so many others, has been adopted for limited purposes having to do with the prohibition of induced abortion, rather than from a real belief in the full human rights of the first few cells after conception.

A related reason why there are so many views and definitions is that they have been sought for such different *purposes.* I indicated above that many of the views about humanity developed in the abortion dispute seem to have been worked out for one such purpose: that of defending a preconceived position on abortion, with little concern for the other consequences flowing from that particular view. But there have been so many other efforts to define humanity and to arrive at the essence of what it means to be human—to distinguish men from angels and demons, plants and animals, witches and robots. The most powerful one has been the urge to know about the human species and to trace the biological or divine origins and the essential characteristics of mankind. It is magnificently set forth beginning with the very earliest writings in philosophy and poetry; in fact, this consciousness of oneself and wonder at one's condition has often been thought one of the essential distinctions between men and animals.

A separate purpose, both giving strength to and flowing from these efforts to describe and to understand humanity, has been that of seeking to define what a *good* human being is—to delineate human aspirations. What ought fully human beings to be like, and how should they differ from and grow beyond their immature, less perfect, sick or criminal fellow men? Who can teach such growth—St. Francis or Nietzsche, Buddha or Erasmus? And what kind of families and societies give support and provide models for growth?

Finally, definitions of humanity have been sought in order to try to set limits to the protection of life. At what level of developing humanity can and ought lives to receive protection? And who, among those many labelled less than human at different times in history—slaves, enemies in war, women, children, the retarded—should be denied such protection?

Of these three purposes for defining 'humanity,' the first is classificatory and descriptive in the first hand (though it gives rise to normative considerations). It has roots in religious and metaphysical thought, and has branched out into biological and archeological and anthropological research. But the latter two, so often confused with the first, are primarily *normative* or prescriptive. They seek to set norms or guidelines for who is fully human and who is at least minimally human—so human as to be entitled to the protection of life. For the sake of these normative purposes, definitions of 'humanity' established elsewhere have been sought in order to determine action —and all too often the action has been devastating for those excluded.

It is crucial to ask at this point why the descriptive and the normative definitions have been thought to coincide; why it has been taken for granted that the line between human and non-human or not yet-human is identical with that distinguishing those who may be killed from those who are to be protected.

One or both of two fundamental assumptions are made by those who base the protection of life upon the possession of 'humanity.' The first is that human beings are not only different from, but *superior to* all other living matter. This is the assumption which changes the definition of humanity into an evaluative one. It lies at the root of Western religious and social thought, from the Bible and the

Aristotelian concept of the "ladder of nature" all the way to Teilhard de Chardin's view of mankind as close to the intended summit and consummation of the development of living beings.

The second assumption holds that the superiority of human beings somehow justifies their using what is non-human as they see fit, dominating it, even killing it when they wish to. St. Augustine, in *The City of God*,[6] expresses both of these anthropocentric assumptions when he holds that the injunction "Thou shalt not kill" does not apply to killing animals and plants, since, having no faculty of reason,

> "therefore by the altogether righteous ordinance of the Creator both their life and death are a matter subordinate to our needs."

Neither of these assumptions is self-evident. And the results of acting upon them, upon the bidding to subdue the earth, to subordinate living matter to human needs, are no longer seen by all to be beneficial. The ancient certainties about man's preordained place in the universe are faltering. The supposition that only human beings have rights is no longer regarded as beyond question.[7]

Not only, therefore, can the line between human and non-human not be drawn empirically so as to permit normative conclusions: the very enterprise of *basing* normative conclusions on such distinctions can no longer be taken for granted. Despite these difficulties, many still try to employ definitions of 'humanity' to do just that. And herein lies by far the most important reason for abandoning such efforts: the monumental misuse of the concept of 'humanity' in so many practices of discrimination and atrocity throughout history. Slavery, witch-hunts, and wars have all been justified by their perpetrators on the ground that they thought their victims to be less than fully human. The insane and the criminal have for long periods been deprived of the most basic necessities for similar reasons, and excluded from society. A theologian, Dr. Joseph Fletcher, has even suggested as recently as last year that someone who has an I.Q. below 40 is "questionably a person" and that those below the 20-mark are not persons at all.[8] He adds that:

> "This has bearing, obviously, on decision-making in gynecology, obstetrics, and pediatrics, as well as in general surgery and medicine."

Here, a criterion for 'personhood' is taken as a guideline for action which could have sinister and far-reaching effects. Even when entered upon with the best of intentions, and in the most guarded manner, the enterprise of basing the protection of human life upon such criteria and definitions is dangerous. To question someone's humanity or personhood is a first step to mistreatment and killing.

We must abandon, therefore, this quest for a definition of humanity capable of showing us who has a right to live. We must seek, instead, common principles for the protection of life that reflect a clear understanding of the harm that comes from the taking of life. Why do we hold life to be sacred? Why does it require protection beyond that given to anything else? The question seems unnecessary at first glance —surely most people share what has been called "the elemental sensation of vitality and the elemental fear of its extinction," and what Hume called "our horrors at annihilation."[9] Many think of this elemental sensation as incapable of further analysis. They view any attempt to say *why* we hold life sacred as an instrumentalist, utilitarian rocking of the boat which may loosen this fundamental respect for life. Yet a failure to scrutinize this respect, to ask what it protects and what it ought to protect, lies at the root not only of the confusion about abortion, but of the persistent vagueness and consequent abuse of the notion of the respect for life. The result is that everyone, including those who authorize or perform the most brutal killings in war, can protest their belief in life's sacredness. I shall therefore list the most important reasons which underlie the elemental sense of the sacredness of life. Having done so, these reasons can be considered as they apply or do not apply to the embryo and the fetus.

B. *Reasons for Protecting Life.*
   1. Killing is viewed as the greatest of all dangers *for the victim.*
   —The knowledge that there is a threat to life causes intense anguish and apprehension.
   —The actual taking of life can cause great suffering.
   —The continued experience of life, once begun, is considered so valuable, so unique, so absorbing, that no one who has this experience should be unjustly deprived of it. And depriving someone of this experience means that all else of value to him will be lost.
   2. Killing is brutalizing and criminalizing *for the killer*. It is a threat to others and destructive to the person engaging therein.
   3. Killing often causes *the family of the victim and others* to experience grief and loss. They may have been tied to the dead person

by affection or economic dependence; they may have given of themselves in the relationship, so that its severance causes deep suffering.

4. All of society, as a result, has a stake in the protection of life. Permitting killing to take place sets patterns for victims, killers, and survivors that are threatening and ultimately harmful to all.

These are neutral principles governing the protection of life. They are shared by most human beings reflecting upon the possibility of dying at the hands of others. It is clear that these principles, if applied in the absence of the confusing terminology of 'humanity,' would rule out the kinds of killing perpetrated by conquerors, witch-hunters, slave-holders, and Nazis. Their victims feared death and suffered; they grieved for their dead; and the societies permitting such killing were brutalized and degraded.

Turning now to abortion once more, how do these principles apply to the taking of the lives of embryos and fetuses?

C. *Reasons to Protect Life in the Prenatal Period.* Consider the very earliest cell formations soon after conception. Clearly the reasons for protecting human life fail to apply here:

This group of cells cannot feel the anguish or pain connected with death, nor can it fear death. Its experiencing of life has not yet begun; it is not yet conscious of the interruption of life nor of the loss of anything it has come to value in life, nor is it tied by bonds of affection to others. If the abortion is desired by both parents, it will cause no grief such as that which accompanies the death of a child. Almost no human care and emotion and resources have been invested in it. Nor is such an early abortion brutalizing for the person voluntarily performing it, or a threat to other members of the society where it takes place.

Some may argue that one can conceive of other deaths with those factors absent, which nevertheless would be murder. Take the killing of a hermit in his sleep by someone who instantly commits suicide. Here there is no anxiety or fear of the killing on the part of the victim, no pain in dying, no mourning by family or friends (to whom the hermit has, in leaving them for ever, already in a sense 'died'), no awareness by others that a wrong has been done; and the possible brutalization of the murderer has been made harmless to others through his suicide. Speculate further that the bodies are never found. Yet we would still call the act one of murder. The reason we would do so is inherent in the act itself and depends on the fact that his life was taken and that he was denied the chance to continue to experience it.

How does this deprivation differ from abortion in the first few days of pregnancy? I find that I cannot use words like 'deprive,' 'deny,' 'take away,' and 'harm' when it comes to the group of cells, whereas I have no difficulty in using them for the hermit. These words require, if not a person conscious of his loss, at least someone who at a prior time has developed enough to be or have been conscious thereof. Because there is no semblance of human form, no conscious life or capability to live independently, no knowledge of death, no sense of pain, one cannot use such words meaningfully to describe early abortion.

In addition, whereas it is possible to frame a rule permitting abortion which will cause no anxiety on the part of others covered by the rule—other embryos or fetuses—it is not possible to frame such a rule permitting the killing of hermits without threatening other *hermits*. All hermits would have to fear for their lives if there were a rule saying that hermits can be killed if they are alone and asleep and if the agent commits suicide.

The reasons, then, for the protection of lives are minimal in very early abortions. At the same time, many of these reasons are clearly present with respect to *infanticide*, most important among them the brutalization of those participating in the act and the resultant danger for all who are felt to be undesirable by their families or by others. This is not to say that acts of infanticide have not taken place in our society; indeed, as late as the 19th century, newborns were frequently killed, either directly or by giving them into the care of institutions such as foundling hospitals, where the death rate could be as high as 90% in the first year of life.[10] A few primitive societies, at the edge of extinction, without other means to limit families, still practice infanticide. But I believe that the *public acceptance* of infanticide in all other societies is unthinkable, given the advent of modern methods of contraception and early abortion and of institutions to which parents can give their children, assured of their survival and of the high likelihood that they will be adopted and cared for by a family.

D. Dividing Lines. If, therefore, very early abortion does not violate these principles of protection for life, but infanticide does, we are confronted with a new kind of continuum in the place of that between less human and more human: that of the growth in strength, as the

Who Shall Count as a Human Being? 101

fetus develops during the prenatal period, of these principles, these reasons for protecting life. In this second continuum, it would be as difficult as in the first to draw a line based upon objective factors. Since most abortions can be performed earlier or later during pregnancy, it would be preferable to encourage early abortions rather than late ones and to draw a line before the second half of the pregnancy, permitting later abortions only on a clear showing of need. For this purpose, the two concepts of *quickening* and *viability*—so unsatisfactory in determining when humanity begins—can provide such limits.

Before quickening, the reasons to protect life are, as has been shown, negligible, perhaps absent altogether. During this period, therefore, abortion could be permitted upon request. Alternatively, the end of the first trimester could be employed as such a limit, as is the case in a number of countries.

Between quickening and viability, when the operation is a more difficult one medically and more traumatic for parents and medical personnel, it would not seem unreasonable to hold that special reasons justifying the abortion should be required in order to counterbalance this resistance: reasons not known earlier, such as the severe malformation of the fetus. After viability, finally, all abortions save the rare ones required to save the life of the mother,[11] should be prohibited, because the reasons to *protect* life may now be thought to be partially present; even though the viable fetus cannot fear death or suffer consciously therefrom, the effects on those participating in the event, and thus on society indirectly, could be serious. This is especially so because of the need, mentioned above, for a protection against infanticide. In the unlikely event, however, that the mother should wish to be separated from the fetus at such a late stage,[12] the procedure ought to be delayed until it can be one of premature birth, not one of harming the fetus in an abortive process.

Medically, however, the definition of 'viability' is difficult. It varies from one fetus to another. At one stage in pregnancy, a certain number of babies, if born, will be viable. At a later stage, the percentage will be greater. Viability also depends greatly on the state of our knowledge concerning the support of life after birth and on the nature of the support itself. Support can be given much earlier in a modern hospital than in a rural village, or in a clinic geared to doing abortions only. It may some day even be the case that almost any human life will be considered viable before birth, once artificial wombs are perfected.

As technological progress pushes back the time when the fetus can be helped to survive independently of the mother, a question will arise as to whether the cut-off point marked by viability ought also to be pushed back. Should abortion then be prohibited much earlier than is now the case, because the medical meaning of 'viability' will have changed, or should we continue to rely on the conventional meaning of the word for the distinction between lawful and unlawful abortion?

In order to answer this question it is necessary to look once more at the reasons for which 'viability' was thought to be a good dividing-line in the first place. Is viability important because the baby can survive outside of the mother? Or because this chance of survival comes at a time in fetal development when the *reasons* to protect life have grown strong enough to prohibit abortion? At present, the two coincide, but in the future, they may come to diverge increasingly.

If the time comes when an embryo *could* be kept alive without its mother and thus be 'viable' in one sense of the word, the *reasons* for protecting life from the point of view of victims, agents, relatives and society would still be absent; it seems right, therefore, to tie the obligatory protection of life to the present conventional definition of 'viability' and to set a socially agreed upon time in pregnancy after which abortion should be prohibited.

To sum up, the justifications a mother has for not wishing to give birth can operate up to a certain point in pregnancy; after that point, the reasons society has for protecting life become sufficiently weighty so as to prohibit late abortions and infanticide.

F. The Slippery Slope. Some argue, however, that such views of abortion could lead, if widely followed, to great dangers for society. This second major argument against abortion appears to set aside the question of when the fetus becomes human. It focuses, rather, on the risks for society—for the newborn, the handicapped, and the aged—which may stem from allowing abortions; it evokes the age-old fear of the slippery slope.[13] Because there are no sharp transitions in the period of fetal development, this argument holds, it would be unreasonable to permit abortion at one time in pregnancy and prohibit it shortly thereafter; in addition, it would be impossible to enforce such prohibitions. Later and later abortions may therefore be allowed, and there will be risks of slipping towards infanticide, euthanasia, even genocide.

The assumption made here is that once we admit reasons for justifying early abortions—reasons such as rape, incest, or maternal illness—nothing will prevent people from acting upon these very same reasons later in pregnancy or even after birth. If abortion is permissible at four weeks of pregnancy, then why not at four weeks and one day, four weeks and two days, and so on until birth and beyond? The reason that this argument possesses superficial plausibility has to do, once more with the concept of 'humanity'. Since all agree that the newborn infant is a human being, and since there are no ways of drawing clear lines before birth in the development of this human being, there appears to be no clear way of saying that the fetus is *not* human. On the assumption that humanity is the *only* criterion, there can then be a slippage from abortion to infanticide, with no clear dividing line between the two. Once more, then, 'humanity' turns out to be at stake. It is the concept providing the "slipperiness" to the slope—the dimension along which no distinctions can be made which make sense and are enforceable.

Once again, here, 'humanity' operates as a premature ultimate, bringing discussion to a dead end too soon. For the discontinuity which is not found in fetal development can be established by society, and indeed has been so established in modern societies permitting abortion. The argument that the reasons *for* aborting may still be declared to exist at childbirth completely ignores the reasons advanced *against* killing. These reasons grow in strength during pregnancy. Sympathy for the victim, grief on the part of those aware of the loss, recoil on the part of those who would do the killing, and a sense of social catastrophe would accompany the acceptance of infanticide by a contemporary democracy.

But, it may be asked, how can one know that these reasons would prevail? How can one be sure that the discontinuity will be respected by most, and that there will not be pressure to move closer and closer to an acceptance of infanticide?

The best way to answer such a question is to see whether that kind of development has actually taken place in one or more of the societies which permit abortion. To the best of my knowledge, the societies which have permitted abortion for considerable lengths of time have not experienced any tendency to infanticide. The infant mortality statistics of Sweden and Denmark, for example, are extremely low, and the protection and care given to all living children, including those born with special handicaps, is exemplary.[14] It is true that facts cannot satisfy those who want a *logical* demonstration that dangerous developments cannot under any circumstances come about. But the burden of proof rests upon them to show *some* evidence of such developments taking place before opposing a policy which will mean so much to women and their families, and also to show why it would not be possible to stop any such development *after* it begins to take place.

The fear of slipping from abortion towards infanticide, therefore, while superficially plausible, does not seem to be supported by the available evidence, so long as a cut-off time in pregnancy is established, either by law or in medical practice, after which all fetuses are protected against killing.[15]

I have sketched an approach to seeking community norms for abortion and tried to show the difficulties and dangers in using considerations of 'humanity' to set such norms. Needless to say, *individual* choices for or against abortion will have to be more complex and influenced by religious and moral considerations.[16] Every effort must be made to show that abortion is a last resort. It presents difficulties not present in contraception, yet it is sometimes the only way out of a great dilemma.

NOTES

[1]The focus in this paper is on abortion as a problem of social policy. Decisions made by individuals must take other factors into consideration. See S. Bok, "Ethical Problems of Abortion," *Hastings Studies,* January 1974; first prepared for the Harvard Interfaculty Seminar on Children, chaired by Nathan B. Talbot. The results and findings of this seminar will be published by Little, Brown, and Company (Boston) and entitled *Raising Children in Modern Urban America: Problems and Prospective Solutions.*

[2]John Noonan, Jr., "An Almost Absolute Value in History," in John Noonan, Jr., ed., *The Morality of Abortion,* p. 51, Harvard University Press, Cambridge, Massachusetts. For a thorough discussion of this and other views concerning the beginnings of human life, see Daniel Callahan, *Abortion: Law, Choice and Morality,* New York: the Macmillan Company, 1970.

[3]"How the Constitution is Amended," p. 56, *Family Planning/Population Reporter,* Vol. 2, no. 3.

[4]Roe v. Wade, *The United States Law Week,* 41, pp. 4227, 4229.

[5]*Ibid.,* p. 4227. For a discussion of this and other positions taken in the 1973 Supreme Court abortion decisions see L. Tribe, Foreword, *Harvard Law Review,* Vol. 87, Nov. 1973, pp. 1-54.

[6]Augustine, *The City of God against the Pagans,* Book I, Ch. XX, Cam-

bridge: Harvard University Press, 1957.

[7]Christopher D. Stone, "Should Trees Have Standing? Toward Legal Rights for Natural Objects," *Southern California Law Review*, Vol. 45, 450-501, provides an interesting analysis of the extension of rights to those not previously considered persons, such as children, and a discussion of possible future extensions to natural objects.

[8]Joseph Fletcher, "Indicators of Humanhood: A Tentative Profile of Man," *The Hastings Center Report*, Vol. 2, no. 5, pp. 1-4.

[9]Edward Shils, "The Sanctity of Life," in D. H. Labby, ed., p. 12, *Life or Death: Ethics and Options*, Seattle: University of Washington Press, 1968. David Hume, *Essay on Immortality*.

[10]William Langer, "Checks on Population Growth: 1750-1850," *Scientific American*, Vol. 226, no. 2, 1972.

[11]Every effort must be made by physicians and others to construe the Supreme Court's statement *(supra)* "If the State is interested in protecting fetal life after viability, it may go so far as to proscribe abortion during that period except when it is necessary to preserve the life or health of the mother" to concern, in effect, only the life or threat to life of the mother. See Alan Stone, "Abortion and the Supreme Court: What Now?" *Modern Medicine,* April 30, 1973, pp. 33-37, for a discussion of this question and what it means for physicians.

[12]For an insightful discussion of this dilemma, see Judith Thomson, "A Defense of Abortion," *Philosophy and Public Policy*, Vol. 1, no. 1, pp. 47-66. My conclusions are set forth in detail in "Ethical Problems of Abortion," (footnote 1).

[13]See S. Bok, "The Leading Edge of the Wedge," *The Hastings Center Report*, pp. 9-11, Vol. 1, no. 3, 1971.

[14]Moreover, Nazi Germany, which is frequently cited as a warning of what is to come once abortion becomes lawful, had very strict laws prohibiting abortion. In 1943, Hitler's regime made the existing penalties for women having abortions and for those performing them even more severe by removing the limit on imprisonment and by including the possibility of hard labor for "especially serious cases." See *Reichsgezetzblatt*, 1926, Teil I, Nr. 28, par. 218, and 1943, Teil I, Art. I, "Angriffe auf Ehe, Familie, und Mutterschaft."

[15]Another type of line-drawing and slippery slope problem is that which would exist if abortions, once permissible, came to be coercively obtained in the case of mothers thought unable to bring up children, or in cases where deformed children were expected. To outlaw abortions out of a fear that involuntary abortions would take place, however, would be the wrong response to such a danger, just as outlawing voluntary divorces, operations, and adoptions on the grounds that they might lead to involuntary divorces, operations, and adoptions, would be. The battle against coercion must be fought at all times, with respect to many social options, but this is no reason to prohibit the options themselves.

[16]See "Ethical Problems of Abortion" (footnote 1).

ROGER WERTHEIMER

Philosophy on Humanity

People often disagree about how a person should act. Yet they agree that whether a person should perform some act depends upon what kinds of things are affected by the act and how those things are affected. For most of us, whether and how an inanimate thing is affected is generally not *in itself* a consideration; we think such effects provide reasons for acting (or refraining) only insofar as they relate to effects on something else such as a human being (e.g., the agent or the object's owner). But, for most of us, the beneficial and harmful effects of a person's act on a human being are *in themselves* relevant considerations; we regard an act's harming some human being (the agent or others) as itself a reason for a person to refrain from that act. That is, we accord an inanimate thing a *dependent moral status*, and a human being an *independent moral status*. The moral status of animals is controversial, but most people believe that, whether independent or not, an animal's moral status is *inferior* to a human being's: though an act's having harmful effects on an animal may itself be a reason for refraining from the act, the reason is of a lower order than the reason provided by an act's having an equivalently harmful effect on a human being.[1]

Let us call the kind of moral status most people ascribe to human beings *human (moral) status*. The term refers to a kind of independent and superior consideration to be accorded an entity, not to the kind of entity to be accorded the consideration, so it is not a definitional truth that human beings have human status. But most people believe that being human has *moral cachet:* viz., a human being has

107

human status in virtue of being a human being (and thus each human being has human status). Call this the *Standard Belief*. That most people accept it is an empirical fact.

Though establishing this fact requires the services of social science, we are already familiar with a sufficiency of evidence, enough so that we may remove most doubts on the matter by eliminating confusions about the data. Among the best batches of data we have is what people say and do and feel regarding the issue of the morality of abortion. Presumably it's common knowledge that few people would say, "What difference does it make whether a fetus is a human being? What's that got to do with the morality of abortion?" People disagree over whether and when abortions are morally objectionable primarily, if not solely, because they disagree over whether and when a fetus is a human being. The other pertinent facts are not much disputed (e.g., facts about the other properties of fetuses and facts about the consequences of aborting and not aborting). So too with the pertinent moral principles. While people may disagree about what overriding considerations may legitimize killing a human being, most people believe that killing a human being is in principle wrong and that, if a fetus is a full-fledged human being, it may be destroyed only for those reasons that justify destroying any other human being.[2] The very structure of this familiar controversy evidences a shared assumption: the Standard Belief.

That structure and thus its value as evidence here may be challenged. Proabortionists often insist that the dispute is due, not to differing beliefs about the humanness of the fetus, but to their allegiance to some consideration antiabortionists deny or deemphasize, such as the mother's rights regarding her own body and welfare. That insistence, however sincere, is rarely reliable testimony. Usually, whatever the alleged moral consideration, it applies in two conceivable cases differing only in that the victim is a fetus in one case and a week or year or ten year old child in the other. And if, as is usual, the proabortionist judges the cases differently—if, for example, he would sanction a mother's destroying her fetus solely because it threatens her with an emotional or economic breakdown, while he balks at her exterminating her week old (or year or ten year old) offspring for the sole same reason—then usually that is good reason for presuming that his beliefs about abortion depend upon his beliefs about the differences between fetuses and children. And usually it can be shown, and (what is not the same thing) often the proabortionist will come to admit that the morally relevant difference for him is that children are human beings and fetuses are not. Sometimes he will first maintain that some other difference (e.g., independent existence) is the morally relevant one, but when he imagines a child similar to a fetus in the alleged relevant respect (e.g., an incubated infant) usually he continues to condone annihilation of the fetus but not the child. And further inquiry usually reveals that his alleged relevant respect actually operates as (part of) his reason for calling a child, but not a fetus, a human being.

However, there are no simple or foolproof procedures for determining what someone believes; they all require a knack, skill and sensitivity for their application, and none is infallible, and not just because people may lie or be self-deceived. The difficulties here are those of explaining a phenomenon, for to ascribe a belief to someone is to explain certain facts about him, to make sense of certain patterns in his behavior (including, but not confined to his speech behavior). What even the most intelligent and sincere of persons *claims* to accept as moral principles usually turns out to be a hodge-podge of rules inconsistent with each other and with his own considered judgments on particular cases. Sometimes we may say he holds contradictory beliefs; other times that what he *really* believes is what he would agree to after proper reflection that clears away confusion or what explains the largest and/or most significant aspects of his behavior. No doubt the criteria for "proper" reflection and for explanatory power are problematic. So too, the distinction between what someone presently believes and what he will agree to on the basis of his present beliefs is difficult to draw and apply if only because attempts to determine what someone believes (e.g., by his reflecting on contrasting cases) may alter his beliefs. Still, there is a clear enough sense in which, whatever else they may believe, most people accept the Standard Belief. That belief is here ascribed to them, not primarily because it matches their reports of their belief on the matter, but because it provides the best account of why they believe that all humans and no animals have human status, and why their arguments over abortion and many other issues take the form they do, and so on. (The "and so on" refers to numerous and diverse facts, only some of which find space for mention here.)

Again, to ascribe a belief is to explain. Whether or not the ascription is made *on the basis of* the person's behavior (self-ascribed beliefs generally are not), the ascription must be testable against the person's behavior for it to be able to explain and make sense of that behavior. To explain the actions of a creature in terms of its beliefs (desires, and the like) is to explain them as the actions of a rational (or at least intelligent) creature—and to do that one must presuppose a theory of rationality. A person's behavior is evidence of some belief only given the assumption that he has certain conative and affective structures and capacities (e.g., certain desires), certain information gathering (perception) and storage (memory) structures and capacities, and also certain physical structures and capacities for action, and further that the world in which he acts has certain physical structures and capacities. But even given this background of facts, his behavior is evidence only within a theory of rational behavior, a system of principles that state what someone would be believing, given the background assumptions, if he behaves in certain ways. Those principles are principles of rational thought and action. So, what and how we do think is determinable only by assuming beliefs about what and how we ought to think. For that matter, determining any of the background facts or any fact at all presupposes the same assumption: an understanding of the physical world requires an understanding of our mental structures and capacities, if only because without the latter one cannot discriminate appearance from reality, the self from the not-self.

A theory of rationality serves two functions. First, its principles may be regarded as statements of natural laws with which to describe, predict, and explain the behavior of an entity given certain background conditions and the assumption that the entity is a rational creature (i.e., an entity operating in accordance with those laws). Secondly, the same principles may be regarded as norms which a rational creature can conform to or violate and by which his activity can be assessed for its rationality. We may "assume" that we are rational (that we can and sometimes do act in conformity with rational principles) if only because we cannot do otherwise: to doubt or deny that oneself is rational is as self-defeating as doubting or denying that oneself exists, for in the very act of doubting or denying one evidences the contrary. Now, a theory explains what is evidence for the theory, and what is explained by the theory is evidence for the theory. Thus, what and how we do think is evidence for the principles of rationality, what and how we ought to think. This itself is a methodological principle of rationality; call it the *Factunorm Principle*. We are (implicitly) accepting the Factunorm Principle whenever we try to determine what or how we ought to think. For we must, in that very attempt, think. And unless we can think that what and how we do think there is correct—and thus is evidence for what and how we ought to think—we cannot determine what or how we ought to think. But that does not undermine the Factunorm Principle, for it is itself something we learn only by thinking and accepting that principle. Of course, we are fallible; sometimes we are mistaken in what or how we think. But that does not undermine the Factunorm Principle, for it is itself something we learn only by thinking and accepting that principle. And if we can learn of our mistakes we can learn from our mistakes, and thus, by thinking and accepting the Factunorm Principle, we can alter and improve what and how we think, gradually approximating to what and how we ought to think. That capacity is the essence of rationality. One essential step in this process is learning that oneself is not special in this regard, that what and how anyone thinks may be evidence for what and how anyone ought to think. Another step is learning that what and how we think in certain circumstances is not much evidence for what and how we ought to think: as a part and prerequisite of the total learning process we continuously develop, refine and apply an elaborate variety of criteria for evaluating the evidentiary value of the processes and products of thought and thus for identifying those we have the best reason to trust and are most likely to be correct (e.g., the person is mature, sane, calm, sober, of at least normal intelligence, possessed of the requisite subsidiary information, without relevant biases, etc.). Thus, when we speak here of common belief or what most people believe, we attend only to those beliefs we cannot find suspect for some relevant defect in the personal history of the belief. And we speak of what *most* people believe just because we have also learned that in disagreements between two groups of persons similar in the other relevant respects, the judgment of the larger group is more likely to be correct; however, while uncertainty increases as the difference in size diminishes, unanimity does not supply certainty. Any such belief, no matter how many people believe it, could be mistaken; and even if something is a necessary truth, we do not necessarily believe it. What and how we do think is *evidence* for rational principles, but a rational principle is not true *because* of what and how we think. A rational principle isn't true by virtue of anything: there neither need be, nor is, nor can be any *foundation* for rational principles.[3]

Put it this way. The goal if philosophy is, as Socrates said, self-knowledge. For philosophy is, in essence, rationality reasoning about rationality. It is the process and product of creatures who are their own paradigms of rationality exercising the very capacities for which they deem themselves rational in the attempt to chart the processes and products of the proper exercise of those capacities. Yet philosophy is not introspective psychology; it is a normative science. The self that the self seeks to know is not, *per se,* the actual self, but the ideal self, the ideally rational self, for it seeks to know how it ought to act (e.g., think) ; how it does act is of interest only insofar as that bears upon how it ought to act. But the self that seeks to know is, ineluctably, the actual self, and its experiences are, ineluctably, its actual experiences, and the only objects it can experience are, ineluctably, the phenomena of the actual self and the rest of the actual world. The ideal self, the norms defining the ideal self, the norms of rationality are not possible objects of experience. The problem of self-knowledge, then, is not just whether and how the actual self can identify the ideal self when its resources are confined to the actual world, but also whether and how the actual self can identify the actual self or anything in the actual or ideal world when any of its operations provide information only insofar as the operation accords with the operations of the ideal self—and when the actual self, in all its operations, is fallible. If the existence of the ideal self is understood on the model of the existence of the actual self, if rational principles need a foundation in some independent reality, then all true knowledge would be impossibly short of some metaphysical-mystical leap. Since there need be no such foundation, knowledge of rational principles is (in principle) attainable through a dialectical process within and between actual selves over time. After all, what we are searching for is only an understanding of our search.

All this, the Factunorm Principle, and the rest, plus more that could be said, is but an elaboration of two "assumptions"; we are rational and it is rational to believe what is believed by rational persons. Of course, not every philosopher acknowledges the Factunorm Principle, let alone the rest of the foregoing. But many have expressed acceptance of that principle, particularly those intent on developing a substantive moral theory, a system of norms of rationality regarding moral matters. By their conscious practice and often by explicit statement, most such philosophers acknowledge that a reason for thinking that some moral belief implied by a theory is true (false) is that the belief is accepted (rejected) by most people. Certainly for most of the most important moral philosophers, conformity with common belief is a test and a touchstone if not the bedrock of moral theory. That is an empirical fact easily established; the texts are public and unequivocal.

That fact, taken with the fact that the Standard Belief is a common belief, might suggest that most if not all philosophers accept the Standard Belief. Yet the fact is they all reject it.[4]

The inevasible question then is: Why do philosophers deny the Standard Belief?

The answer is hard to come by because the question has gone unasked. Philosophers don't explain their denial, for they hardly ever express it; it lies implicit in and entailed by what they do say. Mostly they don't discuss the Standard Belief at all or even demonstrate any awareness of its existence.

The answer is hard to come by as well because objections to the Standard Belief are hard to come by. I know of but two complaints that have ever been raised. One is that the belief that humans have a unique inherent value or dignity is *hubris* and nonsense. The other is that the belief that being a member of the human race is morally relevant is like the belief that being a member of the Aryan race is morally relevant. Both of those claims are true. The trouble is, no one has troubled himself to explain precisely how either of those claims constitutes an objection to the Standard Belief. If it's not obvious now that there is some trouble here, an explanation is forthcoming.

In any case, even if there exists an effective refutation of the Standard Belief, there exists no reason to think such a refutation has motivated philosophers to reject that belief. And even if it has, still, philosophical and common belief do collide here on a most fundamental moral issue, and we need to understand how that fact has passed unnoticed instead of being, as it should be, a philosophical cause célèbre. Philosophers must in general suppose either that their theories imply or are at least consistent with the Standard Belief or that in denying the Standard Belief they conform with common belief. Either or both possibilities must be regularly realized, for otherwise it seems inexplicable that the Standard Belief is routinely rejected with nary a word about it or with words betraying no cognizance of its centrality in common belief. Those two possibilities come to much the same, for the mistakes in both cases share the same cause, a mistaken or misapplied methodology that throws doubt on the philosophers' conceptions of what the common belief is, and on how their theories contrast with it, and, at the same time, on the truth of what those theories affirm.

Let us begin by clarifying the contrast between philosophical and common belief. And let us first remove a verbal similarity that masks a substantive difference, for many a philosopher has *said* (in so many words) that being human has moral cachet. But what he *means* is that being a *person* has moral cachet, that a human being has human status only because and insofar as a human being is a person. By contrast, most people believe a person has human status if the person is a human being.

The term 'human being' is correctly applied to all and only the members of our biological species. That specification is informative but incomplete without criteria for species membership. Being of human parents conceived is a partial criterion; it is explainable without circularity by referring to paradigm cases, but it provides neither a necessary condition (for, e.g., it excludes the original species members) nor a sufficient condition (for, e.g., it includes human terata whom we regard not as human beings but as some unfortunate kind of mutants). But then, the abortion argument supplies sufficient evidence that no neat set of necessary and sufficient conditions for being human is generally agreed upon—which is to say there is no such set. For reasons not discussable here, it would be extraordinary if there were such a set of conditions. Yet disputes about what a human being is or which things are human beings do not indicate the existence of any *linguistic* divergences; on the contrary, such disputes require for their intelligibility that the disputants mean the same thing by the term 'human being.'

In common speech 'person' has various meanings; often it seems freely interchangeable if not synonymous with 'human being' or at least applicable to all human beings though perhaps not only human beings (gods are called persons). But in philosophy 'person' is a theoretical term defined differently in different subspecialties (e.g., ethics, philosophy of mind) and by different theories within each subspecialty. Moral theories generally intend it to be interchangeable with some term like 'entity having human status'. It may be defined by that term, thereby presenting the problem of determining which (ostensibly nonethical) properties are necessary and sufficient for having that status, or it may be defined by some set of (ostensibly nonethical) properties, and then the problem is to determine whether those properties are necessary and sufficient for having that status. The two tactics come to the same. Theories differ over what the essential properties of persons are, but usually they select one or more cognitive or affective capacities such as rationality or sentience or a free will or a sense of justice—but never humanness. However, though 'person' is defined without reference to human beings, since a normal adult human being is the natural paradigm of both a person and a human being, philosophers follow the common practice of freely interchanging 'human being' and 'person'.

The conflict over the Standard Belief is also obscured by significant agreements on which things have human status. Most philosophers grant that no animal has human status (and thus that no property possessed by an animal has moral cachet or that animals do not possess such a property in sufficient degree), and that most human beings and certainly all normal adults have human status. Indeed, many theories seem intended to accord human status to all and (among known things) only human beings. But whatever their intent, none succeeds. They fail in different ways and for different reasons. Most make too stringent a requirement; typically they hold that only some developed (exercisable) capacity has moral cachet, thereby excluding humans whose allegedly relevant capacities are undeveloped, deformed or defunct. When the requirement is reduced to the possession of the original, native capacity alone, still humans with the relevant congenital defects are left out. And here the requirement may be too weak as well as too strong, for normal "infrahuman" fetuses[5] may qualify while congenitally defective adults do not. In other theories the requirement is just too weak, for while every human may qualify, some animals and/or "infrahuman" fetuses qualify as well as and sometimes better than some humans. Here, though the moral status of every human may be independent, it is not superior to that of some nonhuman things. The reverse of this occurs in theories that first account for the moral status of some primary group (usually normal adults) and then admit the rest of the race through their relations (e.g., affectional bonds) to members of the primary group; every plausible suggested relation makes the moral status of the secondary group dependent upon the primary group (e.g., the effects of an act on the interests of an infant get considered only because and insofar as the affections of his parents and other normal adults are affected by effects on his interests). Moreover, with many of the suggested relations, members of the primary group could be so related to a nonhuman things, thereby fitting it for the secondary group.

We need not examine individually each of the many theories (each with its own minor variations) to conclude that each fails to accord human status to all and only human beings. We need only reflect upon the gross disparities between various human beings and upon the close resemblances between some animals (or "infrahuman" fetuses) and some human beings to see that no property, not even a complex disjunct property is possessed by all humans and no animals (or "infrahuman" fetuses) and is plausibly thought to have moral cachet. No property, that is, other than being human.[6]

More importantly, all this is ultimately beside the point, for the opposition over what has moral cachet is not itself and does not entail an opposition over which things have human status. The latter conflicts are avoidable while the former persists. The Standard Belief is consistent with virtually any traditional theory's position regarding which particular things have human status; one need only claim, as many have tried to, that the entity in question—be it fetus, congenital idiot or whatever—is not (or is) a human being. (The plausibility of the claim may vary from case to case (and audience to audience) but the forms of argument employed are remarkably constant: fetuses are likened to parts of their mothers, mongoloids to terata, the permanently comatose to vegetables, slaves to animals, etc.) The Standard Belief is a general principle, and disagreements on principles are evidenced not so much by disagreements over judgments on particular cases ("verdicts") as by differing forms of reasoning employed in reaching those verdicts. Divergencies in verdicts attract more attention because of their more obvious practical import. But it is of more subtle and profound importance that, when arguing about abortion, euthanasia (without consent), infanticide, racial discrimination, and many, many other issues, nonphilosophers find it natural or necessary to claim on one basis or another that the creature in question is (or is not) a human being so that they can then conclude that the creature should (or need not) be regarded and treated as befits one with human status. Philosophers may reach similar verdicts by ascribing moral cachet to some property roughly coextensive with being human, and, since that property may sometimes be relevant in arguments over the humanness of a creature, they may employ similar bases in reaching those verdicts. Still, philosophers employ those bases differently, for *their* arguments bypass the issue of the creature's humanness as essentially irrelevant. Understandably a philosopher might misconstrue this situation, supposing either that his theory entails the Standard Belief and thereby conforms to common belief or that it conforms to common belief while denying the Standard Belief. But actually all such theories entail competitors to the Standard Belief and thereby reject common belief. In fine, a theory lacking the Standard Belief is comparable, not to a theory that would punish arsonists more severely than murderers, but to one that determines whom to punish and how severely without employing the notion of desert at all.

Traditional philosophers are liable to be misled about such matters because they practice a curious kind of doublethink: while regarding the verdicts of common belief as data against which to test their theories, they have not treated the principles of common belief as an independent form of evidence. Theorists have been concerned to formulate principles which, when taken with the facts of any situation, generate the same conclusion a competent moral judge would reach when faced with the same facts, but beyond this they have displayed little concern over whether their principles reflect the reasoning by which a competent moral judge reaches his conclusions. At minimum, theorists rarely mention the relevant evidence, so there's little reason to think they have been moved by it or have even noticed it.

This practice is indefensible. Philosophers cannot, with consistency, respect our verdicts without respecting our operative principles, our forms of reasoning. For, first, our verdicts include judgments about people's motives and characters as well as about their actions and institutions, and if, as I assume, a moral theory is meant to provide us with a system of reasons we could employ when deciding how to act, then those reasons must be measured against our verdicts regarding a man's motivation and character and thus regarding his principles, as well as against the verdicts on the actions directed by those motivating principles. Secondly and more directly, it makes no sense to regard our verdicts as data for testing putative rational principles unless one takes those verdicts to be the output of the operation of rational principles. Any plausible reason for accepting our verdicts as evidence *for* or *against* presumed rational norms will rely on those verdicts being evidence *of* rational norms.

No doubt, unless a difference in principles is *possible, determinable,* and *important* independently of differences in the verdicts they imply, none of this matters.[7] Such a difference is as possible as extensional equivalence with intentional dissimilarity. The difference can be of the form: 'In situation A, do X' *vs.* 'In situation B, do X' where A and B regularly coincide; or 'In situation A, do X' *vs.* 'In situation A, do Y' where doing X and doing Y regularly coincide in A. Besides, the implied verdicts of different principles would count as the same for the purposes of a moral theory as long as their differences were marginal as judged by the considerations bearing on the assessment of the theory: e.g., the divergencies were restricted to fact situations possible only in a world quite unlike ours in very general respects, or to fact situations for which no one verdict is firmly and confidently accepted by most people.

Earlier I said that a difference in principles is evidenced, independently of any difference in verdicts, by a difference in the forms of reasoning employed in reaching the verdicts. This difference will seem unimportant if one takes it to consist solely in that people with different principles are disposed to utter different sound patterns when justifying their verdicts. But surely that can't be the whole difference, for if it were there would cease to be any difference in the meanings of the different utterances. Surely, even if we were certain someone would invariably do the right thing though always for the wrong reasons, we would still care what his reasons were and we could still consider them the wrong reasons. Or rather, to turn this around, in an important respect a person can't do the right thing for the wrong reason, for *what* someone is doing depends not just on his bodily movements in the physical world, but also on the intentions, motives and reasons with which he acts—what he takes himself to be doing— and thus on the concepts and principles with which he explains and justifies his behavior. The acts motivated by different principles may satisfy the same verdicts and be physically the same while the nature and character of the conduct—what act is performed—may differ just in virtue of the acts' being motivated by different principles. Our principles define our acts as well as direct them; they change the meaning of the movements we make as well as moving us to make changes in our movements.

This difference in the meaning of the movements is not made manifest in the movements themselves. Rather, for persons to have different principles is, in essence, for them to regard different facts as relevant to their own and other people's lives and conduct or for them to regard the facts as relevant in different ways. This is not (necessarily) a difference in the facts or verdicts the persons *can be brought* to believe or deny, but rather in what they *are naturally disposed to* and *actually do* believe and deny. The difference is in the items and aspects of their world which they notice, attend to, consider, in what and how they perceive, think about, understand.[8] And those differences are as much a cause as a consequence of differences in what persons care about, are interested in, appreciate and desire, in what and how they love and fear. Such differences are manifested directly and indirectly (via their bearing on motivation and intention) as differences in behavior, much of which is left unregulated by any of a person's principles.

So the conduct evidencing acceptance of a principle need not be conduct in accordance with the principle. That most people believe that being human has moral cachet is revealed not just by the way they argue about issues such as abortion. It is reflected as well in the fact that they perceive, regard, and identify themselves and each other principally and essentially, not as accords with any of the prime philosophical categories, but as human beings. Of course, we do not always so identify ourselves, for the properties of a thing that serve to identify it vary with the purposes for which the identification is made and thus also with the background of beliefs with which it is made. However, the beliefs involved here are rational beliefs and the purposes are not the special purposes we happen to have on special occasions but the general purposes we have in virtue of being rational and thus being capable of self-identification and requiring it. Our reasons for identifying ourselves as human beings are our reasons for accepting the Standard Belief.

As a step toward understanding this, let us take as a rough statement of the notion of human status the dictum, G: You$_1$ are to do unto others$_a$ as you$_2$ would have others$_b$ do unto you$_3$. The dictum is addressed to you$_1$, any rational agent, because, like any rational principle, G is addressed and applies to all and only those who can listen and apply it, rational agents. So too, the others$_b$ are all the other rational agents, and when G is addressed to any of them, you$_1$ are one of the others$_b$. However, while you$_1$=you$_2$=you$_3$, neither you$_2$ nor you$_3$ need be rational agents; you$_2$ need only be what might be called a subjunctively rational creature. So too, the others$_a$ need not be rational agents; they include all but not necessarily only the others$_b$. The others$_a$ comprise the class of those with human status; or rather, they plus yourself$_3$ comprise that class. The question of what has moral cachet is the question of how the others$_a$ are to be identified. To ask it is to ask what it would be rational for you$_2$ to identify yourself$_3$ as so that you$_3$ are among the others$_a$ when G is addressed to any of the others$_b$. That is, it would be rational for you$_1$ to accept and act upon G only if you$_2$ filled in G by identifying the others$_a$ in such a way that you$_3$ could not be excluded from the others$_a$ when the others$_b$ act upon G. And for that very reason it would be irrational for you$_1$ to accept any of the philosophical alternatives to the Standard Belief, because, although you$_1$ are rational, you$_1$ are not necessarily rational and so you$_3$ could become or have been nonrational. Any of your$_1$ cognitive or affective capacities could become or could have been different without altering your$_1$ identity, so the individual whose interests are your$_1$ own could remain constant while those principles would not require the consideration of his (=your$_3$) interests. By contrast, being human is an essential property of anything possessing it. You$_1$ could not be or have been other than a human being and still be identifiable as you$_3$.[9] The Standard Belief is a common belief because it enables all and only those known creatures to whom G can be addressed to rationally accept G, for it ensures that each and every one of them has a rational claim to the consideration of his or her interests throughout his or her lifetime.[10]

Various aspects of all this need further attention. Consider first the paradigmatic moral question: How would you like (or, have liked) it if somebody did (or, had done) that to you? The applicability of that question and the arguments employing it is as broad and as narrow as the criteria for personal identity; the question and arguments can make sense in all and only those situations in which you could still be you. That is to say, among other things, that a rational principle is a law-like generalization, and thus must be interpretable as sustaining subjunctive and contrary to fact conditionals. This helps explain what might otherwise seem odd, that in assessing the rationality of the

Standard Belief and its alternatives what you could have been but no longer can become is just as relevant as what you presently are and what you still can become.[11]

Next consider the prime argument of the antiabortionists. Its power derives from the fact that any human being is identifiable as the same entity as far back as the zygote and no farther. Its weakness is that, while the zygote is undeniably the *same entity* as the later adult, it no more follows that the zygote is the *same human being* than it follows that the still later corpse is the same human being. When and how to date the inception and demise of the human being as distinct from the human body is a further question, and as things stand the question regarding inception has no correct answer. Yet it may seem that, since you have interests in protecting your body come what may or might have been, it would be rational for you to replace the Standard Belief with a principle identifying yourself in terms of your body: e.g., being of woman conceived has moral cachet. After all, that too is an essential property of yourself, and how would you like it if someone had blinded you for life by wounding you while in the womb? To this the proabortionist can properly reply that, first, while *you* have interests regarding your body, your body and its parts have no interests of their own, and in its earliest stages a fetus is only a body and not a self at all; *it* doesn't have any interests, so if that body is destroyed before any self is formed, no one's interests need be harmed. Secondly, even in the later stages when the fetus seems undeniably a creature—even here where the antiabortionist's argument is unquestionably compelling—though there may be some sort of self with interests of its own, that self is not a human self and is not identical with the self of the eventual human being;[12] so if the fetal creature is destroyed before it becomes a human being, no human being's interests need be harmed. And someone who insists on saying that in destroying a fetal body or fetal creature one is harming the interests of a *potential* human being, suffice it to reply that you$_1$ have no good reason to accord human status to nonexistent human beings, however potential they may be, because one thing you$_1$ could never be identical with is anything that never exists. (N.B. Such "entities" are not made of the same stuff as *future* human beings.) The structure of this whole argument is highlighted by the contrast between destroying a fetal body or creature and "merely" damaging one, thereby damaging a later human being. For the true antiabortionist the former is clearly the more serious crime; for the proabortionist the latter is. For both, as the aptness of the proabortionist's rejoinders reveal, the logic of their positions requires the Standard Belief.

Next consider the moral status of animals. Though each of us is essentially a primate, a mammal, an animal, and a living thing, none of us is a nonhuman thing and neither is any other known rational creature. Doubtless some animals are quite clever and can act for a reason, but none is rational, none is among the others$_b$ who can accept and act upon a rational principle like G. That might seem beside the point since, though they may never master a few cute cognitive tricks, many humans never do either, and the interests and sufferings of animals are as real as ours. To this it should be said that to suffer, even to suffer a harm at the hands of another, is not *ipso facto* to suffer a wrong. More, to deny animals human status is not to deny them every substantial moral status, though precisely what the proper status is for each kind of thing is an enormous and enormously difficult question that may have no complete answer. In any case, since none of them can accord human status to any of them, let alone to us, and since none of us is one of them, none of us can have the reason to treat them as we are to treat ourselves that we have for treating ourselves that way. This is not sheer selfishness on our part, for, be it noted, if the argument for the Standard Belief goes through, it does so whatever our desires and interests may be as long as we have some at all (and that we do is presupposed by our being rational creatures). Obviously, insofar as the interests of animals move our sympathies we have reason to protect them, but even if we were carried away to fulfill their interests as fully as our own, that wouldn't sustain an independent moral status for them.[13]

But suppose we could and did sharpen the wits of a gnu in a zoo, enough so that it sued for its emancipation with as much eloquence as you please. Would we be obliged to manumit it?—and every other gnu too? Nice questions these.[14] But let us avoid them for now, except to note that the Standard Belief affirms only that being human is sufficient for having human status, and thus that no property inessential for being human is necessary. The Standard Belief does not deny that being human is not necessary or that some other properties may be sufficient. And common belief does affirm both of these claims, but in a complex way contrary to philosophical convictions. For example, whatever may be true of our gnu, we would probably think it proper to accept as moral equals extraterrestrial travelers who, except for their origins, differed from human beings no more than Tibetans differ from Teutons. On the other hand, it's far from clear that we would feel constrained to accord moral equality to a realization of the typical sci-fi monster—an argute fifteen-and-a-half-foot purple praying mantis oozing goo from every orifice—but our responses to such stories suggest that we might well not, especially if the creature has substantial homnivorous or sadistic impulses, which, after all, are compatible with the philosophers' pet properties. However, the realm of imagination is a treacherous place to investigate the structures of common belief: beliefs about what people's beliefs are regarding some conjecture are usually conjectures, and frequently people have no belief regarding the conjecture. Far better to look into the hard data history richly supplies, especially that regarding racial discrimination.

We need to look there anyway since it may seem objectionable that our account is tantamount to a justification of racism. After all, the fact that humanness is an essential property does not distinguish the Standard Belief from other principles that pick out essential properties defining natural kinds to which we belong. We have explained why principles that would place us in more inclusive kinds than humanity (e.g., primates, animals, living things) won't do, but we have yet to object to principles that place us in more exclusive kinds. Clearly, the progenitors you have are the only ones you could have had, and, for all that has been said so far, you could identify yourself by your race, tribe, clan, ancestral line, or family. Just as clearly, people throughout history have done precisely that and have lived by the correlative moral principles, and have thereby lived in a variety of complex caste systems.

But let us be clear here. It's hardly an objection that our account justifies principles such as: Being an Aryan (or an Apache or a McFarland) has moral cachet. After all, each such principle happens to be true, for they are *all* implied by the Standard Belief, and they are all mutually compatible. The Standard Belief is only the most general expression of these, its "corollaries." What is objectionable is the distinctively racist or caste belief that Aryans (or whatever) are a *superior* kind of creature, that they have an inherent *value* or *worth* lacked by nonAryans, and that in virtue of this difference in *value* Aryans are entitled to accord full human status to themselves and to deny it to non-Aryans. But that distinctively racist belief has no *logical* connection with the Standard Belief or its corollaries. It is, however, connected through the *psychodynamics of rationality:* the structure of the operations of the rational self in its attempts to develop and maintain self-esteem, an evaluation by the self of that which the self identifies itself as being. An investigation of those operations (which cannot be undertaken here) would uncover the rational structures underlying and motivating racism and caste systems. Our account cannot be employed to justify racism, and it is hardly a fault that it fits nicely into an explanation of the pervasive power of the fact of lineage, of common blood, of membership in a family, ancestral line, clan, tribe or race. Egalitarians engaged in counteracting the evils of caste systems may require a rhetoric that derogates those systems by explaining them as products of rank irrationality unalloyed with any elements of rationality other than that guiding the crassest self-interest. But a philosopher is untrue to his trade when he uses the excuse of the political ideologue to explain away those complex social forms with all the wisdom of a village atheist. His overeager egalitarianism serves no one, least of all himself, for by failing in his proper study he thereby risks irrelevance.[15] He also risks—to put it kindly—unintended irony when he helps himself to such metaphors as "the family of man" or "the brotherhood of man" while defending principles that would drain those slogans of all rhetorical force.[16] The literature of philosophy is rife with such ironies. Perhaps the supreme irony is that egalitarian philosophers who reject the Standard Belief and all racist beliefs, those same philosophers happily embrace the claim that human beings have an inherent value and dignity. Yet that claim stands to the Standard Belief in precisely the same relation as racist beliefs stand to the corollaries of the Standard Belief, and is just as false and ultimately incoherent as those racist beliefs.[17]

NOTES

[1] Reasons may differ in kind and degree, and most of us think the superiority of our moral status involves both sorts of differences. Aside from those who attribute some supranatural feature to an animal (e.g., sacredness, the possession of a human soul), even vegetarians and antivivisectionists generally acknowledge not only that we may require a *greater* sacrifice from a person to prevent harm to a human being than to prevent an equivalent harm to an animal, but also that an animal *may,* but a human being *may not* be destroyed

when he is unable and others are unwilling to care for him. (In any case, a human's having a superior status is compatible with, e.g., the propriety of rescuing a drowning pet poodle instead of a drowning Adolph Hitler, since a thing's moral status is not the only morally relevant fact about it.) Since the particular form of the superiority of the moral status accorded human beings will not be at issue here, it need not be specified.

[2] A fuller treatment of these and related matters touched upon herein appears in my "Understanding the Abortion Argument," in *Philosophy and Public Affairs*, Fall 1971 (I,1).

[3] Apparently a failure to appreciate this has led many philosophers to deny the Factunorm Principle for fear that it entailed subjectivism or relativism and thereby required an inappropriate foundation for rational principles. On this, see my *The Significance of Sense*, Ithaca: Cornell University Press, 1972, pp. 160-172. The main thrust of that work is to show that if the Factunorm Principle is applicable for any rational principle it applies to moral principles as well.

[4] Anyway, all (save one) that I know of. But different philosophers reject it in different ways, some by accepting (explicitly or implicitly) some incompatible alternative, some by denying (explicitly or implicitly) that it and its alternatives could be genuinely true or false.

[5] An "infrahuman" fetus (a human fetus that is not (yet) a human being) might have a moral status comparable to an animal's, independent but inferior to a human beings. For many people, a human fetus has, in virtue of being a *human* fetus, an independent status superior to any animal's, yet, in virtue of being a human *fetus*, its status is inferior to a human being's.

[6] This claim has a class of pseudo-exceptions, *species normal properties:* a property (indirectly) attributable to every member of a natural kind if it is (directly) attributable to any normal member of that kind. It is fully proper to say that human beings are, e.g., rational bipeds, albeit some things properly called human beings can't reason or have one or three legs due to congenital malformation or subsequent deformation. A mongoloid, no matter how idiotic, is still a human being, and, in the species normal sense, a rational creature. A natural kind (species) is specifiable by the properties of its normal members without regarding its abnormal members. (More specifically, unless developmental stage properties are intended, the species normal properties are the properties of the normal *mature* members; e.g., humans have thirty two teeth.) Whatever the importance of the conceptual machinery operating here (and it may be considerable), clearly a theory cannot match common belief by appealing to species normal properties while denying the Standard Belief, since the predication of, e.g., rationality to certain human beings, is based solely on their being human.

[7] But then, if none of this matters, one might wonder what is at stake in the competition between rival traditional theories, for the arguments in their debates have generally been concerned at bottom only with how the implied verdicts of each theory compare with those of common belief. Any contrasts there may be on that score are controversial with each side claiming coinci-

dence with common belief. And if, as is rarely denied, the area of coincident verdicts is vastly greater than that of potential clash, a reputedly high-minded and deep struggle would start to smack of petty wrangling.

[8]So too for the philosopher: his acceptance of his theoretically derived principles (moral and extramoral) expresses itself in what he notices, attends to, etc., in his data, common belief. Yet actually philosophers virtually never bother to look at other people's beliefs anyway, in spite of their acknowledging common belief as evidence. Instead they look into their own heads, presumably on the assumption that their own considered judgments are as trustworthy as anyone's so they have no need to look further—a dubious assumption since what is there to be seen may well be their philosophical theory or its effects in their beliefs. (Many philosophers liken philosophy to psychotherapy, but few have learned caution from the fact that patients in therapy often unconsciously manufacture symptoms to fit their therapist's diagnosis.) A more plausible assumption is that their own beliefs are no more and (for the reason just given) perhaps somewhat less trustworthy than the beliefs of other competent moral judges. Unfortunately, whether a philosopher looks at his own or at other people's beliefs, he is likely to look at them through the filter of his theory. And, as psychologists tell us, look as you may, what you see is largely determined by what you believe and are thus prepared to see. To be sure, the alterations of the theorist's beliefs and perceptions may be an improvement, not a perversion, and it is possible to determine which they are. But it's not easy. Nor is it easy to be cognizant of such alterations—and this may help explain why philosophers don't notice the conflict of their theories with common belief.

[9]For the nonce, a complete elucidation and defense of the essential-accidental distinction is not essential. For one thing, it suffices here that, in an unproblematic sense, it is less possible for you to be or have been other than human than it is for you to be or have been other than rational or the like. For another thing, Saul Kripke has personally assured me that being human is an essential property.

[10]An instructive pseudoexception: some cultures have cast out some of their members (e.g., the insane) denying them human status on the ground that they were possessed by demons. The logic of the explanation requires that the outcast was no longer himself, no longer a human being, and that this transformation was effected by supranatural powers.

[11]More generally, this feature of rational principles explains why, for human beings unlike animals, the facts and possibilities of the past can be reasons for acting just as well as the facts and possibilities of the present and future can. A failure to appreciate this vitiates many a moral theory: utilitarianism's inability to make sense of punishment is only the most obvious example. A rational creature cannot live by consequences alone, and no creature can have an adequate comprehension of consequences or control his conduct by such comprehension without being rational.

[12]The proabortionist's position can be only as plausible as this premise is.

[13]Perhaps nothing said here can persuade the unpersuaded since none of it

is likely to dispel the pervasive and profound misconceptions about the very nature of morality that likely underlie their dissatisfaction. Let me here just give warning--however blunt and crabbed it may be—that morality, if it is to make any sense at all, can be only an aspect of rationality and neither a presupposition nor a consequence of it. Our moral principles are among our means of understanding our world, ourselves, and their relations. So our moral status is not something any of us or anything else does or could merit, be worthy of or deserve in consequence of some splendid trait, talent or achievement. It's not a prized position of rights, privileges, and powers awarded for excellence in some cosmic competition. Nor is it a first class citizenship in a community created for and confined to the protection and promotion of our interests. We are "entitled" to our moral status and animals to theirs only in the sense that we are entitled to our human nature and they to theirs.

[14] Beliefs in transmigratory selves raise similar yet importantly different issues, because, unlike the above, they do not suppose a change in the behavior of the beast or its physical (e.g., brain) structure. It is not clear whether such beliefs suppose or require that your self could be other than a human self.

[15] Recently at least two philosophers have published defenses of abortion that allow as how infanticide is also at worst imprudent. Query: Will their essays create anything comparable to the public outrage generated by the now infamous work of Jensen and Herrnstein? Not bloody likely. Why not, for their assault on the conscience and intellect of civilized people is surely no less brutal and blundering? Well, without discounting numerable other salient differences, part of the answer is that Jensen and Herrnstein are social scientists, and, for good reasons and bad alike, we listen when social scientists, even those of minor distinction, speak out on matters touching upon public policy. Their counterparts in philosophy are not invited onto the stage. (It was eras ago, back when philosophers and social scientists were the same men, that the counsels of philosophers were sought and paid for.) Why is this? Just look at a typical philosophical performance: Abortion, an issue inspiring no unanimity among any random class of persons (as is evidenced by the turbulent condition of laws on the matter), provides the occasion for a blithe dismissal of a prohibition endorsed by a monolithic consensus and enforced by every present Western legal system. Once again a philosopher has thrown the baby out with the bath water (and the very premeditation of the performance only deepens the onlooker's despair); and once again, having walked upon the stage, the philosopher turns his back to his audience (and then walks off, for he has no responsibilities for what follows). And then, when the crowd remains unmoved except to laughter and derision, the philosopher deems it benighted. But the explanation of the crowd's response is not what the philosopher says, but *that* he says it. At least since Socrates philosophers have been regarded with hostile suspicion or amused contempt because, at least since Socrates, they have regarded others with hostile suspicion or amused contempt. They are not listened to because they do not listen. That may be an instance of a psychological law, but here the point is also that philosophers are not listened to because what they say is not worth listening to, and is not because they do not listen (to anyone but themselves) and so they are in no position to speak (to anyone

but themselves).

16 Probably the least discussed and most badly treated matter in the literature of moral philosophy is the one that matters most in most people's lives: familial relationships. That's not surprising since that literature lacks a theory that could say much that would be both interesting and true. The familiar philosophical models for understanding or justifying the special regard we accord familial relations are inadequate to the task. That regard must be treated as a phenomenon of rationality, for we don't take imprinting quite as well as ducks do, and neither do we have the mechanisms by which lost lambs are reunited with their mothers: our natural family has a hold on us whoever brings us up, and we find out who our real relations are by being *told*. (It helps here to imagine your reaction if one fine day an elderly and utterly strange gentleman approached you with unimpeachable evidence that he is your real father.) But neither are our relatives like ordinary benefactors, business partners or friends; the special regard goes beyond reciprocity, love or likeness—as often as not, those things are lacking, and even when present they can't explain the special regard for natural parents as opposed to adopted, foster or step parents. Let us admit that a family forms a small (exogamous) caste. It can be understood and justified in terms of the special role the family has in determining an individual's identity. We identify with our relations, not (or not just) because we are akin to them, but because we are a kin to them. I, personally, am largely unmoved by the fact that the human race has gotten itself onto the moon or that blacks dominate in my favorite sports, but I can't imagine what it would be like to be incapable of pride or embarrassment at the achievements and antics of those in my immediate family. (That is no sign of logical impossibility; it goes deeper than that, for there are logical impossibilties I can imagine.)

17 I gratefully acknowledge the support for this work provided by the Guggenheim Foundation.

LAURA PURDY
and MICHAEL TOOLEY

Is Abortion Murder?

This essay deals with the morality of abortion. We shall argue that abortion is morally unobjectionable, and that society benefits if abortion is available on demand. We begin by setting out a preliminary case in support of the practice of abortion. Then we examine moral objections and show why these objections are unsound. We conclude by considering what properties something needs in order to have a serious right to life, and we show that a human fetus does not possess those properties. Thus since there is no moral objection to abortion, the practice must be viewed as both permissible and desirable, in the light of the advantages outlined in the first section of our paper.

I. *Preliminary Considerations in Support of Abortion*

One way of approaching the abortion question is to envision two possible societies, one where strict anti-abortion laws are in force, the other where abortion is unrestricted. In imagining these two societies, we suppose that all other factors are the same, and that the societies otherwise resemble the United States in their social arrangements.

To flesh out these images, we must make some empirical assumptions, which philosophers are no more qualified to evaluate than is the ordinary educated individual, since it is not the main business of philosophy to ascertain facts. However, such assumptions cannot be avoided in moral and political philosophy, unless one is uninterested in the outcomes of various courses of action. About the facts relevant to the issues discussed in this section there is room for disagreement, for we are dependent upon sciences that are as yet incomplete and upon common sense. But while the accuracy of the following pictures is contingent upon future investigation, the major features of the pictures seem plausible, in the light of present knowledge and theory.

The first society is much like that which has existed in the United States up until the present, where abortion has been generally unavailable, either because of restrictive legislation or because of de facto unobtainability. The second society is very different. In it, abortion is freely available. We contend that, as a result, individuals in that society suffer less unhappiness than those in the first society.

Let us consider, in concrete terms, why this is the case. First of all, men and women in our second world can enjoy sex more, since anxiety regarding contraceptive failure will no longer exist. Moreover, pregnancies can be timed so that no child is neglected, reducing stress on all concerned. As a result, couples can plan on temporary or permanent childlessness when necessary or desirable to achieve life goals. In addition, if pregnancy threatens the health—either physical or mental—of the mother, or of other parties, or unduly strains the marriage, it can be safely terminated. Last, and most important perhaps, illegal abortions, now a significant factor in the maternal death rate, can be replaced by legal abortions, thus saving the lives of very many women.

That abortion on demand would reduce frustration and unhappiness among the young is equally evident. When abortion is readily available we can prevent the birth of babies who would otherwise enter the world with gross physical or mental abnormalities and who would face short and unhappy lives. We can also ensure that only wanted children will be born. Since parents who sincerely desire a child are more apt to provide for its physical, intellectual, and emotional needs, it is probable that children will be better cared for than at present. This change should be especially significant in light of our growing awareness of the problem of child abuse.

It also seems reasonable to believe that members of society who do not belong to families availing themselves of abortion will benefit. It is generally frustrated and unhappy individuals who turn to crime, violent or otherwise. Happy people, if not necessarily constructive citizens, are at least not destructive ones. Thus readily available abortions, by eliminating sources of frustration and unhappiness, should improve the social environment for everyone. Secondly, abortion, by making childbearing completely voluntary, will help keep the population in check. The importance of this with respect to education and the environment, and thus the impact upon the general quality of life, need not be labored.

It seems reasonable to conclude then, on the basis of our present knowledge, that the second society will be much happier than the first. At this point two questions arise. The first is empirical: "Is abortion on demand in fact the *best* way to satisfy the needs and desires of members of society? Mightn't some third type of society be superior to both of the possibilities we have so far considered, as measured in terms of the happiness of its members?" The second is moral: "Even if members of the second society are on the whole happier than members of the first, does it follow that the second society is morally preferable to the first? Are there not other factors that should be taken into account, such as the rights of the unborn, that tell in favor of the first society?"

We will consider the moral issues raised by the second question in sections II and III. Our discussion in this section will be confined to the first question.

The issue, then, is this. May there not be alternative social arrangements, not involving abortion, that would result in even greater happiness? Those who are wary of the practice of abortion on demand sometimes suggest that the same ends can be achieved as follows. First, society should ensure that everyone has access to safe and completely reliable methods of contraception. Secondly, there should be legislation to cope with the social welfare problems that are created or aggravated by unwanted or defective children.

This alternative presupposes the existence of a foolproof contraceptive having no undesirable side effects. At present no such device exists. It is true that if a perfect method of contraception were developed, it would dissolve much of the abortion problem. However, at least two problems would remain. First, pregnancy, even though initially desired, sometimes has a serious negative effect upon the mother or other people. We will still need abortion to handle cases of this sort. Secondly, some fetuses turn out to be grossly deformed, or otherwise seriously defective. If abortion is not available, what is likely to happen to such defective children? Proper care is expensive, and if the societies we are envisaging do resemble the present day United

States, then we know that to do the job adequately will be thought to impose too great a sacrifice upon parents and taxpayers. This fact cannot be swept under the rug; it must enter any realistic assessment of the available options. As the real alternative to abortion here, the defective person will face life in an uncaring environment, where physical needs will be only barely met, and where emotional needs will generally go unfulfilled. Only if drastic changes in social legislation were to occur would such individuals have the opportunity to lead a protected life and to develop fully their potentialities. Thus it is not possible to achieve, by contraception and social legislation, all of the benefits that can be realized by abortion.

We must now consider two important objections to our position. The first is that in evaluating the happiness of society, one should take into account the happiness of the fetus, and we have failed to do this.[1] We have considered only the happiness of other members of society. So that, while abortion may increase the happiness of these other members, it certainly does not satisfy the fetus's desires and so contribute to its happiness.

Our response to this is that it is a mistake to attribute to a fetus a significant range of desires. A fetus may have a few very rudimentary desires, such as a desire not to feel pain, but it is incapable of having most of the desires that adult humans can have.

How can we support this claim that a fetus is capable of having only very elementary desires? Perhaps the place to start is by drawing a distinction between having a desire for some state, and being programmed to act so as to increase the likelihood that the state in question will be attained. Thus, imagine a machine constructed so that when its batteries run down, it searches for an electrical outlet to recharge its batteries. The machine is programmed to behave in ways that tend to bring about certain states, but one could not literally speak of the machine having a *desire* to recharge its batteries. Similarly, imagine a more complex machine that can "recognize" certain situations as threats to its survival, and take action that decreases the likelihood of its being destroyed. Even if such a machine were capable of a wide range of complex and effective survival behavior, it would not make sense to speak of it having a desire for continued existence. Moreover, all plant behavior and that of lower animals provide other examples in which there is complex programmed behavior directed toward some goal, but where the organism has no corresponding desire.

What, then, is required before one can attribute desires to something? Our view is that first, it is not possible to attribute desires to something unless it is capable of *consciousness*. So if a machine is not conscious, one cannot attribute any desires to it, no matter how sophisticated its behavior. Second, the *specific* desires a thing can have are limited by the concepts it possesses. The justification for this claim is as follows. The fundamental way of describing a given desire is as a desire that a certain proposition be true.[2] But one cannot desire that a certain proposition be true unless one understands it, and since one cannot understand it without possessing the concepts involved in it, it follows that the desires one can have are limited by the concepts one possesses.

A slightly different way of developing this point is this: if something is to have any desires at all, it must possess consciousness. But to have a specific desire it is not enough to be conscious and to be disposed to bring about certain states. The migration of birds, for example, enables them to achieve a certain end, and it certainly seems likely that they are to some extent conscious. Yet it is implausible to attribute to them a desire for those states that their migratory behavior makes possible. What is needed is a specific connection between consciousness and the goal towards which the behavior is directed. One speaks of a desire only where the organism is capable of recognizing that his behavior is directed towards certain ends: where the organism is incapable of being aware of the object of its behavior, one does not attribute the corresponding desire to it. To be aware of a certain state as the aim of one's behavior presupposes that one possesses concepts that can be employed to characterize that state.

Given this account of the conditions an organism must satisfy if it is to have desires, the justification for our claim that a fetus has at best extremely simple desires should be clear. In the early stages of the development of a human organism it has no mental life at all, i.e., no consciousness, and hence no desires. At later stages, it is reasonable to think that the fetus has some sensations, but its mental life is still very limited. Thus if one compares, say, a human fetus with a chimpanzee fetus, there are no grounds for holding that the mental life of the former is significantly richer than that of the latter. This means that one should not attribute desires to a human fetus which one would be unwilling to attribute to a chimpanzee fetus. The upshot is that one cannot consistently object to abortion in the case of humans, on the grounds that the destruction of the fetus violates some desires that the fetus has, unless one would also object to abortion in the case of chimpanzees.

Moreover, there seem to be no grounds for attributing complex desires to fetuses, human or otherwise. In particular, it seems absurd to attribute to any fetus a desire for continued existence, since to have such a desire it would have to have a conception of what it is to be a continuing subject of experiences and other mental states.

Are there any desires that a fetus has which might be violated by abortion? It appears reasonable to say that fetuses can feel pleasure and pain. Thus abortion might violate a fetus's desire to avoid pain. As it is certainly undesirable to inflict suffering upon any living organism, abortion should be carried out so as to inflict as little pain as possible upon the fetus. If this is done, we do not think that the fetus has any desires that are violated by abortion.

To sum up, our response to the first objection is this: we certainly agree that in choosing policies and institutions, one should take into account everyone affected. So in particular, if the fetus had desires which were adversely affected by abortion, it would be unfair not to take those desires into account. But we have argued that, as a matter of fact, the fetus is incapable of having desires that will go unsatisfied if it is destroyed, providing that action is carried out painlessly.

This brings us to the second objection. It involves the suggestion that while the consequences of isolated acts of abortion do benefit society, this would not be true if abortion were to become a *generally accepted practice*. It is precisely the latter issue that one is interested in.

It has often been suggested that general acceptance of abortion would have disastrous consequences; however, no convincing evidence has been offered in support of this contention. Antiabortionists usually attempt to sway unreflective people with vague claims that abortion will lead to the "denigration of humanity," or to an "erosion of respect for the sanctity of life." Such emotion-laden appeals are in the same intellectual category as politicians' rhetoric about patriotism and the family. Both are designed to encourage unthinking acceptance of a position that would fare ill if exposed to impartial, rational scrutiny.

It is possible, however, to divest the claim of its illicit emotional appeal. When this is done, the underlying suggestion appears to be that if one permits the killing of some humans, viz., fetuses, then respect for human life will decrease, so that other classes of humans, such as the handicapped and the elderly, become candidates for elimination. But this conclusion rests upon intellectual and moral confusion. Specifically, it rests upon a failure to get clear about the conditions something must satisfy if it is to have a serious right to life. To advocate abortion is *not* to suggest that one allow violations of one's moral principles when it happens to be socially convenient. The proabortionist's position is that the *fundamental* principle involved here is that it is seriously wrong to kill, not human beings, but *persons*. If it is seriously wrong to kill a human being it is *because* he is a person, not because he is a human being. And our contention is that fetuses are not persons, but only *potential* persons. Once one realizes that it is persons who have a right to life, and that abortion is morally unobjectionable because fetuses are not persons, there is no danger that one will conclude that it is morally acceptable to kill other humans, such as handicapped and elderly ones, who are persons. When the moral principles relevant to abortion are clear, it is apparent that general acceptance of the practice should not have any undesirable consequences of the sort envisioned by the antiabortionist.

This completes our defense of the claim that where abortion is viewed as morally permissible and is available on demand, people are happier than they would otherwise be. We can now proceed to consider the views of those who hold that abortion should be prohibited even if it is the case that to do so will result in significant frustration and unhappiness. Most antiabortionists feel that there are moral considerations involved in the issue of abortion that far outweigh considerations of human happiness. In view of what is at stake, this is not a claim to be lightly advanced. By lobbying for the prohibition of abortion, the antiabortionist is in effect assuming responsibility for the consequences of those actions. As we have emphasized above, these consequences are deeply disturbing. If antiabortionists prohibit abortion, they will be responsible for untold human misery. They will be responsible for lessened enjoyment of sex; for frustration caused by inconvenient pregnancies and childbearing; for ill health, either physical or mental, of mothers or other persons; for deaths of women resulting from pregnancies and illegal abortions; for child abuse; for crimes committed by frustrated or improperly socialized individuals;

and for the stunted life of everyone if overpopulation seriously curbs our freedoms or lowers the quality of life. The ardent antiabortionist must shoulder the burden of responsibility for these things since, had he acted otherwise, they would not have existed. What considerations, then, can the antiabortionist point to that outweigh the suffering produced by the prohibition of abortion?

In reply to the accusation that the responsibility for this catalogue of woes lies on his shoulders, the antiabortionist will argue that these evils are necessary in order to avoid a much greater evil. Fetuses have a right to life. They have a right to be born and to have the opportunity to become adults. To destroy them by abortion is seriously wrong, and in comparison with it the miseries enumerated above pale into insignificance. Fetuses are human beings, and to kill a human being is murder.

II. *Refutation of "Pro-Life" Objections to Abortion*

The "pro-lifer's" contention is that the fetus has a serious right to life, comparable to that of a normal adult human being. This claim deserves very careful consideration, since if the fetus did have a serious right to life, then indeed it would be necessary to suffer the evils enumerated above. It would be no more justifiable to kill a fetus to avoid threats to someone's health, to eliminate frustration and unhappiness, or to curb population growth, than it would be to kill an adult. Abortion would be justified, if at all, only to save the life of the mother.

In the next two sections we will show that there is no satisfactory support for the claim that the fetus has a right to life, and that, on the contrary, there are excellent reasons for holding that it does not. Before developing our case, however, it will be worthwhile to comment upon the framework of our discussion, even though this requires a brief digression into meta-ethics.

There is an important distinction between *deontological* ethical systems, and *consequentialist* ones. Some moral principles deal with rights or duties, while others are concerned with the intrinsic desirability of different states. A central question in meta-ethics is whether there is any relation between these two types of principles. The consequentialist holds that the best action is the one that maximizes the existence of intrinsically desirable states. This enables him to derive all principles dealing with rights and duties from principles specifying what states are intrinsically desirable together with empirical information about the consequences of actions. In contrast, the deontological view is that such derivation of principles dealing with rights and duties is not possible.

Antiabortionists almost always approach the issue of abortion from the latter perspective. They treat rights in general, and the right to life in particular, as incapable of being derived from more fundamental principles dealing with the intrinsic desirability of various states of affairs. If pressed to defend their principles, they may contend that they are "self-evident." Alternatively, they may appeal to "moral intuition"—thereby implying that those who disagree with them are morally blind. Another common strategem is to cite their favorite religious authority. None of these invocations is conducive to rational discussion of the issues.

In contrast, if one adopts a consequentialist approach to ethics, the question of abortion can be dealt with in a much more fruitful way. Whereas deontological ethical theories involve a number of unrelated principles dealing with obligations and rights, consequentialism bases its ethical claims upon a very few principles specifying what states are intrinsically valuable. Since the consequentialist cannot view the right to life as underived, he must offer some account of it, and in doing this, he will be able to determine whether a human fetus has a right to life.

The following discussion will be formulated in terms of rights, despite the fact that we are inclined to think that a consequentialist outlook is correct, and that a discussion of abortion and the right to life in a consequentialist framework would lead to a deeper understanding of the issues. For this is an essay in ethics, and we want our arguments to be neutral with respect to meta-ethical controversies.

Let us now examine the critical contention that a fetus has a serious right to life. What *grounds* do antiabortionists offer in support of this claim? A survey of antiabortion literature provides us with the following considerations meant to support the moral claim that a fetus has a serious right to life:

(1) A fetus resembles an adult human.
(2) A fetus is alive.
(3) A fetus is a distinct individual.
(4) A fetus inside a human mother is itself human.

We will show that none of these considerations constitutes adequate grounds for attributing a right to life to the fetus.

The following typical passage illustrates the first appeal:

> At the moment of conception, of course, the new life does not look like a baby. But within a few weeks visible changes occur, and the new life *does* begin to look like a baby. From about two weeks onwards, the unborn child can respond to moments of stress. The heart is pumping between the eighteenth and twenty-fifth day. By the fourth week the backbone is complete. By eight weeks the child has all his organs — legs, arms, feet, hands — he looks like a human being.[3]

This reference to the physical resemblance of the fetus to adults has considerable emotional impact, and it is no accident that it figures prominently in "pro-life" attacks upon abortion. Descriptions such as that quoted above are reinforced by pictures of "unborn children" and by bottled fetuses "murdered" by abortionists.

Does the antiabortionist really believe that such resemblance is morally relevant? It is hard to believe that he does. If pig fetuses resembled adult humans, would it be seriously wrong to kill pig fetuses? Or if human fetuses looked like frogs, not adult humans, would abortions be morally permissible? Surely not. The antiabortionist is opposed to abortion at any time after conception, and it is simply false to say that a fertilized human egg cell looks like an adult human being.

Why then the great emphasis upon resemblance? Perhaps resemblance seems relevant because it appears to support the claim that the fetus is a human being. But if "human being" simply means an organism belonging to the biological species *homo sapiens,* the claim that a fetus developing inside a human mother is a human being is trivial. While if to call something a human being is to assert something more than this, namely, that it also has a right to life, then the fact that the fetus resembles adult human beings in *certain physical* respects does not show that it has a right to life. As we will argue later, psychological properties, not physical ones, determine whether something has a right to life.

In our opinion the appeal to resemblance is an attempt to gain support by appealing to the emotions of people, instead of by presenting carefully reasoned argument. Sometimes antiabortionists protest that there is nothing in principle wrong with such emotional appeal.

Is Abortion Murder? 139

Is it ethically objectionable to use films of atrocities to impress upon people the immorality of actions occuring in war? Surely not. But then how can it be ethically objectionable to use pictures of murdered fetuses in order to rally support against abortion?

This response is quite confused. In one case there is clear agreement about the relevant moral principles, and one is simply pointing out that events prohibited by those principles are occurring. In the other there is puzzlement, or disagreement, about what moral principles apply. The antiabortionist, rather than offering rational argument in support of his view is using considerations that are irrelevant to whether the fetus has a right to life, to sway emotions. The situation would be comparable if a vegetarian, rather than arguing for the view that it is wrong to kill animals, were to go about showing gory pictures of slaughtered animals.

We can dismiss the second condition—that since the fetus is alive, it is wrong to kill it—rather quickly. Expressions such as "respect for the sanctity of life," "pro-life movement," and so on, suggest this line of thought, although only in very unsophisticated discussions is this claim explicitly advanced. There are all sorts of living things we do not hesitate to kill, from viruses and bacteria up to complex animals such as chickens and cows. The reply may be that while it is not wrong to destroy life in general, it is wrong to destroy human life. We will consider this view shortly.

A third consideration advanced by antiabortionists is that the fetus is a distinct individual.[4] This suggestion must be clarified before it can be evaluated. The fetus is not distinct in the sense of being physically unconnected to other organisms. Nor is it a separate individual in the sense that it is capable of existing independently of other organisms, at least for most of its development. The idea is presumably that although the fetus is dependent upon another organism, much like an ordinary parasite, it is still a biological unity that contains within itself factors that determine the direction of its development.

As it stands, this consideration has no force. Animals belonging to nonhuman species are distinct individuals in this sense, and most people have no moral qualms about destroying them.[5] So it is not sufficient to claim that the fetus is a distinct organism. If there is a point here, it must be that it is a distinct *human* organism.

Thus most of the "pro-life" arguments seem to boil down to the fourth and final claim—that a fetus developing inside a human mother is a member of *homo sapiens,* and this feature confers upon it a right to life. The first part of the claim is uncontroversial. A fetus developing inside a human mother is certainly an organism belonging to *homo sapiens.* What is incorrect is the contention that membership in a particular biological species in itself endows an organism with a right to life.

We can show this as follows. Some things, normal adult human beings for example, have a right to life. Other living things, such as carrots and flies, apparently do not. How is this difference to be explained and justified? If we grant some things a right to life, while denying others such a right, there must be some morally relevant difference between the two classes of objects. What might this be?

Since most people, rightly or wrongly, tend to hold that only human animals have a serious right to life, it is tempting to suppose that membership in the biological species *homo sapiens* is the relevant property. Most anti-abortionists succumb to this temptation. However, a little reflection shows that this is not a justifiable answer.

First of all, membership in a species is defined by the ability to interbreed and produce fertile offspring. Suppose then we discover Yahoos —animals that look like us, and with whom we can interbreed, but whose brains are much smaller, and whose intellectual qualities are comparable to those of chickens. They could not perform any of the intellectual tasks—such as language learning and problem solving— of which human beings are capable. It is difficult to see why we should treat Yahoos any differently than chickens. Yet they would belong to our species. Hence it cannot be that an organism has a serious right to life because of membership in a particular species. Another way of seeing this is to notice that there might be individuals to whom we would ascribe a right to life, even though they were not humans. If there were a God, he would probably not belong to our species, yet surely it would be wrong to kill him without good reason. Science fiction provides us with many examples. Olaf Stapledon's Sirius is a dog as intelligent and as capable of moral behavior as most humans.[6] When prejudiced individuals hound him to death, we feel enraged and saddened, for his destruction is as wrong, and for the same reason, as that of an adult human being.

Why do we ascribe a right to life not merely to normal adult humans, but also to deities, and to animals such as Sirius? Surely it is because they have certain characteristics in common. These cannot be tied up with physical appearance, or with membership in some biological species. The normally relevant properties are *psychological* ones.

It seems then, that the antiabortionist is wrong to hold that it is a *basic* moral principle that human beings have a right to life. If a given organism enjoys a right to life, it does so not because it is a member of of biological species *homo sapiens*, but because it has psychological traits, as yet unspecified, possessed by normal adult human beings. Once we recognize this, the question is whether fetuses have these psychological traits, or whether it is true only that they will *later* come to possess them. If the latter is the case, there seems to be no reason to think that fetuses have a serious right to life.

Is it possible to justify the contention that a human fetus does not possess the psychological traits that adult humans have and which confer upon them a serious right to life? We believe that it is. The clearest way of doing this is to determine, as we will do in the next section, precisely what the relevant psychological properties are. But even without doing that we can argue that a fetus lacks the relevant properties. One can ask whether there is any reason for holding that the mental life of a human fetus is significantly different from that of a nonhuman fetus such as a chimpanzee. We contend that there is no evidence that this is so. Therefore, unless one is prepared to hold that it is seriously wrong to kill nonhuman fetuses, it seems that one cannot maintain that it is seriously wrong to destroy human fetuses.

There is, however, a last line of argument open to the extreme antiabortionist. Even if a human fetus does not possess the relevant psychological characteristics, it is possible to contend that the fetus has a right to life in virtue of the fact that it will *later* come to develop those properties. Thus the "pro-lifer" might try to defend his position by appealing to the following *potentiality principle:*

> If there are any properties possessed by normal adult human beings which endow any organism possessing them with a serious right to life, then at least one of those properties is such that it is wrong to kill any organism that potentially possesses that property, simply in virtue of the organism's potentiality. (An organism possesses a property potentially if it will come to have it in the normal course of its development.)

This principle is exposed to three telling objections. The first is that if one accepts the potentiality principle, one ought to accept the generalized version that differs from it in only two respects. First, in the generalized version the term "organism" is replaced by the expression "system of causally interrelated objects," on the grounds that it is not morally relevant whether the potentiality resides in a single organism, or in a system of individuals that are so interrelated that they will causally give rise to something possessing the property in question, if not interfered with. Secondly, the generalized version prohibits *any* action that prevents a system from developing the morally relevant property which it potentially possesses, rather than only prohibiting actions which destroy the possessor of the potentialities. To refuse to accept the latter change would force one to admit that a two-step abortion is morally permissible, where one first destroys the potential in the fetus to later develop the relevant psychological features, and then kills the fetus. And surely no "pro-lifer" wants to be driven to this conclusion.

If one accepts the generalized potentiality principle, one must conclude that some methods of contraception are as seriously wrong as abortion, since they involve actions that prevent certain systems (human spermatazoa and unfertilized egg cells) from developing potentialities they otherwise would have developed. It is true that some antiabortionists will find this a cheering conclusion. But there are many more conservatives on abortion who would want to reject the view that artificial contraception can be wrong. Such a combination of positions cannot be defended. One must either accept the claim that some methods of contraception are seriously wrong, or else abandon the potentiality principle, and with it the conservative position on abortion.

Our second argument shows that the potentiality principle, even in its ungeneralized form, leads to even more disturbing consequences. Before we can state this argument we must defend the following moral symmetry principle:

> Let C be any causal process that normally leads to some outcome E. Let A be any action that initiates process C, and B be any action, involving no risk to the agent and a minimal expenditure of energy, which stops process C before E occurs. Assume further that actions A and B do not have any other morally significant consequences, and that E is the only part or outcome of process C that is morally significant in itself. Then there is no moral difference between intentionally performing action B and intentionally refraining from action A, assuming identical motivation in the two cases.

Some philosophers would reject such a symmetry principle, arguing that it is worse to kill someone deliberately than to refrain from saving his life. We feel that this objection is unsound, and that its initial plausibility rests upon a failure to consider the motivation likely to be associated with the two kinds of actions. To kill a person deliberately usually indicates that one *wanted* the person dead, whereas this is not usually true when one merely refrains from saving someone's life. But our moral symmetry principle deals only with cases in which the motivation is the same. One should consider situations such as the following. Jones wants to kill Smith and has acquired a grenade for that purpose. He has pulled out the pin and is about to throw it at Smith. Compare now the following courses of action. In the first, Jones throws his grenade at Smith and it explodes, killing Smith. In the second, just as Jones's arm is moving forward, he notices that someone else has thrown a grenade at Smith. The grenade lands on a trap door near Smith. Jones realizes that there is a button at his fingertips which, if pushed, will open the trap door and save Smith's life. Jones does not throw his grenade, since he sees that Smith is going to be killed anyway, and he can save his grenade for another day. Wanting to see Smith killed, he intentionally refrains from pushing the button. The grenade goes off, killing Smith. Are we to say that there is a significant difference between the wrongness of Jones's behavior in these two cases? It seems unintuitive to do so. Hence, initial appearances notwithstanding, our moral symmetry principle appears to be perfectly reasonable.

Given this principle, we can now set out our second objection to the potentiality principle. One need simply take as process C the development of a fertilized human egg cell, prior to the time when it acquires those psychological properties that confer a serious right to life. Process C will thus encompass the life of the organism before birth, since we saw earlier that there is no reason to believe that a fetus possesses the morally relevant properties. Action B can then be any action of destroying the fetus. Any action that leads to conception, and thus initiates process C, can be chosen as action A, providing that its only morally significant consequence is that it leads to process C. The symmetry principle then asserts that, given identical motivation, there is no moral difference between intentionally performing action B and intentionally refraining from action A. That is to say, there is no moral difference between abortion and intentionally refraining from procreation. Hence if the extreme conservative view of abortion were correct, one would be forced to conclude that conception at every possible opportunity was a serious duty! Few indeed would accept this consequence. It is therefore necessary to reject the potentiality principle.

Our third argument against the potentiality principle turns upon the following example. Suppose that technology has advanced to the point where it is possible to construct humans in the laboratory out of inorganic compounds. Suppose further that it is possible to freeze living beings and then to thaw them out without damaging them, and to program beliefs, desires, and personality traits into organisms by bringing about certain brain states. Given these techniques, imagine now that we construct an adult human in the laboratory. We program in a set of beliefs, desires, and personality traits. If we then thaw it out, we will have a conscious adult human with a distinct personality. But what if, because of all this work, we have developed ravenous appetites, and rather than thawing it out, we grind it up for hamburgers? Our action might be economically unwise, and subject to culinary objections, but would it be open to moral criticism? In particular, would we be guilty of murdering an innocent person? We think most people would agree that the answer to this question is no. Until the organism has been brought to consciousness, and until it envisages a future for itself and has desires about such a future there is nothing *prima facie* wrong about destroying it. Thus it is false that something can have a serious right to life in virtue of its potentialities. So we can bid adieu to the potentiality principle, and with it, the final "pro-life" objection to abortion.

III. *When Does an Organism Have a Right to Life?*

We have shown that there is no reason to believe a human fetus possesses those psychological traits that confer a right to life. But we have not yet indicated precisely what those properties are. We will discuss this now in our final section.

Our view is as follows: an organism can have a right to life only if it now possesses, or possessed at some time in the past, the capacity to have a desire for continued existence. An organism cannot satisfy this requirement unless it is a person, that is, a continuing subject of experiences and other mental states, and unless it has the capacity for self-consciousness—where an organism is self-conscious only if it recognizes that it is itself a person.

The basis for our contention is the claim that there is a conceptual connection between, on the one hand, the rights an individual can have and the circumstances under which they can be violated, and, on the other, the desires he can have. A right is something that can be violated and, in general, to violate an individual's right to something is to frustrate the corresponding desire. Suppose, for example, that someone owns a car. Then you are under a *prima facie* obligation not to take it from him. However, the obligation is not unconditional: if he does not care whether you drive off with his car, then *prima facie* you do not violate his right by doing so.

A precise formulation of the conceptual connection in question would require considerable care. The most important point is that violation of an individual's right to something does not always involve thwarting a *present* desire, that is, a desire that exists at the same time as the action that violates the right. Sometimes the violation of a right involves thwarting a *past* desire. The most dramatic illustration is provided by the rights of dead persons, since here the individual whose right is being transgressed no longer exists. A more common example is that of people who are temporarily unconscious. When a person is unconscious, he does not have any desires. Yet his rights can certainly be infringed upon. This presents no problem when one takes past desires into account. The reason that it is wrong to kill a temporarily unconscious adult is that in the period before he became unconscious, he had a desire to go on living—a desire which it is possible to satisfy.

Violation of an individual's right may also involve frustrating a *future* desire. The most vivid example of this is the case of rights of future generations. Most people would hold that for those living today to use up all of the world's resources would violate the rights of future individuals. Here, as in the case of the rights of a dead person, the violation of an individual's rights occurs at a time when the individual does not even exist.

However, it is very important to notice that what is relevant are the desires that individuals will *actually have* at some time in the future. The desires that individuals would have *if* they were to exist at certain times at which, as a matter of fact, they will not exist, are not relevant. The need for this restriction is brought out by the example used at the end of the previous section of this paper. If one were to consider the desires that something would have if it were to exist at a later time it would be wrong to destroy the frozen human being we had constructed in the laboratory. Even though it has never been conscious, if it were thawed out, it would not want to be destroyed. Rights of future generations provide a second example. Suppose we know with certainty that no future generation will ever exist. Then there is no objection to using up the world's resources now. But if one were obliged to take into account the desires future individuals would have if they were to exist, it would be wrong to use up the world's resources.

A complete account of the connection between rights and desires would also have to take into consideration unusual cases, where an individual is in an emotionally unbalanced state, or where a person's desires have been affected by lack of relevant information, or by his being subjected to abnormal physiological or psychological factors. We shall ignore these, and confine ourselves to paradigm cases of violations of an individual's rights.[7] When this is done, we can say that first, an individual cannot have a right to something unless there can be actions that would violate it. Second, an action cannot violate an individual's right to something unless it wrongs him by depriving him of the thing in question. And thirdly, an action can wrong an individual by depriving him of something only if it violates his desire for that thing. The desire is generally a present desire, but it may be a past or future desire. It follows that a person cannot have a right to something unless he is at some time capable of having the corresponding desire.

Let us now apply this to the case of the right to life. The expression "right to life" misleads one into thinking that the right concerns the continued existence of a biological organism. The following example shows that this interpretation is inadequate. Suppose that we could completely reprogram an adult human so that it has (apparent) memories, beliefs, desires, and personality traits radically different from those associated with it before the reprogramming. (Billy Graham is reprogrammed as a replica of Bertrand Russell.) In such a case, however beneficial the change might be, it is true that *someone* has been destroyed, that someone's right to life has been violated, even though no biological organism has been killed. So the right to life cannot be construed as merely the right of a biological organism to continue to exist.

How then can the right in question be more accurately described?

A natural suggestion is that the expression "right to life" refers to the right of a person—a subject of experiences and other mental states—to continue to exist. However, this interpretation begs the question against certain possible positions. It might be that while persons have a right to continue to exist, so do other things that are only potentially persons. A right to life on this view would be either the right of a person to continue to exist or the right of something that is only potentially a person to become a person.

We concluded above that something cannot have a specific right unless it is capable at some time of having the corresponding desire. It follows from this together with the more accurate analysis of the right to life that something cannot have a right to life unless it is capable at some time either of having a desire to continue to exist as a person, or of having a desire to become a person. If something has not been capable of having either of these desires in the past, and is not now capable, then if it is now destroyed, it will never have possessed the capacity in question. Hence an organism cannot have a right to life unless it is now capable, or was capable at some time in the past, of having a desire to continue to exist as a person or a desire to become a person.

But recall now the discussion of desires in Section I. We showed that one's desires are limited by the concepts one possesses. Therefore one cannot have a desire to continue to exist as a person or a desire to become a person unless one has the concept of a person. The question we must now ask is whether something that is not itself a person could have the concept of such an entity. It seems plausible to hold that it could not. This means that something that is not a person cannot have a desire to become a person. Hence the right to life is confined to persons.

This brings us to our final requirement: an organism cannot have a right to life unless it is capable of self-consciousness, where an organism is self-conscious only if it recognizes that it is itself a continuing subject of experiences and other mental states. To justify this requirement, let us ask whether a person can fail to recognize that it is a person. If the answer were negative, it would follow from the requirement just established that an organism cannot have a right to life unless it possesses self-consciousness.

It is unclear, however, that something necessarily possesses self-consciousness if it is a person. Perhaps a person might fail to notice this fact about himself. Even if this is possible, it seems reasonable to believe that if something is a person, then it is *ipso facto capable* of acquiring the concept of a person, and of recognizing that it is itself a person. Thus even if something can have a right to life without having been self-consciousness, it appears that it cannot have such a right without ever having possessed the capacity for self-consciousness.

Thus, the psychological characteristics that bestow a right to life upon an organism are these: it must be a person, capable of self-consciousness, of envisaging a future for itself, and of having desires about its own future states.

We began by setting out a preliminary case for abortion. Then we examined attempts by antiabortionists to overturn that case by arguing that abortion is wrong because it violates the fetus's right to life. We showed that the arguments antiabortionists offer in support of this claim are unsound, and that the contention itself is false. Our central point was that neither an organism's potentialities, nor membership in a particular species, serves to confer a right to life. An organism has a right to life only if it has certain psychological traits possessed by normal adult human beings, but not by fetuses.

Next we considered what properties endow an organism with a right to life. We defended the view that something can have a right to life only if it possesses, or has possessed, the capacity to have a desire for continued existence. We then argued that to satisfy this requirement, an entity must be a person capable of self-consciousness.

The issue of abortion thus ceases to be puzzling. A human fetus does not have a right to life because it does not have the capacity for self-consciousness; it cannot conceive of itself as a continuing subject of experiences; it cannot envisage a future for itself, nor have desires about such a future. A fetus is not a person, but only a potential person. Hence there is no moral objection to abortion. To prohibit it is to inflict unjustified suffering and death upon society.

NOTES

[1] For the sake of brevity, we shall use the term "fetus" in an extended sense to refer to an organism in either the embryonic or fetal stage of development.

[2] In everyday life one often speaks of desiring things, such as an apple or a newspaper. Such talk is elliptical, the context together with one's ordinary beliefs serving to make it clear that one wants to eat the apple and read the newspaper. Thus if one wanted to provide a completely explicit description of an individual's desires, one would use sentences such as "John wants it to be

the case that he is eating an apple in the next few minutes." This is why the fundamental way of describing a given desire is not as a desire for some object, but as a desire that a certain proposition be true.

[3] See page 352 of "The Question of Abortion," The Committee For Human Life, pages 351-359 in *Declaration of U.S. Policy of Population Stabilization by Voluntary Means,* U.S. Government Printing Office, Washington, D.C., 1972.

[4] See page 331 of *Declaration of U.S. Policy of Population Stabilization by Voluntary Means.*

[5] It is quite possible, however, that people ought to have moral qualms about killing nonhuman animals, for it may well be that adult members of other species have a serious right to life. For a brief discussion of this question, see pages 64-65 of "Abortion and Infanticide," in *Philosophy & Public Affairs,* Volume 2, Number 1, Fall, 1972.

[6] Olaf Stapledon, *Sirius,* Secker and Warburg, 1944.

[7] For an account of rights that takes into consideration these cases, see Michael Tooley, "A Defense of Abortion and Infanticide," in *The Problem of Abortion,* edited by Joel Feinberg, Belmont, California, 1973.

R. B. BRANDT
The Morality of Abortion[1]

The term "abortion" is used in this discussion to refer to deliberate removal (or deliberate action to cause the expulsion) of a fetus[2] from the womb of a human female, at the request or through the agency of the mother, so as in fact to result in the death of the fetus but with insignificantly small risk to the life or health of the mother. The question I raise is roughly whether abortion in that sense is morally wrong. I am not raising the question whether abortion should be prohibited by law. That is a very different question, and I am confining myself to the moral issue. There is another question I am not raising: whether a fetus should be removed, *irrespective* of the preferences of the mother, when there is good reason to think the child will be seriously defective, mentally or physically. Since it is a grave responsibility to bring a human being into the world, I think this latter is an important question; but I do not propose to discuss it here.

The question must be made more precise. First, let us distinguish the question whether abortion is morally wrong from the question whether a person who does it is morally blameworthy, that is, whether even if and when abortion is morally wrong there can be considerations which morally excuse the agent. (Some persons might use alternative language, saying that, even if abortion is morally wrong, it might be that a person who performed an abortion has sometimes not, in the total circumstances, committed a "sin"; but I prefer to avoid this term, with its theological overtones.) Let me explain how this might be. Suppose a physician performs an abortion in the sincere belief that in the circumstances it is his moral obligation to do so, and at some risk to his professional standing; I would think it highly likely that he is morally blameless (unless his having the belief is itself culpable), even though the abortion was wrong. Again, the temptations for an unwed mother to commit an abortion on herself might be so strong that we might say her act was morally blameless, even though in fact wrong—since an action can hardly be morally blameworthy unless it shows a defect of character, and her act might not show a defect of character. Now I do not wish to discuss the question when a person may be morally blameworthy for performing an action. What I do wish to discuss is whether acts of abortion are morally wrong in the sense that their agents *would* be morally blameworthy *unless* their actions were *excused* (not justified, but excused) in some way. This question seems to me the most controverted one today.

The question I wish to discuss, however, is even narrower than this. There are some persons who are absolutists about abortion; that is, they hold that abortion in the sense explained above is *universally* and *unconditionally* morally wrong. This position is widely held, especially by writers in the Catholic Church. I do mean to discuss this issue by implication, but the thesis I wish to discuss is a weaker thesis than this one. I am going to question the weaker thesis, and *a fortiori* I shall be questioning the stronger thesis. The thesis I wish to discuss is the thesis that abortion as above explained is *prima facie* morally wrong. Let me explain. Persons who hold this weaker thesis are prepared to concede that, although abortion is usually and normally morally wrong, there are circumstances in which it is not. For instance, it is sometimes held that if an abortion is necessary to save the life of the mother, or if it is highly likely that the infant will be seriously defective, or if the mother already has crippling responsibilities so that her other children will suffer if another child is born (etc.), then an abortion is morally justified. But they hold that an abortion is *prima facie* wrong; or, in other words, they hold that there is a *prima facie* obligation not to bring about an abortion. (What I mean here by saying there is a "*prima facie* obligation" to do A, is that there is an obligation to do A, everything considered, except in the presence of a *prima facie* obligation to do something which is incompatible with doing A.) Thus the position is that there is always a *prima facie* moral obligation not to cause the death of a fetus, and that, *unless* there is a stronger *prima facie* moral obligation to do something which is incompatible with meeting the obligation not to kill the fetus, it is morally wrong to perform the abortion. So, generally, it is morally wrong to perform an abortion except where there is some moral obligation which can be met only by taking such action. Evidently, the stronger view that it is unconditionally and morally wrong to perform an abortion is untenable unless one believes it is at least morally wrong to do so and there are no conflicting and stronger moral obligations which can be met only by performing an abortion.

I wish to discuss the question whether it is *prima facie* morally wrong to perform an abortion (or *prima facie* obligatory not to do so), viz., whether abortion is wrong except when it is called for by *moral obligations*. Since the preferences of the mother may not constitute a moral obligation, what I am asking is, in part, whether there is anything morally objectionable about performing an abortion for no other reason than that the mother wants it, or, perhaps better, does not want to continue a pregnancy or have the responsibility of rearing a child.

I shall confine my attention to abortions not later than the third month, partly because I think such abortions are the primary object of contemporary controversy, and partly because I think it may make a difference if the abortion occurs, say, in the six or seventh month.

In what follows I shall discuss the issue on two levels. In the first section I shall make no assumption about what moral principles are or about how to decide whether a particular moral principle is acceptable; I shall argue in a very commonsense way. I shall maintain that there is not an unrestricted *prima facie* obligation not to kill, but only a *prima facie* obligation not to kill in certain types of cases; and I shall tentatively suggest a general formulation of a restricted principle which would have the effect of not implying that there is a *prima facie* obligation not to cause an abortion. In the second section I shall attempt to answer my question about abortion on a deeper level, at which explicit assumptions are being made about what a moral principle is and how the acceptability of one may be decided, by inquiring whether a rule prohibiting abortions, except where there are conflicting other moral rules, would be a part of a rational moral system.

It is convenient to begin with comments on the views of Pope Pius XI, as expressed in his encyclical *Casti Connubii* (1930), although he is there asserting not just the *prima facie* wrongness of abortion but its absolute wrongness. He affirms:

But can any reason ever avail to excuse the direct killing of the innocent?

For this is what is at stake. The infliction of death whether upon mother or upon child is against the commandment of God and the voice of nature: "Thou shalt not kill." The lives of both are equally sacred, and no one, not even public authority, can ever have the right to destroy them. It is absurd to invoke against innocent human beings the right of the State to inflict capital punishment, for this is valid only against the guilty. Nor is there any question here of the right of self-defense, even to the shedding of blood, against an unjust assailant, for none could describe as an unjust assailant an innocent child. Nor, finally, does there exist any so called right of extreme necessity which could extend to the direct killing of an innocent human being.

Pope Pius presents his moral principle as being both a commandment of God and the expression of the "voice of nature." His reason for saying that the prohibition is a commandment of God seems to be simply that the Bible asserts that God has said, "Thou shalt not kill." It does not, however, follow from agreement that there is a commandment not to kill that there is a divine commandment not to cause abortion. The question remains: Was this kind of killing intended? The Commandment as reported in the Bible is a very summary statement, requiring interpretation. As it stands, it might be taken to forbid killing of animals, capital punishment, action necessary for self-defense, euthanasia to relieve extreme pain, and suicide. The Church has not, I believe, proposed understanding of the Commandment as forbidding *all* killing. Exceptions must be admitted. But which ones? The question whether God prohibits abortion is not settled by appeal to the Biblical Commandment until it has been shown whether abortion falls among the admissible exceptions.

Abortion, incidentally, is not explicitly mentioned in the New Testament, although it is forbidden as early as the *Didache* (c. 80 A.D.) and by the early Church Fathers. Prohibition of abortion as being morally wrong is not part of the Jewish tradition, and it is far from universal among human societies.

Pope Pius XI also said that abortion is contrary to the "voice of nature"; this contention is too obscure and difficult to justify discussion in this brief essay.

If, like the Pope, we accept the injunction, "Thou shalt not kill," because it is believed to be God's commandment, the question of how it should be interpreted must presumably be answered by arguments to determine what God really does command, or how God intends his commandment to be interpreted. Actually, the Pope interprets the principle (1) as not applying to the killing of animals, (2) as applying to the killing of a human fetus, (3) as not applying to the killing of a "uninnocent" human being, where "uninnocent" is apparently construed as meaning "guilty of a capital crime," and (4) as not applying to killing in self-defense.

Let us now set aside the contention that the general injunction "Do not kill" should be accepted because it is God's commandment; we can then ignore matters of exegesis of Biblical texts, theological arguments, etc. Let us rather consider how the injunction must be construed, if it is to be viewed as a principle of *prima facie* moral obligation and is to be restricted so as to be compatible with what appear to be firm intuitive moral convictions.

One might ask, "Why should we discuss this more general principle at all, when all we want to know is whether it is *prima facie* wrong to perform an abortion?" To this the answer is that the above injunction, in some interpretation, is probably accepted by everyone, whereas no principle directly about abortions enjoys such status. One way to show that abortion is *prima facie* wrong would be to show that the only reasonable construction of the above principle is such that it would be inconsistent to accept it and at the same time to condone abortion as not even being *prima facie* wrong.

There is, of course, a difficulty in using the above injunction to settle the abortion question. For anyone who denies that abortion is *prima facie* wrong will presumably insist on an interpretation of the general injunction about killing, such a prohibition of abortion will not follow from it. So, if an argument from a general injunction against killing to a prohibition of abortion is to succeed, the defender of abortion must somehow be brought to accept a relatively unrestricted injunction against killing.

It can be and may properly be argued that a proponent of permitting abortion is going to find it much harder to show reasonable grounds for restricting a general principle about killing human beings intentionally, when construed as only a principle of *prima facie* moral obligation, than when construed as an absolute principle. For instance, probably most people today would accept the view that a fetus may be aborted if absolutely necessary to save the life of the mother, this view, if accepted, is a counterexample to the view that it is unconditionally and always wrong to perform an abortion. But this view is by no means necessarily a counterexample to the thesis that abortion is only *prima facie* wrong. In this case there presumably is a *prima facie* moral obligation to save the life of the mother; hence it could be argued that there is a *prima facie* obligation to avoid the abortion, but because of the stronger *prima facie* obligation to save the life of the mother, an abortion would not be wrong. How might one show that there is not an unrestricted *prima facie* obligation to avoid abortion?

Let me begin by pointing out that it *may* be that any plausible *prima facie* principle about killing will require restriction. To see this, it is convenient to consider the matter of keeping promises. It has been maintained that there is a *prima facie* moral obligation to keep *all* promises as such, although there are of course promises which, everything considered, morally ought to be broken, e.g., promises of a rather trivial sort which could be kept only at the cost of serious injury to someone. But, on reflection, it seems that some promises have not even a *prima facie* force (corresponding, perhaps, to contracts which courts regard as essentially null and void). Consider a promise made under duress (when the person had no right to try to extract the promise), or a promise made as a result of a deliberate misrepresentation of the facts to the promise for the purpose of extracting the promise, or an old promise made to a person who has since violated all his obligations to the promisor. It is at least plausible to say that such promises have no moral force at all; there is not even a *prima facie* obligation to keep them—surely one need not discover that one has a stronger moral obligation to do something incompatible with keeping the promise, in order to be free of an obligation to keep such promises. So, if we are going to formulate a sound general principle about a *prima facie* obligation to keep promises, the principle must be restricted to promises that do not have certain voiding properties.

The very same thing could be true about killing. It could be that there are types of situations, and kinds of human beings, such that it is not wrong to destroy them, even in the absence of a *prima facie* obligation to do something which requires that. Are there, or are there not? I propose one example that seems clear.

Suppose a human being has suffered massive brain damage in an accident. He is unconscious, and it is quite clear he will never regain consciousness—his brain is beyond repair. His body, however, can be kept alive by means known to science, more or less indefinitely. Is there a *prima facie* obligation to keep this being alive, or to refrain from terminating its existence? I believe there is no such thing.

Critics may say that this instance is no support for the claim that there is no unrestricted *prima facie* obligation not to kill—indeed not even support for the claim that there is no unrestricted absolute obligation not to kill. For, they may say, all that is here in question is the withdrawal of artificial means of sustaining life; when these are withdrawn, nature is allowed to take its course, and the man dies. He is not *killed*.

This criticism is, however, without force. (1) If it seems convincing to some because an abstention from providing help seems very different from actively killing, we must point out that acts and abstentions are morally not different; morally it is as wrong to allow a man to die when one could have saved his life by lifting a finger, as it is to kill him. In both cases one is responsible for the death. (2) If it seems convincing because "allowing nature to take its course" is very different from "interfering with nature"—what happens in an abortion—we must point out that interference with a natural process has never been shown to have a moral standing different from abstention from using some artificial means. We certainly think we must use artificial means to save an ill person pain; in fact, all surgery and medication might be viewed as interfering with nature.

(3) In any case the criticism can be met by pointing out that we believe a moral proposition to which it clearly does not apply: that in case the injured man's vital organs are needed for another person, it is permissible to operate and remove them, even when this terminates his life there and then. In other words, we think it permissible directly to bring about the death of a person in some circumstances, and not merely to allow nature to take its course. It may be said that all this retort shows is that the obligation not to kill is not absolute, but only *prima facie*. But I suggest we feel that there is *no moral issue* about a lethal operation in this total situation. (I admit, however, that some persons apparently feel qualms, and hence the device is used of defining "medically dead" so that the injured man is declared to be already dead.)

I suggest, then, that it is at least quite plausible to say there is no *prima facie* obligation not to bring about the death of a man injured in this way. Hence any plausible general statement about the *prima facie* obligation not to kill must be restricted so as to take this fact into account.[3]

Can we formulate a more general restriction, of which the above example may be viewed as an instance, on the *prima facie* obligation not to kill? One logically possible view is one apparently espoused by William James: that there is no moral claim where there is no *sentience*. James wrote:

> Take any demand, however slight, which any creature, however weak, may make. Ought it not, for its own sake, to be satisfied? If not, prove why not. The only possible kind of proof you could adduce would be the exhibition of another creature who should make a demand that ran the other way. The only possible reason there can be why any phenomenon ought to exist is that such a phenomenon actually is desired.

The implication of James's principle seems to be: it is *prima facie* wrong to kill a being that wants to live, or that has desires which can be satisfied only if it is alive. But the fetus is not sentient; it has no wish or desire, is insufficiently developed to be capable of any. Since the fetus has no desires at all, it is not *prima facie* wrong to destroy it. (Moreover, if the mother wishes that she not bear a child, or have the lifelong responsibilities that go with bringing up a child, that *is* a reason, according to James, why what she wants should be done.) So, if we follow James, we might assert: It is *prima facie* wrong to kill human beings, except those which are not sentient and have no desires, and except in reasonable defense of self or others against unjust assault. Doubtless this suggestion is only a rough first approximation, which needs amendment and complication—as it surely does, since we do not wish to hold that it is not wrong to kill a person who is asleep or in a coma (and in that sense is not "sentient"). It seems clear, however, that a restricted principle can be formulated along the suggested line, which is not obviously a less acceptable principle than the one which affirms an unrestricted *prima facie* obligation not to cause the death of any human being.

It is sometimes argued, in criticism of the restriction of the right to life to sentient, desiring beings, that if one accepts such a restriction one then has no reason in principle not to withdraw the right to life from babies, the elderly, the feeble-minded, and indeed anyone it is socially inconvenient to have around. But, it is said, such a withdrawal of a *prima facie* right to life is morally intolerable. What is necessary in order to avoid this dread slippery slope is to espouse the right of human beings to life in the most unrestricted way.

But in what sense is there "no reason in principle" not to withdraw the right to life from babies, etc.? A child has sentience, desires, and memory, even if in rather undeveloped form at first. An old person has all the feelings and awareness any of us has (and persons of any age would feel anxiety if they knew they were up for execution beyond a certain age). The feeble-minded, again, have some sort of life with value, at least on the same level as the higher subhuman species. So what could be meant by saying there is "no reason in principle"?

It would, of course, be a complete mistake for anyone to argue that the restriction proposed could not be accepted because then *no line* could be drawn between this restriction and the unacceptable ones. A line can be drawn; we have already drawn it by distinguishing the types of cases. Indeed, one can draw lines rather more sharply, if one wishes. Since it is a matter of observation and inference when "sentience" begins, some finer lines in the form of behavioral criteria need to be drawn, which I do not know how to draw. Some writers draw a line at implantation, a proposal that would permit morning-after pills but not abortion thereafter. The Church has sometimes drawn a line at the moment of "quickening." My point is that there is no problem about distinguishing the proposed restriction of the right to life from other quite different restrictions and also that the restriction I have suggested can be, and needs to be, formulated somewhat more sharply.

Another argument is sometimes used: as a practical matter the permission of abortions will weaken respect for human life generally, so in effect we encourage murder in general by permitting abortion even in the early stages. This argument is a claim about empirical fact, and one would like to see evidence which supports it. I should suppose that actually we make a very sharp distinction between a virtually formless fetus in its early stages and a sentient human being; surely a woman who requests an abortion might not dream of killing an adult. The difference is so great that an explanation is needed why we should think that attitudes toward the killing of a fetus might generalize to the killing of the already born.

Some kind of Jamesian principle about when it is *prima facie* wrong to kill a human being, then, seems not open to some objections that have been raised. Of course, I have only put it forward as a suggestion; all I have done by way of support for it is to have offered an example which is a counterexample to an unrestricted right to life of "innocent" persons not engaged in an unjust assault.

We shall now approach the question of the *prima facie* wrongness of abortion on a more fundamental level where, if we are fortunate, we may hope to find more decisive reasoning. This effort will at least disclose some problems which are intriguing.

I shall do this by assuming, as a useful meaning to be assigned to the expression "*A* is *prima facie* wrong," a definition the value of at least some variant of which has grown on moral philosophers in recent years. The proposal is that "*A* is *prima facie* morally wrong" be assigned the meaning:

> *A* would be prohibited by a rule of the moral code the currency of which for their society would be preferred over all others by all persons who
> (A) expected to live a lifetime in that society,
> (B) were rational at least in the sense that their preferences were fully guided by all relevant available knowledge, and
> (C) had some general benevolence, the degree and extent being compatible with the restriction that the preference of each be rational.

There are some alternative proposals which some philosophers might prefer to substitute for (C). For instance, we might have

> (C') were impartial in the sense that (and this is a restriction on (B)) their preferences were uninfluenced by information which would enable them to choose a system which would especially advantage them.

I shall conduct my discussion in terms of (C), but it would be interesting for the reader to follow the implications of a choice of (C'),[4] which is a somewhat stronger assumption than (C), since it appears to be equivalent to requiring a degree of benevolence toward all others equal to the degree of the person's "self love," or interest in his own future welfare.

It will naturally be asked: Why is the foregoing proposed as a "useful" meaning to be assigned to "*A* is *prima facie* wrong"? A full reply would have to be lengthy, but it may be helpful to mention three points. (1) If "wrong" is construed in this way, then intelligent persons must regard moral principles not just as traditional prejudices or commitments but as restrictions or requirements with real point in terms of the welfare of sentient beings. Such persons will tend to respect and support an actual morality to the extent to which it conforms with true moral principles understood in the explained way. (2) If moral principles are construed in the way suggested, intelligent people will be generally disposed to adjudicate conflicts of interest by appeal to them and to recognize that they cannot in decency argue publicly that a claim of theirs deserves public support if it does not comport with such principles. (3) If we identify right and wrong actions in the way the proposed definition suggests, then it is in principle possible to find out, by methods of ordinary reasoning and evidence (but doubtless not in a very simple way), which actions are right or wrong. These considerations seem important in deciding on a useful meaning for moral words; indeed, I think we would be prepared to alter our formulation if we found it could not have the support of these considerations.

There is an ambiguity in the above formulation which needs to be resolved. If what is right or wrong is determined, in the end, by the preferences of "all persons" who meet certain conditions, one will wonder who is to count as a "person." Does this include the mentally defective? children? small babies? fetuses, whom the recent Supreme Court decision has ruled are not persons within the meaning of the law at least during the early months of development? chimpanzees? intelligent dogs? any sentient creatures whatever? The reason for the interest in these questions is that, for instance, it might be that dogs would not prefer the currency of a moral system which committed stray dogs to a gas chamber, whereas such a system might be preferred if dogs do not "have a vote." I point this out, because a person hardly wants to accept the claim that a proposed definition of a moral term is "useful" until he understands it sharply enough to see something of the moral principles it may commit him to.

I propose to construe "persons" to mean "adult human beings with reasonable intelligence." This is not very precise and, if one wanted, one could spell it out as "human beings at least eighteen years of age, and with an I.Q. at the time of at least 110, and not temporarily in a psychotic or neurotic or even a highly emotional state of mind." An advantage of such a construction of "persons" is that our definition then clearly excludes any such bizarre conception as babies (or, worse, animals or fetuses) *expecting* to live a lifetime in a society, and so on. The restricted conception also, I think, does not really have implications different from those of a less restricted conception which in effect "gives a vote" to animals, etc. The reason for this is that if these adults have the benevolence specified in (C), they will presumably take an interest in the welfare of babies, animals, etc. and will prefer a moral system which will give them the same protection these would give themselves if they "had a vote."

What is meant by saying that a person has "benevolence"? The Shorter Oxford Dictionary defines "benevolent" as "desirous of the good of others." Notice that it is defined as desire for the good *of others*, not some abstract goodness or value at large. So far the Dictionary reminds us of the New Testament, which enjoins us to love "thy neighbor as thyself" but does not enjoin loving any abstract good.

But we need to be more specific about "the good" of others, and it is easiest to be so by considering first the notion of "self-love." We all of us have what have been called "particular" desires, like the desire to eat a certain French pastry or to be praised for a certain achievement. There is also a desire of a different kind, just to be in *some state or other* which one likes (notice how one can motivate a child by promising him "something nice" without telling him what it is to be), and a desire not to be in any state one dislikes such as fatigue, feeling hungry, feeling lonely, or in general being uncomfortable. Let us call this desire "self-love." Obviously one way to gratify one's self-love is by gratifying one's other particular desires; for if we do this we do not suffer the discomfort of hunger or longing, and we get to enjoy the consummatory experience associated with these desires.

We can think of benevolence as a desire like self-love, but directed at the inner states of *other* persons. Being benevolent is not sharing another person's particular desires; if another person wants a French pastry, benevolence does not imply that I shall be motivated by the prospect of his eating a French pastry in the way in which he is. Like self-love, benevolence is a desire for another person to be in a state he likes, one of joy or satisfaction or comfort and not in a state he dislikes, like fatigue, hunger, or other distress. Benevolence, then, is a positive interest in another's being in a state which he likes and a negative interest in his being in a state which he dislikes.

States of joy and distress are not limited to human beings; correspondingly people who are benevolent take an interest in the joy and distress, are motivated at least to relieve the misery of animals, and to some extent to satisfy them.

What is meant by the term "general" in clause (C)? This is a requirement that the benevolence be directed not merely to specific preferred individuals like one's own wife or children or even compatriots. How far must benevolence reach in order to be "general"? We probably do better not to try to make any further definitional specification of this for the purpose of application of clause (C). It is perhaps enough that (C) already specifies that the degree and extent are to be compatible with the preferences of the individual being rational (guided by full available information).

After all these preliminaries about a proposed meaning for "*A* is *prima facie* morally wrong" (or "is *prima facie* morally obligatory"), it is time to get back to our question about the morality of abortion. Our question whether abortion is *prima facie* morally wrong may now be construed as the question whether abortion as defined (destruction of a fetus within the first three months when this is wanted or undertaken by the mother) would be forbidden by the rules of the moral system which rational persons, with the benevolence specified, would prefer to any other moral system. This question may not be easy to answer.

At first it may seem that of course benevolent persons would not want a fetus destroyed, and hence that they would prefer a moral system which forbade this. But matters are not quite that simple.

There is an important distinction to be made. It seems very plausible that rational persons with some benevolence will take a favorable interest in the well-being of future generations, in that of persons who live in the future. (Obviously intelligent benevolent persons do, as we can notice from all the present concern about the environment and conservation of resources.) But it is one thing to take an interest in persons, living now or in the future, being deprived of happiness or brought joy; it is quite another thing to take an interest in the being *brought into being* of a sentient creature which, *if* produced, will be happy and enjoy well-being. It is not impossible for one to be strongly interested in the welfare of all actual persons, present or future, but be totally indifferent to whether a person *is produced* who, *if* produced, will be happy. We must remember that *no person is frustrated or made unhappy or miserable by not coming to exist.* No one is *deprived* by non-birth as a sentient being. So it is possible that a person take a strong interest in the welfare of actual (present or future) persons, but that he be left cold by the idea of producing more happy people. Producing somebody who would be unhappy (say, because of physical defects) would presumably be unacceptable to a benevolent person; but *failing* to produce a happy person would seem not necessarily unacceptable to a benevolent person.

The implication of this distinction for the morality of abortion is obvious. Suppose we construe abortion as the prevention of the *coming into being* of a person (perhaps one who will be happy, if he is brought into being). Then it would be a mistake to infer from the fact that rational benevolent people will presumably want a moral system which protects the life and happiness and welfare of sentient creatures that they will want a moral system which forbids the *prevention of the coming into being* of some sentient creatures.

It may be objected that the preceding paragraph misunderstands the nature of abortion. It may be said that a fetus is an *already existing person,* so that its destruction is not merely preventing the coming into being of a person, but is incompatible with the protection of the happiness and welfare of sentient beings, just as much as the murder of an adult. I shall come back to this—and argue that the preceding paragraph does not misunderstand the nature of abortion.

First I want to consider how we might argue that rational benevolent persons would want a moral system which did *not* forbid abortion (or, if you like, would want a system which forbids killing human beings but with an exceptive clause about fetuses in the first three months). How will rational benevolent people make up their minds on a point of this sort? Presumably they will count up all the probable harms to people and the benefits to people, if one rule or its opposite is adopted. They will ask: Will it do more good to sentient creatures, in terms of happiness in the long run, to have current a rule forbidding abortions or not to have such a rule? Now the first thing they will notice is that "abortion" has been defined as the destruction of a fetus *instigated by the mother*. If it is so instigated, there will normally, or always, be a reason. Mothers do not want abortions for no reason at all. Either they cannot afford another child or another child is a risk to the health of the mother or a child will be an unwanted burden and so on. It will be agreed that it can be assumed that if a mother wants an abortion, then it is her judgment that from her point of view there will be more harm than good in the arrival of the offspring. That fact will be a harm, something which counts against having a rule forbidding abortion. Is there usually a *public* benefit from the arrival of another child? Doubtless in a country with a manpower shortage, the more children the better. But at the present time, for most of the world, there are too many people already. Another mouth to feed, or someone to pollute the air by driving another car, is not a benefit to others. It looks as if other people would be better off if those who are not wanted anyway did not make it to existence. Average welfare is obviously related to population size; there is an optimum size at which the average welfare is maximal. The addition of people beyond this optimal point has the effect of reducing the welfare of somebody else. In most countries the population is already such that the optimal population has been exceeded. So, will benevolent people want to insist that a fetus be permitted to develop and be born, when the nonexistence of the extra person would bring the population nearer the optimal? It looks as if, from the point of view of the general public, there is no reason to prefer a moral rule forbidding abortion.

Someone might, unwisely, reply to this as follows: "In consistency you should permit a few murders. After all, a murder does somebody good—the murderer, or else he would not be doing it. And it does bring the population down." The answer to this objection is, however, obvious. If murders are permitted, then nobody can feel secure. Even if there would be some public benefit from certain murders, they cannot be permitted without rendering human life so precarious as to be of no account. The situation is very different in the case of abortion. The fetus has not the foresight to feel insecure; it suffers no pain, has no worries. It is *not yet* a sentient, intelligent being. So there is not the reason against a policy of terminating a fetus that there is against permitting a murder.

Nevertheless, it may be claimed that the above line of argument, counting the harm or good to persons arising from a moral rule about abortions, has overlooked an important point: the future happy life of the fetus itself. Suppose it *is* true that another person will slightly reduce the welfare of persons who will exist whether this person, whose existence is being deliberated, comes into being or not. Must not *its* happiness be counted too? Possibly that is a good to be considered so great that its development must be allowed, even if an additional person will somewhat diminish the well-being of other persons.

Should the supposititious happiness of the prospective extra person be counted or not? I have questioned above whether benevolent persons *would* count it, on the ground that no *person* is harmed, or deprived of happiness, if the fetus is not permitted to *become* a human person. So we are brought back to the controversial point I raised at the conclusion of making what I said was an "important distinction": whether, in some sense appropriate to our issue, the fetus is already a person. What we want to know is whether somebody is being deprived or harmed by the act of abortion, which admittedly prevents the fetus from developing into a human being with a possibly happy life. I said I would return to this question. I shall now try to meet it head on.

I am going to argue that it is mistaken to suppose that the fetus is, in an appropriate sense, *the same person* as the child who will occur after the development of the fetus, and birth. And, if it is not the same person as the person which begins at some later time, then it is not, in an appropriate sense, now a person at all—and hence we cannot say that somebody is harmed or deprived by the abortion.

This claim may seem puzzling, and it may seem initially that any argument to support it is bound to be contrived. I think, however, that we can see the force of the claim by considering a possible situation which is closely parallel. Suppose I were seriously ill, and were told that, for a sizable fee, an operation to save "my life" could be performed, of the following sort: my brain would be removed to another body which could provide a normal life, but the unfortunate result of the operation would be that my memory and learned abilities would be wholly erased, and that the forming of memory brain traces must begin again from scratch, as in a newborn baby. Now, how large a fee would I be willing to pay for this operation, when the alternative is my peaceful demise? My own answer would be: None at all. I would take no interest in the continued existence of "myself" in that sense, and I would rather add the sizable fee to the inheritance of my children. It is true that in some sense "I" would continue to exist; obviously my *brain* would. But it looks as if something is missing which is necessary for personal identity in an important sense. The important thing that is missing seems to be *memory;* if the latter person cannot remember my present and earlier experiences at all, then he is as good as a new person from my point of view. And I cannot see the point of forfeiting my children's inheritance in order to start off a person who is brand new except that he happens to enjoy the benefit of having my present brain, without the memory traces. It appears that some continuity of memory is a necessary condition for personal identity in an important sense.[5]

How does the above example bear on the situation of the fetus?

Let us compare the physical components. In the case of the operation, one part of the first body (the brain) is transferred relatively intact (except for memory traces) into a different body; in the case of the fetus, one whole body at the earlier stage grows, through ingestion of new materials, into a structure quite different at the later stage (although a structure already determined by the genetic components there at the earlier stage). In both cases the total body at the first stage is qualitatively very different from the total body at the second stage. But in the operation case one part is identical in the two bodies at different times, whereas in the case of the fetus there is development, involving ingestion of new materials, from one stage into a very different later stage (although we say, in view of the continuity of development, that it is "the same body").

In a most important respect, however, the two cases are exactly similar; in both there is a complete break between the two body-stages as far as *memory* is concerned. The person who exists after birth will not recall any events of the first three months of fetal life, just as, after the operation, the new memory will contain no recollections of experiences up to the time of the operation. In saying this, of course, I am affirming as a fact what conceivably might not be true. I believe that (a) there are *no conscious experiences* at all in the fetus in the first three months, or else that (b) even if there are, they cannot be recalled by the baby which gets born. (I would also defend a stronger position about the intermediate stages, but there seems no point in doing so here.) Thus I think that if a fetus could consider the importance to it of the existence of the baby after birth, that existence would seem no more important than the existence of the life of the person with "my brain" after the hypothesized operation seems important to me. If I am right in my suggestion above that some continuity of memory is a necessary condition for personal identity in an important sense, then that important condition for personal identity is lacking in the case of the fetus just as in the case of the operation.

As a result, I would say I was not being harmed, or deprived, if it was decided just to let me die in peace rather than perform the operation transferring my brain to another body. For similar reasons it appears to make no sense to say that the fetus is harmed, or deprived, if steps are taken so that it does not develop into a normal baby. In that sense, we can say that the fetus is not now a person at all, in the important sense. (We might say that since it is not the same person as the later baby, in the important sense, and since it is obviously not *some other* person, it follows that it is not a person at all in any important sense.)

How does this conclusion bear on our question? What we were trying to decide is whether rational, somewhat benevolent persons would prefer a moral system which would prohibit the destruction of a fetus when the abortion is wanted by the mother. Now, we agreed that benevolent persons take an interest in the present and future happiness and well-being of other persons. But we earlier raised the question whether it followed from this that they would take an interest in the preservation of the fetus—since this seems to be an interest in the *addition of another person.* It seemed to be one thing to want the future happiness and welfare of a person who does or will exist, and another to want to produce another being which, if produced, would be happy and enjoy well-being. Our most recent discussion about the conditions of personal identity has been such as to sustain this distinction. It appears from this discussion that no person is being harmed or deprived by the termination of a fetus, nor being benefited by its continuance so that a baby is born. So it is one thing to want all persons to be happy and not miserable; it is quite another thing to want that there develop, from non-persons such as fetuses or ova or whatever, persons who will be happy or unhappy. Whereas it is clear that a benevolent person wants all persons to be happy and not miserable, now or in the future, it is not obvious that a benevolent person wants sentient beings *brought into being* at all, much less that he will want them to be brought into being at a cost to others who already do or will exist, such as the mother or other persons whose standard of living may be reduced by the appearance of another human being.

It is not impossible that there should be some other reason for thinking that, after all, benevolent beings would want fetuses protected from destruction because of the happiness that would come into the world if they are so protected, or even that benevolent beings would want as many sentient creatures produced as possible, provided that if they were born their lives would be happy, or lives of positive welfare, that is, above the indifference point.[6]

NOTES

[1] The following paper is a revision of one of the same title, published in

The Monist 56 (1972), pp. 504-26. The first part is substantially identical with the first part of the *Monist* paper; the second part has been completely altered and rewritten, although the most important idea is the same. I am grateful to the editors of the *Monist* for their permission to republish the parts of that article that reappear here.

[2] I shall use this term in a general sense to denote an unborn, potential human being, at any stage from the moment of conception until birth.

[3] We would feel differently if we knew that, after nine months' treatment, the man would regain consciousness and live a normal life. One might say this difference of view is relevant to abortion. All I want to say here, however, is that the case as described is an exception to any unrestricted rule about a *prima facie* obligation not to kill.

[4] The original article in the *Monist*, of which the present paper is a reformulation, adopted this reading, and considered also a further possible reading. See the *Monist* 56 (1972), pp. 513 ff

[5] The following question has been put to me: Suppose you knew that the operation was going to be performed, and you had a choice whether a very severe pain was going to occur to this "descendant" of you, or to someone entirely different. Would you prefer the pain to occur to the totally different person? — the suggestion being that, if the answer is affirmative, we do after all think there is some important sense of identity between this later self and our present self. I am inclined to think that the right answer to the question is "no preference," and that any tendency to give a different answer arises from failing to get the hypothesized situation clearly in mind.

[6] I do not believe that anything I have said shows that it is impossible that there be some other reason supporting conclusions of this sort.

APPENDIX

QUESTION CXVIII.

OF THE PRODUCTION OF MAN FROM MAN AS TO THE SOUL.*

(In Three Articles.)

We now consider the production of man from man: first, as to the soul; secondly, as to the body.

Under the first head there are three points of inquiry: (1) Whether the sensitive soul is transmitted with the semen? (2) Whether the intellectual soul is thus transmitted? (3) Whether all souls were created at the same time?

First Article.

WHETHER THE SENSITIVE SOUL IS TRANSMITTED WITH THE SEMEN?

We proceed thus to the First Article:—

Objection 1. It would seem that the sensitive soul is not transmitted with the semen, but created by God. For every perfect substance, not composed of matter and form, that begins to exist, acquires existence not by generation, but by creation: for nothing is generated save from matter. But the sensitive soul is a perfect substance, otherwise it could not move the body; and since it is the form of a body, it is not composed of matter and form. Therefore it begins to exist not by generation but by creation.

Obj. 2. Further, in living things the principle of generation is the generating power; which, since it is one of the powers of the vegetative soul, is of a lower order than the sensitive soul. Now nothing acts beyond its species. Therefore the sensitive soul cannot be caused by the animal's generating power.

Obj. 3. Further, the generator begets its like: so that the form of the generator must be actually in the cause of generation. But neither the sensitive soul itself nor any part thereof is actually in the semen,

---

*Aquinas, Thomas, *Summa Theologica,* literally translated by Fathers of the English Dominican Province, London: Burns Oates and Washbourne, Ltd. 1922 (N.Y. Benziger Brothers, 7 East 51st St., N.Y. 10022.)

for no part of the sensitive soul is elsewhere than in some part of the body; while in the semen there is not even a particle of the body, because there is not a particle of the body which is not made from the semen and by the power thereof. Therefore the sensitive soul is not produced through the semen.

Obj. 4. Further, if there be in the semen any principle productive of the sensitive soul, this principle either remains after the animal is begotten, or it does not remain. Now it cannot remain. For either it would be identified with the sensitive soul of the begotten animal; which is impossible, for thus there would be identity between begetter and begotten, maker and made: or it would be distinct therefrom; and again this is impossible, for it has been proved above (Q. LXXVI., A. 4) that in one animal there is but one formal principle, which is the soul. If on the other hand the aforesaid principle does not remain, this again seems to be impossible: for thus an agent would act to its own destruction, which cannot be. Therefore the sensitive soul cannot be generated from the semen.

On the contrary, The power in the semen is to the animal seminally generated, as the power in the elements of the world is to animals produced from these elements,—for instance by putrefaction. But in the latter animals the soul is produced by the elemental power, according to Genesis i. 20: *Let the waters bring forth the creeping creatures having life.* Therefore also the souls of animals seminally generated are produced by the seminal power.

I answer that, Some have held that the sensitive souls of animals are created by God (Q. LXV., A. 4). This opinion would hold if the sensitive soul were subsistent, having being and operation of itself. For thus, as having being and operation of itself, to be made would needs be proper to it. And since a simple and subsistent thing cannot be made except by creation, it would follow that the sensitive soul would arrive at existence by creation.

But this principle is false,—namely, that being and operation are proper to the sensitive soul, as has been made clear above (Q. LXXV., A. 3): for it would not cease to exist when the body perishes. Since, therefore, it is not a subsistent form, its relation to existence is that of the corporeal forms, to which existence does not belong as proper to them, but which are said to exist forasmuch as the subsistent composites exist through them.

Wherefore to be made is proper to composites. And since the

generator is like the generated, it follows of necessity that both the sensitive soul, and all other like forms are naturally brought into existence by certain corporeal agents that reduce the matter from potentiality to act, through some corporeal power of which they are possessed.

Now the more powerful an agent, the greater scope its action has: for instance, the hotter a body, the greater the distance to which its heat carries. Therefore bodies not endowed with life, which are the lowest in the order of nature, generate their like, not through some medium, but by themselves; thus fire by itself generates fire. But living bodies, as being more powerful, act so as to generate their like, both without and with a medium. Without a medium—in the work of nutrition, in which flesh generates flesh: with a medium—in the act of generation, because the semen of the animal or plant derives a certain active force from the soul of the generator, just as the instrument derives a certain motive power from the principal agent. And as it matters not whether we say that something is moved by the instrument or by the principal agent, so neither does it matter whether we say that the soul of the generated is caused by the soul of the generator, or by some seminal power derived therefrom.

Reply Obj. 1. The sensitive soul is not a perfect self-subsistent substance. We have said enough (Q. XXV., A. 3) on this point, nor need we repeat it here.

Reply Obj. 2. The generating power begets not only by its own virtue, but by that of the whole soul, of which it is a power. Therefore the generating power of a plant generates a plant, and that of an animal begets an animal. For the more perfect the soul is, to so much a more perfect effect is its generating power ordained.

Reply Obj. 3. This active force which is in the semen, and which is derived from the soul of the generator, is, as it were, a certain movement of this soul itself: nor is it the soul or a part of the soul, save virtually; thus the form of a bed is not in the saw or the axe, but a certain movement towards that form. Consequently there is no need for this active force to have an actual organ; but it is based on the (vital) spirit in the semen which is frothy, as is attested by its whiteness. In which spirit, moreover, there is a certain heat derived from the power of the heavenly bodies, by virtue of which the inferior bodies also act towards the production of the species as stated above (Q. CXV., A. 3, *ad* 2). And since in this (vital) spirit the power of the soul is concurrent with the power of a heavenly body, it has been said that *man and the sun generate man.* Moreover, elemental heat is employed instrumentally by the soul's power, as also by the nutritive power, as stated (*De Anima* ii. 4).

Reply Obj. 4. In perfect animals, generated by coition, the active force is in the semen of the male, as the Philosopher says (*De Gener. Animal.* ii. 3); but the fœtal matter is provided by the female. In this matter the vegetable soul exists from the very beginning, not as to the second act, but as to the first act, as the sensitive soul is in one who sleeps. But as soon as it begins to attract nourishment, then it already operates in act. This matter therefore is transmuted by the power which is in the semen of the male, until it is actually informed by the sensitive soul; not as though the force itself which was in the semen becomes the sensitive soul; for thus, indeed, the generator and generated would be identical; moreover, this would be more like nourishment and growth than generation, as the Philosopher says. And after the sensitive soul, by the power of the active principle in the semen, has been produced in one of the principal parts of the thing generated, then it is that the sensitive soul of the offspring begins to work towards the perfection of its own body, by nourishment and growth. As to the active power which was in the semen, it ceases to exist, when the semen is dissolved and the (vital) spirit thereof vanishes. Nor is there anything unreasonable in this, because this force is not the principal but the instrumental agent; and the movement of an instrument ceases when once the effect has been produced.

Second Article.

Whether the intellectual soul is produced from the semen?

We proceed thus to the Second Article:—

Objection 1. It would seem that the intellectual soul is produced from the semen. For it is written (Gen. xlvi. 26): *All the souls that came out of* Jacob's *thigh, sixty-six.* But nothing is produced from the thigh of a man, except from the semen. Therefore the intellectual soul is produced from the semen.

Obj. 2. Further, as shown above (Q. LXXVI., A. 3), the intellectual, sensitive, and nutritive souls are, in substance, one soul in man. But the sensitive soul in man is generated from the semen, as in other animals; wherefore the Philosopher says (*De Gener. Animal.* ii. 3) that the animal and the man are not made at the same time, but first of all the animal is made having a sensitive soul. Therefore also the intellectual soul is produced from the semen.

Obj. 3. Further, it is one and the same agent whose action is directed to the matter and to the form: else from the matter and the form there would not result something simply one. But the intellectual soul is the form of the human body, which is produced by the power of the semen. Therefore the intellectual soul also is produced by the power of the semen.

Obj. 4. Further, man begets his like in species. But the human species is constituted by the rational soul. Therefore the rational soul is from the begetter.

Obj. 5. Further, it cannot be said that God concurs in sin. But if the rational soul be created by God, sometimes God concurs in the sin of adultery, since sometimes offspring is begotten of illicit intercourse. Therefore, the rational soul is not created by God.

On the contrary, It is written in *De Eccl. Dogmat.* xiv. that *the rational soul is not engendered by coition.*

I answer that, It is impossible for an active power existing in matter to extend its action to the production of an immaterial effect. Now it is manifest that the intellectual principle in man transcends matter; for it has an operation in which the body takes no part whatever. It is therefore impossible for the seminal power to produce the intellectual principle.

Again, the seminal power acts by virtue of the soul of the begetter, according as the soul of the begetter is the act of the body, making use of the body in its operation. Now the body has nothing whatever to do in the operation of the intellect. Therefore the power of the intellectual principle, as intellectual, cannot reach to the semen. Hence the Philosopher says (*De Gener. Animal.* ii. 3): *It follows that the intellect alone comes from without.*

Again, since the intellectual soul has an operation independent of the body, it is subsistent, as proved above (Q. LXXV., A. 2): therefore to be and to be made are proper to it. Moreover, since it is an immaterial substance it cannot be caused through generation, but only through creation by God. Therefore to hold that the intellectual soul is caused by the begetter, is nothing else than to hold the soul to be non-subsistent, and consequently to perish with the body. It is therefore heretical to say that the intellectual soul is transmitted with the semen.

Reply Obj. 1. In the passage quoted, the part is put instead of the whole, the soul for the whole man, by the figure of synecdoche.

Reply Obj. 2. Some say that the vital functions observed in the embryo are not from its soul, but from the soul of the mother; or from the formative power of the semen. Both of these explanations are false; for vital functions such as feeling, nourishment, and growth cannot be from an extrinsic principle. Consequently it must be said that the soul is in the embryo; the nutritive soul from the beginning, then the sensitive, lastly the intellectual soul.

Therefore some say that in addition to the vegetative soul which existed first, another, namely the sensitive soul, supervenes; and in addition to this, again another, namely the intellectual soul. Thus there would be in man three souls of which one would be in potentiality to another. This has been disproved above (Q. LXXVI., A. 3).

Therefore others say that the same soul which was at first merely vegetative, afterwards through the action of the seminal power, becomes a sensitive soul; and finally this same soul becomes intellectual, not indeed through the active seminal power, but by the power of a higher agent, namely God enlightening (the soul) from without. For this reason the Philosopher says that the intellect comes from without. —But this will not hold. First, because no substantial form is susceptive of more or less; but addition of greater perfection constitutes another species, just as the addition of unity constitutes another species of number. Now it is not possible for the same identical form to belong to different species. Secondly, because it would follow that the generation of an animal would be a continuous movement, proceeding gradually from the imperfect to the perfect, as happens in alteration. Thirdly, because it would follow that the generation of a man or an animal is not generation simply, because the subject thereof would be a being in act. For if the vegetable soul is from the beginning in the matter of offspring, and is subsequently gradually brought to perfection; this will imply addition of further perfection without corruption of the preceding perfection. And this is contrary to the nature of generation properly so called. Fourthly, because either that which is caused by the action of God is something subsistent: and thus it must needs be essentially distinct from the pre-existing form, which was non-subsistent; and we shall then come back to the opinion of those who held the existence of several souls in the body:—or else it is not subsistent, but a perfection of the pre-existing soul: and from this it follows of necessity that the intellectual soul perishes with the body, which cannot be admitted.

There is again another explanation, according to those who held that all men have but one intellect in common: but this has been disproved above (Q. LXXVI., A. 2).

We must therefore say that since the generation of one thing is the corruption of another, it follows of necessity that both in men and in other animals, when a more perfect form supervenes the previous form is corrupted: yet so that the supervening form contains the perfection of the previous form, and something in addition. It is in this way that through many generations and corruptions we arrive at the ultimate substantial form, both in man and other animals. This indeed is apparent to the senses in animals generated from putrefaction. We conclude therefore that the intellectual soul is created by God at the end of human generation, and this soul is at the same time sensitive and nutritive, the pre-existing forms being corrupted.

Reply Obj. 3. This argument holds in the case of diverse agents not ordered to one another. But where there are many agents ordered to one another, nothing hinders the power of the higher agent from reaching to the ultimate form; while the powers of the inferior agents extend only to some disposition of matter: thus in the generation of an animal, the seminal power disposes the matter, but the power of the soul gives the form. Now it is manifest from what has been said above (Q. CV., A. 5; Q. CX., A. 1) that the whole of corporeal nature acts as the instrument of a spiritual power, especially of God. Therefore nothing hinders the formation of the body from being due to a corporeal power, while the intellectual soul is from God alone.

Reply Obj. 4. Man begets his like, forasmuch as by his seminal power, the matter is disposed for the reception of a certain species of form.

Reply Obj. 5. In the action of the adulterer, what is of nature is good; in this God concurs. But what there is of inordinate lust is evil; in this God does not concur.

THIRD ARTICLE.

WHETHER HUMAN SOULS WERE CREATED TOGETHER AT THE BEGINNING OF THE WORLD?

We proceed thus to the Third Article:—

Objection 1. It would seem that human souls were created together at the beginning of the world. For it is written (Gen. ii. 2) : *God rested Him from all His work which He had done.* This would not be true if He created new souls every day. Therefore all souls were created at the same time.

Obj. 2. Further, spiritual substances before all others belong to the perfection of the universe. If therefore souls were created with the bodies, every day innumerable spiritual substances would be added to the perfection of the universe: consequently at the beginning the universe would have been imperfect. This is contrary to Genesis ii. 2, where it is said that *God ended* all *His work.*

Obj. 3. Further, the end of a thing corresponds to its beginning. But the intellectual soul remains, when the body perishes. Therefore it began to exist before the body.

On the contrary, it is said (*De Eccl. Dogmat.* xiv., xviii.) that *the soul is created together with the body.*

I answer that, Some have maintained that it is accidental to the intellectual soul to be united to the body, asserting that the soul is of the same nature as those spiritual substances which are not united to a body. These, therefore, stated that the souls of men were created together with the angels at the beginning. But this statement is false. Firstly, in the very principle on which it is based. For if it were accidental to the soul to be united to the body, it would follow that man who results from this union is a being by accident; or that the soul is a man, which is false, as proved above (Q. LXXV., A. 4). Moreover, that the human soul is not of the same nature as the angels, is proved from the different mode of understanding, as shown above (Q. LV., A. 2; Q. LXXXV., A. 1): for man understands through receiving from the senses, and turning to phantasms, as stated above (Q. LXXXIV., AA. 6, 7; Q. LXXXV., A. 1). For this reason the soul needs to be united to the body, which is necessary to it for the operation of the sensitive part: whereas this cannot be said of an angel.

Secondly, this statement can be proved to be false in itself. For if it is natural to the soul to be united to the body, it is unnatural to it to be without a body, and as long as it is without a body it is deprived of its natural perfection. Now it was not fitting that God should begin His work with things imperfect and unnatural, for He did not make man without a hand or a foot, which are natural parts of a man. Much less, therefore, did He make the soul without the body.

But if someone says that it is not natural to the soul to be united to the body, he must give the reason why it is united to a body. And the reason must be either because the soul so willed, or for some other reason. If because the soul willed it,—this seems incongruous. First, because it would be unreasonable of the soul to wish to be united to the body, if it did not need the body: for if it did need it, it would be natural for it to be united to it, since *nature does not fail in what is necessary*. Secondly, because there would be no reason why, having been created from the beginning of the world, the soul should, after such a long time, come to wish to be united to the body. For a spiritual substance is above time, and superior to the heavenly revolutions. Thirdly, because it would seem that this body was united to this soul by chance: since for this union to take place two wills would have to concur,—to wit, that of the incoming soul, and that of the begetter.— If, however, this union be neither voluntary nor natural on the part of the soul, then it must be the result of some violent cause, and to the soul would have something of a penal and afflicting nature. This is in keeping with the opinion of Origen, who held that souls were embodied in punishment of sin. Since, therefore, all these opinions are unreasonable, we must simply confess that souls were not created before bodies, but are created at the same time as they are infused into them.

Reply Obj. 1. God is said to have rested on the seventh day, not from all work, since we read (Jo. v. 17): *My Father worketh until now;* but from the creation of any new genera and species, which may not have already existed in the first works. For in this sense, the souls which are created now, existed already, as to the likeness of the species, in the first works, which included the creation of Adam's soul.

Reply Obj. 2. Something can be added every day to the perfection of the universe, as to the number of individuals, but not as to the number of species.

Reply Obj. 3. That the soul remains without the body is due to the corruption of the body, which was a result of sin. Consequently it was not fitting that God should make the soul without the body from the beginning: for as it is writen (Wisd. i. 13, 16): *God made not death ... but the wicked with works and words have called it to them*

ABORTION LAW REFORM: THE ENGLISH EXPERIENCE[1]

H. L. A. HART*

At the present time there are strong pressures both for and against reform of the existing law relating to abortion in Victoria. In his Southey Lecture, Professor Hart examines the achievements and failings of the recent English legislation. In an analysis of the statistics available since the passing of the Abortion Act of 1967, he indicates the various effects which the legislation appears to have produced in such areas of social and legal concern as illegitimacy, maternal mortality and illegal abortion. He also makes mention of the 'political' aspects of abortion law reform, in a discussion of the attitudes of the various branches of the British medical profession. The lecture presents a broad over-view of the problems likely to be encountered by legislatures contemplating the adoption of similar measures.

I INTRODUCTION

In offering to a Melbourne audience these reflections on the recent English experience of abortion law reform, I wish first to make a disclaimer and also to declare my hand. I am not here with the impudent aim of urging upon you the need for similar law reform in Victoria, nor am I here with the equally impudent aim of urging you to keep your law unchanged. Instead, my aim is to describe as clearly as I can some of the many different aspects of this problem which have been forced upon our attention in England and which are, I think, likely to be of importance wherever the legalisation of abortion is debated.

*M. A. (Oxon); formerly Professor of Jurisprudence at Oxford University.

So much then for my disclaimer. I declare my hand simply by saying that, had I been a member of Parliament when the English Abortion Act of 1967 was enacted, I would certainly have voted for it. I shall however end my lecture by drawing two morals from our experience in England of the new law. These are not criticisms of its main principles, but attribute certain unsatisfactory features of its operation to two principal failings in our legislation which should certainly be avoided by other countries, if and when they engage in similar reforms.

The study of the changes produced by the Abortion Act 1967 which came into force on 27 April 1968 will I am sure occupy the specialists of many different disciplines for years to come. The change was a very large scale phenomenon, as can be seen from the figures available for the last four years. Before the Act the largest number of legal abortions performed in National Health Service hospitals was 9,700 in 1967,[2] but in the first eight months of the Act's operation the figure for legal abortions performed in N.H.S. hospitals and licensed private clinics was 23,641; in the next year, 1969, the figure was 54,819, in 1970 it rose to 86,565 and in 1971 to 126,774.[3] This being the magnitude of the phenomenon, it is not surprising that there are problems here, some of them very difficult, for the lawyer, the student of politics, the demographer and sociologist, the moral philosopher and various branches of the medical profession. The study of this subject is indeed an inter-disciplinary study *par excellence*.

II LAW AND STATISTICS

As a lawyer I shall start with the law. Before 1968 the English law in relation to abortion was very similar to what it is now in Victoria. The English Offences Against the Person Act 1861 section 58 made it a felony punishable with imprisonment for life for a woman to abort herself or for another to abort her. The Act contained no explicit exceptions for cases where this was done solely to save the life of a mother, but such an exception was in effect read into section 58 of the Act as an interpretation of the meaning of the word 'unlawfully' used in the formulation of the offence. This step was taken in 1939 in the famous case of *R v. Bourne*[4] in which it was held that an abortion was permitted if it was done in the honest belief on adequate grounds that it was necessary to save the life of the mother; and the construction given to this exception was that if a doctor was of the opinion, on reasonable grounds and with adequate knowledge, that the probable consequence of the continued pregnancy would be to make the mother 'a physical or mental wreck', he would not be guilty of the offence. English law also includes a separate provision in the Infant Life (Preservation) Act 1929 (which is still law) making it an offence punishable with imprisonment for life to cause the death of a child capable of being born alive but subject to the proviso that no person shall be guilty of the offence unless it is proved that the act which caused death was not done in good faith for the purpose only of preserving the life of the mother. The interpretation given in *Bourne's* case to the word 'unlawfully' was based on this proviso in the 1929 Act.

Except that the maximum penalties are different, the law in England in relation to abortion, thus interpreted, was before the new Act very similar to the law under section 65 of the Victorian Crimes Act 1958 as interpreted by the decision of Mr Justice Menhennitt in *R. v. Davidson* in 1969.[5] This, like the English decision in *Bourne's* case, in effect made an exception for cases where an abortion was performed if the probable consequence of a continued pregnancy would be to make the woman a physical or mental wreck. Though similar[6] in result, the interpretation in *Davidson's* case of the Victorian statute was reached by a different route from that followed in the English *Bourne* decision since section 10 of the Victorian Crimes Act 1958, which is the counterpart of the English Infant Life (Preservation) Act 1929, did not contain the proviso on which the interpretation in *Bourne's* case of the word 'unlawfully' was based.

The Abortion Act of 1967 made great changes in English law. The core of the Act is the provision in section 1(1) that no offence under the law relating to abortion will be committed by the termination of a pregnancy by a registered medical practitioner if two registered medical practitioners are of opinion, formed in good faith, that either (a) the continuance of the pregnancy would involve risk to the life of the pregnant woman or of injury to the physical or mental health of the woman or of any of the existing children of the family greater than if the pregnancy were terminated, or (b) that there is substantial risk that if the child were born it would suffer from such physical or mental abnormalities as to be seriously handicapped. The Act also provides in section 1(2) that in determining whether there is the relevant risk of injury to health, account may be taken of the woman's actual or reasonably foreseeable environment, and it stipulates in section 1(3) that operations must take place either in a N.H.S. hospital or in an approved place.

The main provisions of the new legislation are the foregoing. The Act however also provides in section 1(4) that a single medical practitioner may terminate a pregnancy if this is immediately necessary in order to save the life of the mother or to prevent a grave permanent injury to her physical or mental health. To such emergency cases the requirement of the opinion of two registered practitioners and the restriction of the place of operations to N.H.S. hospitals and approved places do not apply. The Act also contains in section 4(1) a conscience clause to relieve those who have conscientious objections from the duty to take any part in treatment authorised by the Act, but this is subject to the proviso of section 4(2) that this is not to relieve a doctor of any duty he may otherwise have to save the life or prevent grave permanent injury to the physical or mental health of the mother.

The main point to bear in mind in considering this legislation is that section 1(1) of the Act permits the termination of a pregnancy on the ground that its continuance would involve risk to life or injury to the health of the woman or of any existing children of her family greater than if the pregnancy were terminated. The risk of injury to health, it is important to notice, need neither be grave nor immediate. It is under the provisions of this wide clause concerning the risk of injury to the mother's health (not life) that the vast majority of legal abortions have in fact been done.[7]

Before discussing the new law I shall consider for a moment the operation of the old. There were two salient features: first, prosecutions were very rarely brought against the pregnant woman who aborted or attempted to abort herself or allowed others to abort her, and secondly, the number of prosecutions and convictions for aborting or attempting to abort a woman were always minute in comparison even with the minimum estimate (10,000 *per annum*) of the amount of illegal abortion which had been mentioned in any serious discussion of the subject.[8] Thus in the years 1949-63 the average number of convictions for England and Wales was 54 and in the years 1964-69 it varied between 65 (for 1965) and 52 (for 1969).[9] The figures for illegal abortions reported as known to the police were similarly small and in the five years before the Act (1962-67) averaged 243 *per annum*.[10]

These minute law enforcement figures of course raise a question as to what the social function of the old law was, or was supposed to be.

In considering this question it is necessary to distinguish what may be called the direct function of the law consisting in the suppression of the practice of abortion from the indirect function of the law consisting in the promotion of certain good results through the dissemination of the general knowledge that the law exists and its principles are endorsed by the authority of the State. It is necessary to make this distinction, in discussing the function of the law against abortion, in order to make room for the contention which was frequently put forward in support of the old law[11] that even if it largely failed in its direct function (since the scale of illegal abortions was so great) it yet may be the case that the law performed indirectly the beneficial function of maintaining a general respect for the sanctity of human life, since this respect may have been strengthened by the knowledge that the State by its law against abortion bears witness to and symbolises society's commitment to the value of human life even in the case of the *foetus in utero*.

Plainly this contention as to the indirect function of the law cannot be simply dismissed, but it is exposed to some serious counterarguments and in any sober estimate of the social costs and benefits of the law at least two further facts have to be taken into account. The first of these facts is simply that a law so widely disregarded as was the old law was never an effective witness to the sanctity of life, but was an impotent gesture which, because of its impotence, harmfully blurred the line between respectable and criminal behaviour. Thus (to use again the minimum estimate mentioned above), if only 10,000 women *per annum* were illegally aborted then in 25 years a quarter of a million women, drawn from many different segments of society, together with those who operated on them would have involved themselves in the breach of a criminal law the seriousness of which was marked by the fact that the maximum penalty provided for the offence which it defines was imprisonment for life. Secondly, the law against abortion differs from many other criminal laws which are also widely disregarded such as *e.g.* the law against careless driving, in the very important respect that offences against it may be not merely individual criminal acts but may also be part of a high profit criminal industry. This offers targets for the blackmailer and corrupting temptations to law enforcement agencies. It has indeed been asserted that 'there seem to be no general criminal rackets flourishing on the basis of illegal abortion'.[12] But recent experience in Victoria has provided much melancholy evidence that serious corruption of the police is to be found among the consequences of restrictive abortion law.[13]

I turn now to the new law. In considering the 1967 Act it is important to observe that it represents a compromise; it does so because in its subordinate provisions it recognises, partly and indirectly, both a more conservative and a more radical opinion as to the permissibility of abortion than the principles on which its main provisions rest. Thus the conservative view that abortion is permissible only to save the life of the mother or to prevent grave injury to her health, is partially reflected in the qualified conscience clause (section 4(1)) which, while exempting a doctor from the duty to participate in operations authorised by the Act, if he has conscientious objections, also provides that this shall not affect the duty to participate in such an operation if it is necessary to save the life or to prevent grave permanent injury to the physical or mental health of the pregnant woman. On the other hand the Act as finally passed does not, as many reformers hoped it would, directly reflect the radical view that certain social, non-medical indications might be recognised as sufficient grounds for abortion, since it does not include the so-called 'social' clause which formed part of the Bill as originally drafted. This clause provided that a pregnancy might be lawfully terminated if the pregnant woman's capacity as a mother would be severely strained by the care of a child or another child as the case may be. Instead the Act preserves the general principle that the indications for abortion must always be medical in the sense of relating to risks to life or health, but partly recognised the more radical opinion by its provisions that risk of injury to the health of the existing children of the pregnant woman's family and substantial risks of the birth of a seriously handicapped child are grounds for termination[14] and also by its provision that, in determining the risk to health either to the woman or her children, account might be taken of the woman's actual or reasonably foreseeable environment.

Does the law honestly interpreted provide 'abortion on demand'? That it does has been claimed not only by uninformed members of a lay public, but by at least one serious student of the legal and medical aspects of abortion who has argued that, as a matter of law, the new Act, at least in the case of early pregnancies, does permit abortion on demand.[15] His argument is simply that the Act, in providing that an operation is permissible if the risk to the mother's life through continuance of the pregnancy is greater than if the pregnancy were terminated, has thereby specified a condition which is always satisfied if the abortion is performed in the early weeks of the pregnancy in a N.H.S. hospital: for in such cases the statistical risk to the mother's life of an abortion will not be greater and may indeed be less than the normal risks of pregnancy. It is then argued that this being so, any doctor on the basis simply of these general comparative risks would be justified in terminating in hospital any early pregnancy. It is, however, quite clear that even if the comparative risks are as they are assumed to be in this argument,[16] the Act has not been, and will not be, interpreted in the way required by the argument. Doctors are required by law when terminating a pregnancy to certify the particular ground on which they do this and, while an overwhelmingly large number of terminations under the Act are certified as being done to prevent injury to the health of the mother, only a very small proportion are certified as done on account of risks to her life. These amounted in the years 1968, 1969 and 1970 only to 5 *per cent*, 4 *per cent* and 3 *per cent* respectively of the total. In each such case the doctor is required to specify on the certificate the disease, obstetric or otherwise, which is the ground for the termination of the pregnancy.

It is clear therefore that doctors do not regard the risk to the mother's life as an available ground for terminating an early pregnancy simply because of the comparative statistical risks. In 1969 the then president of the Royal College of Obstetricians and Gynaecologists, Sir John Peel, expressly repudiated this 'statistical interpretation' on the footing that the relevant risk to life through continued pregnancy must be some risk to which the individual woman is found to be exposed other than the normal statistical risks of child birth.[17]

In any case, the Act does not compel a doctor to operate; it entitles him to operate if the two opinions required by the Act are forthcoming, unless these were not formed in good faith. A doctor would be criminally liable for a refusal to terminate a pregnancy where the Act permits it, only if he were guilty of criminal negligence in disregarding a risk of death or serious injury to the woman and she died as a result. In such a case the doctor could be convicted of manslaughter. It is less easy to describe with confidence the civil liability of a doctor[18] for damages if a pregnancy which he has refused to terminate results in post-natal injury to the health of the mother or the existing children of her family or in the birth of a seriously handicapped child. It seems clear that he would be liable in such cases if he had failed to consider seriously all the risks indicated by the Act or if, after considering them, he refused to operate and the plaintiff is able to show that a reasonably careful doctor, after balancing all the factors referred to in the Act, would have concluded as a matter of medical judgment that the operation ought to be performed in the interests of the woman and her family. Some apprehensions were felt by doctors that they might be unduly exposed by the Act to actions for negligence for clinical errors of judgment in cases of refusal to advise a termination or to perform the operation. In fact no such actions have yet been instituted in the English courts.[19]

Though the legal position is as stated here, in practice the Act notwithstanding its careful and much debated wording has, for reasons explained in section VI *infra,* produced a situation where few women, able and willing to pay the very high fees sometimes demanded, will have much difficulty in obtaining an abortion in a private clinic licensed under the Act. But in the N.H.S. hospitals the position is very different and for most women abortion is certainly not yet available on demand.[20]

III POLITICS AND OPINIONS

Let me now turn from law and statistics to politics and moral opinions. The Abortion Act 1967 was the eighth Bill presented to Parliament designed to alter the law on this subject and was passed into law under a Labour government. It was a private member's Bill but drafting assistance and government time were given for its debate, without which no Bill as controversial as this could have succeeded. In this respect the Abortion Act resembled three other measures enacted under the Labour government: the Murder Act 1965 which abolished the death penalty for murder, the Sexual Offences Act 1967 which removed homosexual acts between consenting adults in private from the scope of the criminal law, and the Divorce Law Reform Act 1969 which greatly altered the law of divorce in England. A free vote was allowed in each of these cases and members of both parties were found voting both for and against these measures, but it seems very unlikely that these legislative changes would have been made under a Conservative government.[21] It is perhaps a paradox that the most noteworthy achievements of a Labour government, which might have been expected to make its prime objective the reduction of social and economic inequalities, should have in fact been these considerable changes in the criminal law affecting primarily matters of morals and private life.

In one important respect, however, the Abortion Act differs from the other measures mentioned above, each of which had been preceded by an elaborate governmental inquiry either in the form of a Royal Commission or a Departmental Committee.[22] For the last governmental inquiry in England into abortion law was the Interdepartmental Committee of 1939 under the chairmanship of Lord Birkett. This Committee which recommended the codification of the law as interpreted by the decision in *Bourne's* case but no other changes, was obviously much influenced by the then prevailing fears of a falling population, and had little to say that is relevant to contemporary conditions. Hence nothing was done, before the Act came into force in 1968, to explore the size of the likely demand for operations if the law was relaxed, and to investigate and plan ways and means of providing for it by reorganization and extension of hospital and other medical resources.

The changes in the abortion law brought about by the 1967 Act were in very large measure made possible by the pressure exerted by a voluntary society, the Abortion Law Reform Association.[23] This was founded by a group of women as long ago as 1936, and had made a number of unsuccessful attempts to obtain a change in the law including the organization of support for some of the private members' Bills, which were presented unsuccessfully to Parliament since 1952. The A.L.R.A. was predominantly middle class and left of centre in politics. By 1967 two-thirds of its members were women, one-fourth of whom had obtained abortions 'mostly legally'; two-thirds of its members had had some form of higher education and one-fifth were doctors. After a dormant period in its activities new life was given to it in 1961 by the distressing cases of gross deformity found in children born to mothers who had taken the tranquillising drug thalidomide. A further impact was made by the subsequent trial and acquittal in Belgium in 1962 of a mother who had killed her baby born deformed by the drug. From 1963 onwards the A.L.R.A. conducted opinion surveys with great energy and skill especially among doctors, and marshalled considerable support from them by the time the 1967 Bill was debated in Parliament.

I do not propose to make a critical assessment here of the arguments about the morality of abortion which were advanced during the passage of the Act through Parliament. I shall attempt only a description of the opinions which I think were most widely shared by its supporters. In the description of opinions held on this matter it is useful to distinguish three principal conceptions of the moral status and claims to life of the non-viable foetus. The first is that a foetus is a full human person with the same right to life as an adult; the second conception is that it is a person with a moral right to life but a lesser right than that of an independent person and may be destroyed to avoid what may be considered greater evils than the termination of its life. The third conception is that the foetus is not to be regarded as a person at all, but as part of the mother. On this footing if abortions are not to be performed simply on her demand, the restrictions can be justified only on paternalistic grounds and in cases where the operation would be gravely injurious to her life or health and so should be refused by a doctor, just as he should refuse to perform any other dangerous and unnecessary operation on any person.

The attitude not only of many of those who voted for the recent legislation but of a considerable number of the public who supported it was, I think, accurately expressed in simple terms by a Conservative Member of Parliament, Mr Angus Maude, in the first debate on the Abortion Bill as follows: 'I... cannot find it in me and I do not believe I shall ever find it in me to regard the non-viable *foetus in utero* as a human personality. I cannot say I am right to believe this but nobody can say I am wrong. I am therefore left unmoved by the talk of killing unborn babies.'[24] Of course those who share Mr. Maude's attitude were invited by their opponents to consider two sets of facts, one medical and the other legal, tending to show how little difference there may be between the foetus and the independent human being where the attribution of human personality is in question. The medical facts are simply those that show that after the first few weeks the physical structure and indeed appearance to the naked eye of a foetus is remarkably similar to that of a new born baby and that its heart beats are easily detectable. The legal facts are those which show that the law recognises the unborn foetus as having rights to compensation for injuries done to it by third parties which may be enforced by legal proceedings after birth.

I do not think that emphasis on these physical and legal similarities, even when dramatically presented, as they have been by opponents of the relaxation of the law, have converted many to a different view of the moral status of the foetus. This is so I think because underlying the perhaps crude dismissal of the idea that a non-viable foetus is at any stage a person, there is the conviction that the difference between termination of a pregnancy resulting in the death of a foetus and other forms of destruction of human life are so great that the legalisation of the former does not constitute any threat to the general respect for the sanctity of human life in other forms. This differentiation between the destruction of a foetus and other forms of destruction to human life seems to many to be anchored in much human experience, and to account for the facts that only rarely has English law equated any form of abortion with murder, that penalties even for the professional abortionist have rarely exceeded 5 years imprisonment, and that the woman aborting herself or procuring others to abort her is virtually never prosecuted.[25]

It is also a noticeable fact both of human individual psychology and of national character that advocates of liberalisation of the law of abortion are to be found among those most concerned to protect human life in general. Many of those who have campaigned for the relaxation of this law have also been opponents of capital punishment and pacifists, and though this syndrome of attitudes has been denounced as contradictory, it seems to many both consistent and natural and to reflect the radical difference between abortion and the killing of an independent person. Similarly, at the national level, the Scandinavian countries who have been the foremost and most consistent supporters of liberalisation of the law were also among the earliest to abandon capital punishment and are generally pacific in outlook.

However, other supporters of reform have been prepared to distinguish between different stages of the growth of the foetus. While arguing that very early abortions need no justification since the foetus is then a cluster of cells which is no more a person or the possessor of rights than an acorn is an oak tree, they have conceded that after this earlier period it is a person with certain rights to life. Their argument has been that though it is important to draw this distinction, nonetheless the bare fact that the foetus is a person in this later period, with rights not to be destroyed or injured by third parties, does not entail that it has a right against the mother to be maintained in existence by the use of her body which outweighs or limits her right to determine what shall happen to or be done to her body. That it does not follow from the fact that the foetus is a person, that it has a right to obtain by use of the mother's body everything which may be required to keep it in existence is something plainly conceded by those who accept (as the old law accepted) that an abortion is permissible if it is necessary in order to save the life of the mother: the foetus' 'right to life' is not a right to be kept alive at the cost of the mother's life. The argument of some supporters of reform has pushed this principle further, on the footing that, at least in cases where pregnancy was unwanted and reasonable steps were taken to avoid it, the foetus whatever rights it may have against strangers has no right to be kept in existence through the use of the body of a woman who does not wish her body to be used for this purpose.[26]

IV INTENTIONS AND RESULTS

In two principal respects Parliament gave the reformers less than they asked. The Bill, as originally presented to Parliament, included, as I have already mentioned, a purely 'social' clause providing that a pregnancy might be terminated if the pregnant woman's capacity as a mother would be severely overstrained by the care of a child or of another child, and it also included a provision that a pregnancy might be terminated if the mother was a defective or became pregnant while under the age of 16 or as a result of rape. These two clauses were deleted from the Bill. On the other hand the main clause of the original Bill was immensely widened and it is under this much widened clause that nearly three-quarters of the legal abortions have been done. As originally presented this clause seemed merely to codify, so far as risks to the mother's life or health was concerned, the previously existing law, since it provided that there must be a 'serious' risk to life or a risk of 'grave' injury to physical or mental health if risk to her life or health was to be a condition for the operation. However, the Bill in fact emerged from the committee stage without the words 'serious' or 'grave'. I was astonished, when I investigated the Parliamentary history, to find that these words were taken out of the Bill as a result of representations made by the two medical associations, the British Medical Association and the Royal College of Obstetricians and Gynaecologists who expressed the view that if these words were included they would bring into question current medical practices which were regarded by these bodies as acceptable.[27] Both these bodies, however, while assenting to this widened clause, were strongly opposed to the original social clause which was deleted, and were, and are still, opposed to the provision which the Act makes that a pregnancy may be terminated out of consideration for the health of the existing children of the woman's family. Since the Act, both bodies have repeatedly affirmed that though such an operation is now lawful it is not ethical.[28]

The upshot is a curious one. It seems plain to many lawyers that had the main clause been kept as originally drafted with the insertion of the words 'serious' and 'grave', this would have fairly represented, or at least would have been no more restrictive than, the previous law as interpreted in *Bourne's* case according to which an abortion was permitted only if believed necessary to prevent the mother becoming 'a physical or mental wreck'. The medical associations in asking for the deletion of these words did so on the footing that they would bring into question acceptable medical practices current before the Act, yet only three months previously the R.C.O.G. had insisted that in any reform of the law[29] the qualifying words 'serious' and 'grave' should be retained. This seems a clear indication that a practice might be regarded by these professional bodies as ethical even if legal opinion as to its lawfulness was divided. On the other hand, the opposition of these bodies to the clause permitting an operation out of consideration for the health of the woman's existing children has taken the form of a refusal to countenance as ethical what Parliament has declared to be lawful. Some confusion in the relationship between law and professional ethics has thus been generated. However, no disciplinary steps have been taken or are likely to be taken by the professional body against doctors who perform operations permitted by the law.

Among the aims of the reformers three have at all times been paramount. These are the reduction in numbers of unwanted children, particularly illegitimate children, the reduction of maternal mortality through illegal abortion, and the reduction of illegal abortion. Till recently there was little clear or convincing evidence that the Act had significantly advanced these aims, but the three years statistics now available seem to me to justify the conclusion that it has done so and is likely to continue to do so. I consider here the statistics under the heads of the reformers' three main aims.

(a) *Decrease in numbers of illegitimate births*

From 1961 when the number of illegitimate births was 48,490, representing 6 *per cent* of live births, the number of illegitimate births rose steadily until 1967 when the number was 69,928, representing *8.4 per cent* of live births. In 1968, however, during which the Act was in force for eight months, this rise was virtually halted: the numbers of illegitimate births fell to 69,806 and the percentage of live births increased only by *.1 per cent* to *8.5 per cent* which was by far the smallest annual increase yet recorded. In 1969 the number fell to 67,041 and the percentage of live births to *8.4 per cent* and in 1970 they fell again to 64,744 and *8.3 per cent*.[30]

These figures alone afford convincing evidence that the Act has succeeded in reversing the trend and has secured a substantial reduction in the number of illegitimate births. But to appreciate its full effect, it is necessary to extrapolate the previous trend and to compare the actual numbers of illegitimate births for the years since the Act with the estimated numbers of such births which would have occurred had the established trend continued. On the footing that in 1968-70 illegitimate births would have continued to increase at a rate equivalent to the average annual rate of increase for the years 1960-67, the figures (in whole thousands) for 1968-70 would have been 74,000, 78,000 and 82,000 and thus would have exceeded the *actual* figures for these three years by 4,000, 11,000 and 17,000 respectively.

This reduction in numbers of illegitimate births for 1968-70 is, however, considerably less than the numbers of single women known to have obtained legal abortions in these years (*viz* 11,120, 24,499 and 40,734). Part of the difference is accounted for by the success which the Act has had in reversing another established trend, namely, the increasing number of so-called shot-gun marriages where the parents have married after the child has been conceived. From 1961-67 the number of such cases rose from 59,000 to 74,000 and the average annual increase during these years was 2,500. In 1968, though the Act was only in force for eight months of the year, the annual increase fell to 900 and in 1969 there was an actual decrease of 2,000.[31] Had the trend continued, the number of such cases would have exceeded the *actual* number in 1968 by 2,000 and in 1969 by 6,500. Nonetheless, there still remains a difference between the total number of single women legally aborted in 1968-70 and the reductions in illegitimate and shot-gun marriage births. For 1968 and 1969 the difference was between 5,000 and 6,000 but cannot yet be calculated for 1970. The most obvious explanation of the difference between these figures is that some part of it represents single women legally aborted who would have obtained a legal abortion even if the Act had not been passed, and the remainder represents single women legally aborted under the Act who but for the Act would have sought and obtained an illegal abortion. If this is so their transfer from illegal to legal abortion is one way in which the Act has secured yet another of its main objectives, namely the reduction of the amount of illegal abortion.

However, an alternative and more pessimistic interpretation of this remainder of the difference (between the total number of single women legally aborted in 1968-70 and the reductions in illegitimate and shot-gun marriage births) is logically possible, namely, that it represents an increase in the total number of conceptions by single women. Those who hold this view attribute the increase to the Act on the footing that the belief that the Act has made abortions easier to obtain has either led single women who would otherwise not have had intercourse to have it without adequate contraceptives or has led single women who previously used adequate contraceptives to abandon them or become careless in their use.

Most people, myself included, find the hypothesis that many women were caused by the change in the law to change their sexual habits or their use of contraceptives much less credible than the hypothesis that the total number of single women legally aborted comprises many who but for the Act would have sought and obtained an illegal abortion. But fortunately we are not left to our intuitions to choose between these alternatives for, as I shall argue in paragraph (c) below, the hypothesis that there has been a considerable transfer of illegal to legal abortion is well supported by reasonable inferences from the figures now available for deaths from illegal abortion which I shall now consider.

(b) *Decrease in deaths through illegal abortion*

For the eight years before the Act came into force (1960-67) the numbers of deaths certified as due to illegal abortion were 30, 23, 29, 21, 24, 21, 30 and 17 respectively. For the three years since the Act (1968-70) they were 22, 15 and 11 and both in 1969 and 1970 the numbers were lower than in any previous year.[32] This is a striking and of course welcome decline in the figures for mortality but, before it can be attributed to the Act, it is necessary to exclude the alternative explanation that it merely reflects, very imperfectly, a general fall in maternal mortality rates due to general medical improvements. In fact this alternative explanation is not available. A comparison[33] of the annual percentage changes in hospital maternal mortality rates *per* live births for the period 1950-67 with the annual percentage change in deaths from illegal abortion *per* live births show there was so little relationship between the two during this long period that any fall in the former since 1967 could not explain the fall in the latter. In fact, in 1969 the percentage fall in deaths from illegal abortion was *32 per cent* while ordinary maternal deaths fell by *20 per cent*, and in 1970 deaths from illegal abortion fell again by *27 per cent* while ordinary maternal deaths fell only by *5 per cent*.

(c) *Decrease in illegal abortion*

At all times the difficulty of estimating the amount of illegal abortion is formidable. During the debates in Parliament the figure of 100,000 *per annum* for the years before the Act was frequently mentioned but without supporting evidence and much higher figures have also been suggested.[35] A sample poll conducted in 1966 on behalf of the Abortion Law Reform Association among 3,500 women aged between 21 and 35 yielded an estimate of 31,000 *per anum,* but far too few of those polled gave complete answers to permit reliance on this sample estimate.[36]

Scepticism of the common opinion that the numbers of illegal abortions before the Act were very large has been usually based on the small numbers of deaths officially reported as due to illegal abortions. As can be seen from the figures already cited, these ran for many years before the Act at an average of less than 30 *per annum,* and even if these figures are increased by *30 per cent* to allow for the result of the Registrar-General's confidential inquiries into cases of maternal deaths, the average figure was under 40 *per annum*. The sceptical argument[37] was that if a figure as large as say 100,000 illegal abortions was a correct estimate, then the illegal abortionist was successful in operating with a level of mortality considerably less than double that attending normal childbirth; so it was suggested that a figure of 10,000-15,000 illegal abortions *per annum,* yielding a much higher mortality rate might be more realistic.

To this argument (quite apart from the possibility that the number of such deaths might still be under-stated even after allowance for confidential inquiries), the chief and, in my view, convincing objection is that since the earliest form of antibiotics became generally available, the illegal abortionists (many of whom were doctors operating under safe conditions) might well possess enough skill to avoid a rate of mortality very much greater than that attending normal childbirth or legal abortion in a hospital, especially since many of their victims might be rescued from death by transfer to hospital. The greatest risks attending illegal abortion before the Act were not death but serious damage to health or sterility. Hence the low mortality figures are not good evidence that the figure of 100,000 *per annum* illegal abortions was an over-estimate. The most useful statement that can be made by way of a gauge of the amount of illegal abortion is I think, the following. In the three years since the Act (1968-70) the average rate of death for legal abortions carried out in N.H.S. hospitals or authorised clinics was approximately 15 *per* 100,000. If we suppose that illegal abortion was twice as risky as this, then a figure of 30 deaths *per annum* from illegal abortion implies a total of 100,000 illegal abortions, and a figure of 40 deaths *per annum* implies 133,000 illegal abortions. If, as might well be reasonable, we suppose that the risks of death from illegal abortion was less than twice the risk in the case of legal abortion, then the total amount of illegal abortion would have been correspondingly greater.

Although the estimate of the absolute amount of illegal abortion at any time is beset with these difficulties, the striking decrease in the numbers of deaths from illegal abortion since the Act constitutes good evidence that the total amount of illegal abortion has decreased and perhaps by a roughly similar proportion. This would not be so if there were good reasons for thinking that the death *rate per* illegal abortion was considerably less after the Act than it had been before it. We have, however, already excluded in paragraph (b) above the suggestion that the death rate *per* illegal abortion has declined since the Act as the result of medical improvements which have reduced general maternal mortality rates. There remains the abstract possibility that since the Act the proportionate reduction in numbers of illegal abortions has been greater among cases where the operation carried unusually high risks of death than among other cases, so that the reduction in deaths from illegal abortion could not be taken to reflect any similar reduction in illegal abortion generally. But this seems very implausible since any illegal abortionist willing to undertake such cases before the Act would have just as much or as little reason for undertaking them since the Act. In fact, the only plausible argument suggesting a variation since the Act in the death rate *per* illegal abortion points in the other direction to the conclusion that the proportionate reduction in the total amount of illegal abortion may have been greater than the reduction in deaths. For it is most likely that the reduction in the relatively safe and expensive forms of illegal abortion carried out, not in the back streets but by doctors in hygienic conditions, has been greater than the reduction in the relatively risky back street abortions. This is so because the doctor, unlike the back street abortionist, could transfer to the new legal private sector created by the Act and probably could do this with very little alteration in the type of case and clientele with which he dealt. If this is so, the rate of deaths *per* illegal abortion is likely to have increased, since illegal abortions would since the Act includes proportionately more of the risky cases and proportionately less of the relatively safe cases. Hence the decline in the numbers of such deaths may reflect at least a roughly similar proportionate decline in the total numbers of illegal abortions, but in view of the small numbers of deaths, before and after the Act, I would assert only that the amount of illegal abortion must have considerably declined.

This reduction in the total amount of illegal abortion is not only welcome in itself because of the risks of death and the greater risks of ill health and sterility attached to it, but it also strongly supports the conclusion that the difference between the numbers of single women aborted since the Act and the numbers representing the reduction in illegitimate births and shot-gun marriage cases is to a large extent accounted for by a transfer from illegal to legal abortion.

V ATTITUDES OF THE MEDICAL PROFESSION: N.H.S. AND PRIVATE SECTOR

Both before and since the Act there has been a well-marked contrast between the attitudes of the general practitioners on the one hand and that expressed by the spokesmen of the official bodies, the British Medical Association and the Royal College of Obstetricians and Gynaecologists. In the years before the Act both these bodies expressed themselves as opposed to far-reaching changes in the law and, in 1966, the Royal College published a memorandum on legalised abortion[38] in which it urged that the grounds for abortion should be confined to those cases where there were serious risks to the life or grave injury to the physical and mental health of the mother, or where there was a substantial risk of a child being born with physical or mental abnormalities so as to deprive it of any prospect of a reasonable enjoyment of life. During the passage of the Act through Parliament these official bodies generally supported its central clauses and confined their opposition to two points. They denounced as 'unethical' the provision that a pregnancy might be terminated because of the risk to health of the existing children of the woman's family and also maintained a firm opposition to the clause which permitted operations to be performed by and on the certificate of medical practitioners who were neither consultants nor operating under their direction. Since the Act these bodies have maintained their opposition to both these provisions. Efforts to reverse the ruling that the termination of pregnancies out of consideration for the health of the existing children of the mother is unethical notwithstanding its legality were unsuccessfully made at the Annual Representative Meeting of the British Medical Association.[39] Two unsuccessful attempts, both supported by both the professional medical bodies, have been made in Parliament to amend the Act so as to permit operations for abortion only if they are performed by or under the supervision of a consultant gynaecologist in the N.H.S. or by an approved medical practitioner of equivalent status.[40]

By contrast, the general practitioners whose views have been sought by a detailed National Opinion Poll,[41] have given answers which permit the statement that two-thirds of general practitioners are satisfied with the new law or would welcome some further relaxation of the Act so that legal abortion would be easier to obtain, while *28 per cent* would welcome some restrictions. These percentages were almost exactly reversed in the case of consultant gynaecologists in the N.H.S., *30 per cent* of whom in reply to an elaborate questionnaire sent out by the Royal College in 1970 expressed themselves against any restrictions of the Act while the remainder were in favour of its restriction.[42]

It seems, however, that since the Act there has been some modification of opinion on the part of the consultants who, owing to the vastly increased number of referrals, have had to confront and have come to understand more of the problems of women seeking abortion. A considerable number (*88 per cent*) of the consultants who answered the 1970 questionnaire stated that where they had performed an increased number of operations this was in great part due simply to the fact that the number of cases referred to them by doctors had increased, and many found on referral that an operation was justified under the old criteria which they were still using, notwithstanding the passing of the Act. This attitude was expressed by Mr S. Bender,[43] a distinguished consultant gynaecologist, who said that the consultant gynaecologist 'applying the same principles and standards [as before], is now terminating more pregnancies simply because he is seeing more women with, to him, justifiable indications for intervention — women who previously would never have sought medical help because they thought it hopeless to try.' But he added '[f]or every such case . . . there are also several where there is no indication under the Act, as he interprets it but where the patient or her doctor or both understand the law as allowing abortion on demand.' It should be added that among senior consultant gynaecologists there are some ardent defenders of the new law as well as severe critics.

It is important, in assessing the range of attitudes to the Act within the medical profession, to consider the development alongside the N.H.S., where treatment is free, of a private sector where fees are charged for abortion operations in a private clinic licensed under the Act. The number of private clinics now approved and licensed is 52 and the proportion of all legal abortions performed in these clinics rose from *38 per cent* in 1968 to *45 per cent* in 1970.[44] The growth of a vast private sector where often very high fees are charged and large profits may be made by doctors and clinics is due in part to the great regional variation among N.H.S. hospitals in the interpretation of the Act and willingness to apply it. This development is a great disappointment to those many reformers whose concern was not only to liberalise the law but to secure that there should no longer be in effect one abortion law for the rich and another for the poor.

These and other very unsatisfactory features of the operation of the new law led the Government in February 1971 to set up a Committee of Enquiry into the operation of the Act under the chairmanship of a High Court Judge, Mrs Justice Lane. This Committee's terms of reference do not extend to the principles of the Act or the conditions for legal abortion which it lays down, but only to the manner of its operation.[45] The Committee has not yet reported but the main problems to which it will have to address itself are already plainly identifiable and fall to be considered under the two heads of the N.H.S. hospitals and the private clinics.

(a) *N.H.S. hospitals*

The regional variations in the amount of abortion operations performed in N.H.S. hospitals are still very considerable and still tend to reflect the varying attitudes of the local senior gynaecological staff to the liberalisation of the law. Many hospitals where a liberal policy of applying the law prevails have sought to protect themselves from overcrowding by refusing to take cases from outside their normal catchment area; but there has been some overcrowding in some hospitals with regrettable consequences. These include the deferment of many abortion operations until after the thirteenth week of pregnancy when the relatively simple operation is no longer available[46] and also the deferment of other gynaecological cases considered less urgent than abortion. Moreover, in many such hospitals a great distaste has been felt and expressed by a number of staff, especially nurses, who while not refusing to take part in the treatment, nonetheless dislike being involved continuously in this form of work. Owing to the unequal distribution throughout the country, the burden of operations has at times fallen on a small proportion of gynaecologists and in 1970 it was estimated that one-third of all such operations were performed by only one-tenth of N.H.S. gynaecologists.[47]

(b) *Private clinics*

Both overcrowding in some hospitals where the Act is liberally applied and the refusal to perform operations where it is conservatively applied have fostered the growth of the private sector. Much has been written to the discredit of some private clinics licensed under the Act and of those who operate in them and though unfortunately there is room for such criticisms certain discriminations should be made. There are for example some clinics which have been set up by essentially charitable organizations to aid women to find at a moderate fee a private treatment which they could not obtain from the N.H.S.[48]

It is also the case that, though a few of these licensed clinics have failed to obtain a renewal of their licence, there has been little substantial evidence of medical ill-treatment: certainly the amount of mortality from operations in the clinics is no greater than those from operations in the N.H.S. hospitals. There is, however, not the slightest doubt that a large scale racket[49] has developed in this sector and it is a racket which has three tiers. First, very high fees are charged by some of the doctors who operate in some of these clinics; secondly, very high fees may be charged by the clinics themselves, and thirdly, an ancillary network of bureaux and touts has grown up enabling a woman sometimes to obtain a fixed date and place for the operation before she has been examined by any doctors. Foreign women coming from abroad for an operation in a clinic and able to pay fees which are often much higher than those charged to residents accounted in the first quarter of 1971 to some *11 per cent of the total of operations.*[50]

VI LESSONS OF THE ENGLISH EXPERIENCE

The first moral to be drawn from the English experience is that if abortion law reform is to be undertaken it must not be regarded merely as yet another piece of permissive legislation comparable to the relaxation of the law against homosexuality which can be introduced without previous organization and ancillary supports. Liberalization of abortion law in any modern industrial state is a large scale medical and social change which demands careful planning of available resources. It was in England unfortunately the case that there was no such anticipatory planning and, although in 1970 the amount of legal abortion in N.H.S. hospitals was approximately six times that done in 1967 no extra beds, nurses or doctors had been supplied for this work. The Government appeared to think that no expansion in medical services was needed and, indeed, the attitude both of the general public and the great willingness demonstrated since the Act of the general practitioner to refer cases to the hospitals seems to have taken both the Government and consultants by surprise.[51]

The Lane Committee may have much to say on ways of securing a more equitable distribution of the burden on hospitals and will consider suggestions already made for special units and part-time rotas to alleviate its work and for the improved use that could be made of hospital capacity by rearrangement of the division between obstetric and gynaecological beds. It may, however, soon be the case that both the costs and difficulty of providing for large numbers in the N.H.S. will be eased by the further simplification in the new rapidly developing techniques for the operation in the early weeks of pregnancy, and there has already been a noticeable increase in the proportion of operations performed by vacuum aspiration instead of the older dilatation technique.[52]

It is however unlikely even with these latest developments that the N.H.S. hospitals will be able in the next few years to cater without strain for the full demand so that a private sector will no longer be necessary. No doubt the racket will diminish, but it will still present a problem of control and the efficacy of any such controls as stipulation of maximum fees must in the end depend upon the ability of the professional associations to define and enforce standards which, though easy to prescribe on paper, may be empty unless some investigatory machinery is available.

The second and in the long term more important moral to be drawn from the English experience is that no country contemplating the liberalisation of abortion law should legislate for abortion alone. It is of crucial importance that such legislation should be part of a coherent and comprehensive scheme for dealing with the whole problem of unwanted pregnancies and should be accompanied, and if possible preceded by a really effective provision of free contraceptive services and education in their use. Among the mass of information which has come to light since the Act there is plain and depressing evidence that a high proportion of women who became pregnant and later sought abortion, used no contraceptive precautions on the relevant occasion and a smaller, though still large, proportion habitually used none.[53]

Since the National Health Service (Family Planning) Act 1967 local authorities in England have been authorised to set up birth control clinics to give free advice and, when need is demonstrated, to give free equipment; but they are not required to do this, and a large number of local authorities do not provide these services at all, or only do so for married women. Much important work has been done by volunteers in the Family Planning Association, but their scope is limited by their need to charge fees. The work of local authority and Family Planning Association clinics has in some areas been reinforced by hospital-based clinics and services and the Government[54] has supported both voluntary associations and local authorities with increased financial grants. Yet in spite of these efforts it seems clear that a system in which free contraceptive services will be provided only if hospitals or local authorities decide to provide them, cannot cope with the problem. It is not I think an exaggeration to say, as an indication of the change that is required, that any unwanted pregnancy should be regarded as an illness, and the provision of adequate contraceptive education and services should be regarded as a duty of preventive gynaecology. After a slow start the medical associations in England have come to take something like this view of the problem and in April 1966 (when legislation on abortion was impending) the Royal College of Obstetricians and Gynaecologists[55] announced its full support for the provision of free contraceptive advice and materials for all, and also for voluntary sterilisation of both men and women. But much active effort is needed to counter widespread ignorance, irresponsibility and even fear of contraception; a passive system in which free advice and facilities are merely provided for women if they elect to come forward and ask for them will not succeed in penetrating to those areas of society where contraception is most needed. Until this deficiency is remedied, abortion, which should be used only in the last resort to prevent the misery of unwanted pregnancies and unwanted children, will too often be used as the first.

I said at the beginning of this lecture that had I been a member of Parliament in 1967 I would have voted for the Act. I would still do so in spite of the unsatisfactory features in its operation which I have discussed in this section. For the overcrowding in the hospitals and the racket in the private sector are things that can be remedied and controlled without an impossible strain on our resources; in any case they are likely to diminish with the development of new techniques. Regrettable though they are, they seeem to me to be outweighed by the substantial success which the Act has had in reducing the numbers of illegitimate children, the numbers of shot-gun marriage cases, the number of deaths from illegal abortion and the total amount of illegal abortion. But important as these benefits are, I consider no less important the fact that since the Act it has become possible for large numbers of pregnant women who do not wish to continue their pregnancy to lay their case frankly before doctors and to discuss it without shame and without fear.

NOTES

[1] A revised version (including statistics subsequently available) of the Southey lecture for 1970 delivered at Melbourne University in May 1971. Two books on the English experience of abortion law reform have since been published in England: Hordern, *Legal Abortion: The English Experience* (1971) and Hindell and Simms, *Abortion Law Reformed* (1971).

[2] The figures for legal abortion in N.H.S. Hospitals for the four years prior to the Act were respectively 3,300, 4,530, 6,380 and 9,700.

[3] The figures cited here for 1968 to 1970 are from the *Registrar-General's Statistical Review of England and Wales,* Supplement on Abortion. Figures for 1971 are from the *Registrar-General's Quarterly Return for England and Wales* which give provisional figures to be corrected in the later published Annual Review. The rate of increase in the number of legal abortions rose very steeply during the period from April 1968 (when the Act came into operation) until June 1970 but the figures for the last three quarters of 1970 and the first quarter of 1971 (21,082, 22,253, 22,774, and 22,808) showed a comparatively stable annual rate. The sharp increase in 1971 began with the second quarter of that year.

[4] [1939] 1 K.B. 687.

[5] [1969] V.R. 667.

[6] The result, though similar, is not identical since according to *Davidson's* case a person terminating a pregnancy is liable to conviction under s. 65 of the Crimes Act 1958 if it is proved either (a) that he did not honestly believe on reasonable grounds that the operation was necessary to preserve the woman from serious danger to her life or her physical or mental health, or (b) that he did not believe that the operation was in the circumstances proportionate to the need to preserve the woman from such danger. There was nothing corresponding to (b) in the former English law, though in *Davidson* the conception of proportion was said to underlie the decision in *Bourne.*

[7] The percentages of the total numbers of legal abortions for which this was the sole ground in 1968 (8 months), 1969 and 1970 were respectively 71%, 73% and 75%.

[8] See C. B. Goodhart 'The Frequency of Legal Abortion' (1964) 55 *Eugenics Review* 197, 200; but note the discussion of his argument *infra* p. 403.

[8] See C. B. Goodhart, 'The Frequency of Legal Abortion' (1964) 55

[9] Figures from *Home Office Supplementary Statistics relating to Crime and Criminal Proceedings* 1963 onwards. Table 6A.

[10] *Ibid.* Table 4 (a).

[11] *E.g.* Finnis, 'Three Schemes of Regulation' in Noonan (ed.) *The Morality of Abortion* (1970) 184.

[12] *Ibid.* 203.

[13] See Victoria, *Report of the Board of Enquiry into Allegations of Corruption in the Police Force in connection with illegal abortion practices in the State of Victoria* (1971). Two senior members of the Victoria Police Force of more than thirty years standing, Matthews, a former superintendent and Ford, a former officer in charge of the Homicide Squad, were as a result of this

enquiry convicted of conspiring to obstruct the course of justice and sentenced to imprisonment for five years with a minimum of three. Jacobson, a former detective constable of the Homicide Squad of seven years standing was convicted of the same charge and sentenced to three years imprisonment with a maximum of eighteen months.

[14]In the three years 1968-70 operations on the grounds of the health of the existing children of the woman's family represented 4% of the total for each year. Operations on account of the risk of the birth of a handicapped child represented 4%, 2% and 1% of the total for these years respectively.

[15]See C. B. Goodhart, Letter in [1968] 2 *British Medical Journal* 298.

[16]In 1969 there were no deaths from illegal abortion among the 7,427 women on whom the operation was performed in the ninth week of pregnancy or earlier (*Registrar-General's Statistical Review of England and Wales for the Year 1969*, Supplement on Abortion, Tables 22, 32). In 1968 and 1969, Supplement on Abortion, Tables 22, 32). In 1968 and 1969, when the numbers of maternal deaths, other than deaths from abortion, were 18 and 15 per 100,000 of live births respectively, the number of deaths from legally induced abortions were 5 and 10, yielding a rate approximately of 20 and 19 per 100,000 abortions. See *Registrar-General's Statistical Review of England and Wales for the Year 1969*, Pt 1, Table F.1, 463; *Registrar-General's Quarterly Return for England and Wales* (Quarter ended June 1970) Table V, 24; (Quarter ended June 1971) Table V, 26.

[17]See the Proceedings of a Symposium by the Medical Protection Society published under the title *The Abortion Act 1967* (1969) 32.

[18]See the discussion of these legal problems by Howe Q.C. *ibid.* 72.

[19]A New York jury awarded $46,000 damages to the parents of a girl born physically and mentally handicapped after she had been refused an abortion. See *The Sunday Express* 6 October 1968. This was the first decision of its kind in the U.S.A.

[20]No records of refusal of operations for abortions are required to be kept by law or are generally available at present. It is, however, clear that the great regional variations in numbers of operations performed in N.H.S. hospitals in the first two years since the Act, *e.g.* in Birmingham 2.4% of live births, compared with 7.6% in Newcastle for the first six months of 1970 (see 1971 Abortion Law Reform Association *Newsletter*, No. 29, 3), are attributable only to a negligible extent to variations in demand, the major factor being the varying hostility to or sympathy with the policy of the Act among gynaecologists in N.S.H. hospitals. 33% of women wanting an abortion who were seen by the charitable Pregnancy Advisory Service in Birmingham had been recommended for abortion by general practitioners and had either been refused by N.H.S. hospitals or were faced with an excessive waiting period there. (See the accounts of the Pregnancy Advisory Service in Hordern, *op. cit.* 126, 129, 181, and Hindell and Simms, *op. cit.* 216 8.) Refusals of abortions by the N.H.S. to pregnant girls under the age of 16 have been frequently reported (see The Times, 21 June 1971, (2). In 1969 the number of under-age girls who had illegitimate babies exceeded at 1,486 the number of those who had legal abortions (1,231).

[21] See the analysis of voting showing a preponderant Labour support for the Abortion Act in Hindell and Simms, *op. cit.* 165, 201-2.

[22] United Kingdom, *Report of the Royal Commission on Capital Punishment 1949-53* (1953) Cmnd 8932; United Kingdom, *Report of the Committee on Homosexual Offences and Prostitution* (1957) Cmnd 247; United Kingdom, *Report of the Royal Commission on Marriage and Divorce 1951-55* (1956) Cmnd 9678; United Kingdom, *Report of the Law Commission: The Field of Choice* (1966).

[23] See the detailed accounts of this Association in Hindell and Simms, *op. cit.* See also their earlier article, 'How the Abortion Lobby Worked' (1968) 39 *Political Quarterly* 269.

[24] (1966) 732 H.C. Deb. 1118.

[25] According to Coke's *Institutes* III, 50 (repeated in Blackstone's *Commentaries* IV, 198) the abortion of a woman even after 'quickening' is a great 'misprision and no murder'. This is wrongly cited as 'misprision and *so* murder' (my italics) in Louisell and Noonan, 'Constitutional Balance', in Noonan (ed.), *op. cit.* 223. Abortion after quickening was a capital offence in England only between Lord Ellenborough's Act 1803 and the Offences Against the Persons Act 1837.

[26] See Judith Thompson, 'A Defence of Abortion' (1971) 1 *Journal of Philosophy and Public Affairs* 47.

[27] See speech of Lord Stoneham in (1967) 285 H.L. Deb. 988-90. As a result of these representations by the medical bodies the clause emerged from the committee stage without any words qualifying the relevant risks to life and health. The qualification that the risk must be greater than if the pregnancy were terminated was added at the suggestion of Lord Parker, *ibid.* 1431.

[28] [1968] 3 *British Medical Journal* Supplements 25-7.

[29] R.C.O.G., 'Memorandum on Legalised Abortion' [1966] 1 *British Medical Journal* 850.

[30] For these figures see *Registrar-General's Quarterly Return for England and Wales* (Quarter ended June 1971), Tables Ia and Ib.

[31] See *Registrar-General's Statistical Review of England and Wales for the Year 1969*, Pt II, Table UU, 195. The figures for 1970 and 1971 are not yet available.

[32] Ibid. Pt 1, Appendix F1, 463; *Registrar-General's Quarterly Return for England and Wales* (Quarter ended June 1970), Table V, 24; (Quarter ended June 1971) Table V, 26; Ministry of Health, *Report on Confidential Inquiries into Maternal Deaths in England and Wales for 1964-66* which suggests that the official figures may understate the number of deaths.

[33] A regression of the annual percentage change in deaths from illegal abortions *per* live birth run on the annual percentage change in hospital maternity mortality rates *per* live birth in the period 1950-67 shows the R^2 of the regression to be .12. This can be rejected as insignificant at a 1% significance level. I am indebted to Mr David Soskice, Fellow of University College, Oxford for this regression analysis. I am also much indebted to him for drawing my attention to the significance of the figures for the shot-gun marriage cases and for much help with the statistics in general.

[34]Percentages calculated from *Registrar-General's Statistical Review of England and Wales for the Year 1969*, Appendix F.1, 463; *Registrar-General's Quarterly Return for England and Wales* (Quarter ended June 1971), Table V, 26.

[35]Cf. D. V. Glass, *Population Policies and Movements in Europe* (1940) (100,000 'not at all improbable'); Mr. Roy Jenkins, then Home Secretary, in (1966) 732 H.C. Deb. 1141 ('perhaps 100,000'); Dr. Eustace Chester, 'The Law of Abortion' (1950) 72 *Medical World* 495 ('not less than a quarter of a million').

[36]See Hindell and Simms, *op. cit.* 32.

[37]See C. B. Goodhart, 'The Frequency of Illegal Abortion' (1964) 55 *Eugenics Review* 197. In 1964 when Dr Goodhart wrote this article the rate of maternal mortality otherwise than from abortion was 20 *per* 100,000.

[38][1966] 1 *British Medical Journal* 850.

[39][1968] 3 *British Medical Journal* Supplements 25-9.

[40]See (1969) 787 H.C. Deb. 411; (1970) 795 H.C. Deb. 1653.

[41]National Opinion Polls, *Survey of General Practitioners* (1970) 4. 55% of the electorate supported the Act's retention or relaxation.

[42][1970] 2 *British Medical Journal* 529.

[43]*Ibid.* 478.

[44]Percentages calculated from figures given in the *Registrar-General's Statistical Review of England and Wales for the Year 1968*, Supplement on Abortion, Table 1; *Registrar-General's Statistical Review of England and Wales for the Year 1970*, Supplement on Abortion, Table 1A.

[45](1971) 812 H.C. Deb. 318. The terms of reference are '[t]o review the operation of the Abortion Act 1967, and, on the basis that the conditions for legal abortion contained in paragraphs (a) and (b) of subsection (1) and in subsections (2), (3) and (4) of section 1 af the Act, remain unaltered, to make recommendations.'

[46]*Registrar-General's Statistical Review of England and Wales for the Year 1968* Supplement on Abortion, Table 1; *Registrar-General's Statistical Review of England and Wales for the Year 1969*, Supplement on Abortion, Table 1.

[47]Report on R.C.O.G.'s questionnaire in [1970] 2 *British Medical Journal* 529.

[48]See the account of the charitable Pregnancy Advisory Service in Birmingham and London and of the Calthorp Nursing Home in Hordern, *op. cit.* 107-12, 181-2 and Hindell and Simms, *op. cit.* 216-8.

[49]For a vivid and detailed account of this racket see *Daily Telegraph Magazine*, 28 November 1971.

[50][1971] 817 H.C. Deb. 1177.

[51]See Lewis, 'The Abortion Act' [1969] 1 *British Medical Journal* 241.

[52]See Lewis, Lal, Branch and Beard, 'Outpatient Termination of Pregnancies' [1971] 4 *British Medical Journal* 606. According to this account 127 women between 6 and 10 weeks pregnant were aborted by a form of vacuum aspiration operation lasting only 5 to 10 minutes, and were allowed to go home after a period of 2 to 3 hours. Only one patient was required to stay in hospital after the operation and though 16 were readmitted for short periods, no com-

plications were found after careful follow-ups at 3 months.

[53] Among 300 women seeeking abortion in Birmingham in 1968, 45.8% habitually used no contraception and 73.5% used none on the relevant occasion (see Diggory, 'Some Experiences of Therapeutic Abortion' [1969] 1 *The Lancet* 1051).

[54] The Government has announced a trebled grant for these purposes for 1972-73, see [1971] 812 H.C. Deb. 313.

[55] [1966] 1 *British Medical Journal* 850-3.

SUPREME COURT OF THE UNITED STATES

Syllabus

ROE ET. AL. v. WADE, DISTRICT ATTORNEY OF DALLAS COUNTY

APPEAL FROM THE UNITED STATES DISTRICT COURT FOR THE NORTHERN DISTRICT OF TEXAS

No. 70-18 Argued December 13, 1971—Reargued October 11, 1972—Decided January 22, 1973

A pregnant single woman (Roe) brought a class action challenging the constitutionality of the Texas criminal abortion laws, which proscribe procuring or attempting an abortion except on medical advice for the purpose of saving the mother's life. A licensed physician (Hallford), who had two state abortion prosecutions pending against him, was permitted to intervene. A childless married couple (the Does), the wife not being pregnant, separately attacked the laws, basing alleged injury on the future possibilities of contraceptive failure, pregnancy, unpreparedness for parenthood, and impairment of the wife's health. A three-judge District Court, which consolidated the actions, held that Roe and Hallford, and members of their classes, had standing to sue and presented justiciable controversies. Ruling that declaratory, though not injunctive, relief was warranted, the court declared the abortion statutes void as vague and overbroadly infringing those plaintiffs' Ninth and Fourteenth Amendment rights. The court ruled the Does' complaint not justiciable. Appellants directly appealed to this Court on the injunctive rulings, and appellee cross-appealed from the District Court's grant of declaratory relief to Roe and Hallford. *Held:*

1. While 28 U.S.C. § 1253 authorizes no direct appeal to this Court from the grant or denial of declaratory relief alone, review is not foreclosed when the case is properly before the Court on appeal from specific denial of injunctive relief and the arguments as to both injunctive and declaratory relief are necessarily identical. P. 8.

2. Roe has standing to sue; the Does and Hallford do not. Pp. 9-14.

211

ROE *vs.* WADE

Syllabus

(a) Contrary to appellee's contention, the natural termination of Roe's pregnancy did not moot her suit. Litigation involving pregnancy, which is "capable of repetition, yet evading review," is an exception to the usual federal rule that an actual controversy must exist at review stages and not simply when the action is initiated. Pp. 9-10.

(b) The District Court correctly refused injunctive, but erred in granting declaratory, relief to Hallford, who alleged no federally protected right not assertable as a defense against the good-faith state prosecutions pending against him. *Samuels* v. *Mackell,* 401 U. S. 66.

(c) The Does' complaint, based as it is on contingencies, any one or more of which may not occur, is too speculative to present an actual case or controversy. Pp. 12-14.

3. State criminal abortion laws, like those involved here, that except from criminality only a life-saving procedure on the mother's behalf without regard to the stage of her pregnancy and other interests involved violate the Due Process Clause of the Fourteenth Amendment, which protects against state action the right to privacy, including a woman's qualified right to terminate her pregnancy. Though the State cannot override that right, it has legitimate interests in protecting both the pregnant woman's health and the potentiality of human life, each of which interests grows and reaches a "compelling" point at various stages of the woman's approach to term. Pp. 36-49.

(a) For the stage prior to approximately the end of the first trimester, the abortion decision and its effectuation must be left to the medical judgment of the pregnant woman's attending physician. Pp. 36-47.

(b) For the stage subsequent to approximately the end of the first trimester, the State, in promoting its interest in the health of the mother, may, if it chooses, regulate the abortion procedure in ways that are reasonably related to maternal health. Pp. 43-44.

(c) For the stage subsequent to viability the State, in promoting its interest in the potentiality of human life, may, if it chooses, regulate, and even proscribe, abortion except where necessary, in appropriate medical judgment, for the preservation of the life or health of the mother. Pp. 44-48.

4. The State may define the term "physician" to mean only a physician currently licensed by the State, and may proscribe any abortion by a person who is not a physician as so defined. Pp. 34-35, 48.

5. It is unnecessary to decide the injunctive relief issue since the Texas authorities will doubtless fully recognize the Court's ruling that the Texas criminal abortion statutes are unconstitutional. Pp. 51. 314 F. Supp. 1217, affirmed in part and reversed in part.

BLACKMUN, J., delivered the opinion of the Court, in which BURGER, C. J., and DOUGLAS, BRENNAN, STEWART, MARSHALL, and POWELL, JJ., joined. BURGER, C. J., and DOUGLAS and STEWART, JJ., filed concurring opinions. WHITE, J, filed a dissenting opinion, in which REHNQUIST, J., joined. REHNQUIST, J., filed a dissenting opinion.

VII

Three reasons have been advanced to explain historically the enactment of criminal abortion laws in the 19th century and to justify their continued existence.

It has been argued occasionally that these laws were the product of a Victorian social concern to discourage illicit sexual conduct. Texas, however, does not advance this justification in the present case, and it appears that no court or commentator has taken the argument seriously.[12] The appellants and *amici* contend, moreover, that this is not a proper state purpose at all and suggest that, if it were, the Texas statutes are overbroad in protecting it since the law fails to distinguish between married and unwed mothers.

A second reason is concerned with abortion as a medical procedure. When most criminal abortion laws were first enacted, the procedure was a hazardous one for the woman.[43] This was particularly true prior to the development of antisepsis. Antiseptic techniques, of course, were based on discoveries by Lister, Pasteur, and others first announced in 1867, but were not generally accepted and employed until about the turn of the century. Abortion mortality was high. Even after 1900, and perhaps until as late as the development of antibiotics in the 1940's, standard modern techniques such as dilation and curettage were not nearly so safe as they are today. Thus it has been argued that a State's real concern in enacting a criminal abortion law was to protect the pregnant woman, that is, to restrain her from submitting to a procedure that placed her life in serious jeopardy.

Modern medical techniques have altered this situation. Appellants and various *amici* refer to medical data indicating that abortion in early pregnancy, that is, prior to the end of first trimester, although not without its risk, is now relatively safe. Mortality rates for women undergoing early abortions, where the procedure is legal, appear to be as low as or lower than the rates for normal childbirth.[44] Consequently, any interest of the State in protecting the woman from an inherently hazardous procedure, except when it would be equally dangerous for her to forego it, has largely disappeared. Of course, important state interests in the area of health and medical standards do remain. The State has a legitimate interest in seeing to it that abortion, like any other medical procedure, is performed under circumstances that insure maximum safety for the patient. This interest obviously extends at least to the performing physician and his staff, to the facilities involved, to the availability of after-care, and to adequate provision for any complication or emergency that might arise. The prevalence of high mortality rates at illegal "abortion mills" strengthens, rather than weakens, the State's interest in regulating the conditions under which abortions are performed. Moreover, the risk to the woman increases as her pregnancy continues. Thus the State retains a definite interest in protecting the woman's own health and safety when an abortion is proposed at a late stage of pregnancy.

The third reason is the State's interest—some phrase it in terms of duty—in protecting prenatal life. Some of the argument for this justification rests on the theory that a new human life is present from the moment of conception.[45] The State's interest and general obligation to protect life then extends, it is argued, to prenatal life. Only when the life of the pregnant mother herself is at stake, balanced against the life she carries within her, should the interest of the embryo or fetus not prevail. Logically, of course, a legitimate state interest in this area need not stand or fall on acceptance of the belief that life begins at conception or at some other point prior to live birth. In assessing the State's interest, recognition may be given to the less rigid claim that as long as at least *potential* life is involved, the State may assert interests beyond the protection of the pregnant woman alone.

Parties challenging state abortion laws have sharply disputed in some courts the contention that a purpose of these laws, when enacted, was to protect prenatal life.[46] Pointing to the absence of legislative history to support the contention, they claim that most state laws were designed solely to protect the woman. Because medical advances have lessened this concern, at least with respect to abortion in early pregnancy, they argue that with respect to such abortions the laws can no longer be justified by any state interest. There is some scholarly support for this view of original purpose.[47] The few state courts called upon to interpret their laws in the late 19th and early 20th centuries did focus on the State's interest in protecting the woman's health rather than in preserving the embryo and fetus.[48] Proponents of this view point out that in many States, including Texas,[49] by statute or judicial interpretation, the pregnant woman herself could not be prosecuted for self-abortion or for cooperating in an abortion performed upon her by another.[50] They claim that adoption of the "quickening" distinction through received common law and state statutes tacitly recognizes the greater health hazards inherent in late abortion and impliedly repudiates the theory that life begins at conception.

It is with these interests, and the weight to be attached to them, that this case is concerned.

VIII

The Constitution does not explicitly mention any right of privacy. In a line of decisions, however, going back perhaps as far as *Union Pacific R. Co. v. Botsford,* 141 U. S. 250, 251 (1891), the Court has recognized that a right of personal privacy, or a guarantee of certain areas or zones of privacy, does exist under the Constitution. In varying contexts the Court or individual Justices have indeed found at least the roots of that right in the First Amendment, *Stanley v. Georgia,* 394 U. S. 557, 564 (1969); in the Fourth and Fifth Amendments, *Terry v. Ohio,* 392 U. S. 1, 8-9 (1968), *Katz v. United States,* 389 U. S. 347, 350 (1967), *Boyd v. United States,* 116 U. S. 616 (1886), see *Olmstead v. United States,* 277 U. S. 438, 478 (1928) (Brandeis, J. dissenting); in the penumbras of the Bill of Rights, *Griswold v. Connecticut,* 381 U. S. 479, 484-485 (1965); in the Ninth Amendment, *id.,* at 486 (Goldberg, J., concurring); or in the concept of liberty guaranteed by the first section of the Fourteenth Amendment, see *Meyer v. Nebraska,* 262 U. S. 390, 399 (1923). These decisions make it clear that only personal rights that can be deemed "fundamental" or "implicit in the concept of ordered liberty," *Palko*

v. *Connecticut,* 302 U. S. 319, 325 (1937), are included in this guarantee of personal privacy. They also make it clear that the right has some extension to activities relating to marriage, *Loving* v. *Virginia,* 388 U. S. 1, 12 (1967), procreation, *Skinner* v. *Oklahoma,* 316 U. S. 535, 541-542 (1942), contraception, *Eisenstadt* v. *Baird,* 405 U. S. 438, 453-454 (1972); *id.,* at 460, 463-465 (WHITE, J., concurring), family relationships, *Prince* v. *Massachusetts,* 321 U. S. 158, 166 (1944), and child rearing and education, *Pierce* v. *Society of Sisters,* 268 U. S. 510, 535 (1925), *Meyer* v. *Nebraska, supra.*

This right of privacy, whether it be founded in the Fourteenth Amendment's concept of personal liberty and restrictions upon state action, as we feel it is, or, as the District Court determined, in the Ninth Amendment's reservation of rights to the people, is broad enough to encompass a woman's decision whether or not to terminate her pregnancy. The detriment that the State would impose upon the pregnant woman by denying this choice altogether is apparent. Specific and direct harm medically diagnosable even in early pregnancy may be involved. Maternity, or additional offspring, may force upon the woman a distressful life and future. Psychological harm may be imminent. Mental and physical health may be taxed by child care. There is also the distress, for all concerned, associated with the unwanted child, and there is the problem of bringing a child into a family already unable, psychologically and otherwise, to care for it. In other cases, as in this one, the additional difficulties and continuing stigma of unwed motherhood may be involved. All these are factors the woman and her responsible physician necessarily will consider in consultation.

On the basis of elements such as these, appellants and some *amici* argue that the woman's right is absolute and that she is entitled to terminate her pregnancy at whatever time, in whatever way, and for whatever reason she alone chooses. With these we do not agree. Appellants' arguments that Texas either has no valid interest at all in regulating the abortion decision, or no interest strong enough to support any limitation upon the woman's sole determination, is unpersuasive. The Court's decisions recognizing a right of privacy also acknowledge that some state regulation in areas protected by that right is appropriate. As noted above, a state may properly assert important interests in safeguarding health, in maintaining medical standards, and in protecting potential life. At some point in pregnancy, these respective interests become sufficiently compelling to sustain regulation of the factors that govern the abortion decision. The privacy right involved, therefore, cannot be said to be absolute. In fact, it is not clear to us that the claim asserted by some *amici* that one has an unlimited right to do with one's body as one pleases bears a close relationship to the right of privacy previously articulated in the Court's decisions. The Court has refused to recognize an unlimited right of this kind in the past. *Jacobson* v. *Massachusetts,* 197 U. S. 11 (1905) (vaccination); *Buck* v. *Bell,* 274 U. S. 200 (1927) (sterilization).

We therefore conclude that the right of personal privacy includes the abortion decision, but that this right is not unqualified and must be considered against important state interests in regulation.

We note that those federal and state courts that have recently considered abortion law challenges have reached the same conclusion. A majority, in addition to the District Court in the present case, have held state laws unconstitutional, at least in part, because of vagueness or because of overbreadth and abridgement of rights. *Abele* v. *Markle,* 342 F. Supp. 800 (Conn. 1972), appeal pending; *Abele* v. *Markle,* —— F. Supp. —— (Conn. Sept. 20, 1972), appeal pending; *Doe* v. *Bolton,* 319 F. Supp. 1048 (ND Ga. 1970), appeal decided today, *post* ——; *Doe* v. *Scott,* 321 F. Supp. 1385 (ND Ill. 1971), appeal pending; *Poe* v. *Menghini,* 339 F. Supp. 986 (Kan. 1972); *YWCA* v. *Kugler,* 342 F. Supp. 1048 (NJ 1972); *Babbitz* v. *McCann,* 310 F. Supp. 293 (ED Wis. 1970), appeal dismissed, 400 U. S. 1 (1970); *People* v. *Belous,* 71 Cal. 2d 954, 458 P. 2d 194 (1969), cert. denied, 397 U. S. 915 (1970); *State* v. *Barquet,* 262 S. 2d 431 (Fla. 1972).

Others have sustained state statutes. *Crossen* v. *Attorney General,* 344 F. Supp. 587 (ED Ky. 1972), appeal pending; *Rosen* v. *Louisiana State Board of Medical Examiners,* 318 F. Supp. 1217 (ED La. 1970), appeal pending; *Corkey* v. *Edwards,* 322 F. Supp. 1248 (WDNC 1971), appeal pending; *Steinberg* v. *Brown,* 321 F. Supp. 741 (ND Ohio 1970); *Doe* v. *Rampton,* —— F. Supp. —— (Utah 1971), appeal pending; *Cheaney* v. *Indiana,* —— Ind. ——, 285 N. E. 2d 265 (1972); *Spears* v. *State,* 257 So. 2d 876 (Miss. 1972); *State* v. *Munson,* —— S. D. ——, 201 N. W. 2d 123 (1972), appeal pending.

Although the results are divided, most of these courts have agreed that the right of privacy, however based, is broad enough to cover the abortion decision; that the right, nonetheless, is not absolute and is subject to some limitations; and that at some point the state interests as to protection of health, medical standards, and prenatal life, become dominant. We agree with this approach.

Where certain "fundamental rights" are involved, the Court has held that regulation limiting these rights may be justified only by a "compelling state interest." *Kramer* v. *Union Free School District,* 395 U. S. 621, 627 (1969); *Shapiro* v. *Thompson,* 394 U. S. 618, 634 (1969); *Sherbert* v. *Verner,* 374 U. S. 398, 406 (1963), and that legislative enactments must be narrowly drawn to express only the legitimate state interests at stake. *Griswold* v. *Connecticut,* 381 U. S. 479, 485 (1965); *Aptheker* v. *Secretary of State,* 378 U. S. 500, 508 (1964); *Cantwell* v. *Connecticut,* 310 U. S. 296, 307-308 (1940); see *Eisenstadt* v. *Baird,* 405 U. S. 438, 460, 463-464 (1972) (WHITE, J., concurring).

In the recent abortion cases cited above, courts have recognized these principles. Those striking down state laws have generally scrutinized the State's interest in protecting health and potential life and have concluded that neither interest justified broad limitations on the reasons for which a physician and his pregnant patient might decide that she should have an abortion in the early stages of pregnancy. Courts sustaining state laws have held that the State's determinations to protect health or prenatal life are dominant and constitutionally justifiable.

IX

The District Court held that the appellee failed to meet his burden of demonstrating that the Texas statute's infringement upon Roe's rights was necessary to support a compelling state interest, and that, although the defendant presented "several compelling justifications for state presence in the area of abortions," the statutes outstripped these justifications and swept "far beyond any areas of compelling state interest." 314 F. Supp., at 1222-1223. Appellant and appellee both contest that holding. Appellant, as has been indicated, claims an absolute right that bars any state imposition of criminal penalties in the area. Appellee argues that the State's determination to recognize and protect prenatal life from and after conception constitutes a compelling state interest. As noted above, we do not agree fully with either formulation.

A. The appellee and certain *amici* argue that the fetus is a "person" within the language and meaning of the Fourteenth Amendment. In support of this they outline at length and in detail the well-known facts of fetal development. If this suggestion of personhood is established, the appellant's case, of course, collapses, for the fetus' right to life is then guaranteed specifically by the Amendment. The appellant conceded as much on reargument.[51] On the other hand, the appellee conceded on reargument[52] that no case could be cited that holds that a fetus is a person within the meaning of the Fourteenth Amendment.

The Constitution does not define "person" in so many words. Section 1 of the Fourteenth Amendment contains three references to "person." The first, in defining "citizens," speaks of "persons born or naturalized in the United States." The word also appears both in the Due Process Clause and in the Equal Protection Clause. "Person" is used in other places in the Constitution: in the listing of qualifications for representatives and senators, Art. I, § 2, cl. 2, and § 3, cl. 3; in the Apportionment Clause, Art. I, § 2, cl. 3;[53] in the Migration and Importation provision, Art. I, § 9, cl. 1; in the Emolument Clause, Art. I, § 9, cl. 8; in the Electors provisions, Art. II, § 1, cl. 2, and the superseded cl. 3; in the provision outlining qualifications for the office of President, Art. II, § 1, cl. 5; in the Extradition provisions, Art. IV, § 2, cl. 2, and the superseded Fugitive Slave cl. 3; and in the Fifth, Twelfth, and Twenty-second Amendments as well as in §§ 2 and 3 of the Fourteenth Amendment. But in nearly all these instances, the use of the word is such that it has application only postnatally. None indicates, with any assurance, that it has any possible pre-natal application.[54]

All this, together with our observation, *supra,* that throughout the major portion of the 19th century prevailing legal abortion practices were far freer than they are today, persuades us that the word "person," as used in the Fourteenth Amendment, does not include the unborn.[55] This is in accord with the results reached in those few cases where the issue has been squarely presented. *McGarvey* v. *Magee-Womens Hospital,* 340 F. Supp. 751 (WD Pa. 1972); *Byrn* v. *New York City Health & Hospitals Corp.,* 31 N. Y. 2d 194, 286 N. E. 2d 887 (1972), appeal pending; *Abele* v. *Markle,* —— F. Supp. —— (Conn. Sept. 20, 1972), appeal pending. Compare *Cheaney* v. *Indiana,* —— Ind. ——, 285 N. E. 265, 270 (1972); *Montana* v. *Rogers,* 278 F. 2d 68, 72 (CA7 1960), aff'd *sub nom. Montana* v. *Kennedy,* 366 U. S. 308 (1961); *Keeler* v. *Superior Court,* ——Cal. ——,

470 P. 2d 617 (1970); *State* v. *Dickinson,* 23 Ohio App. 2d 259, 275 N. E. 2d 599 (1970). Indeed, our decision in *United States* v. *Vuitch,* 402 U. S. 62 (1971), inferentially is to the same effect, for we there would not have indulged in statutory interpretation favorable to abortion in specified circumstances if the necessary consequence was the termination of life entitled to Fourteenth Amendment protection. This conclusion, however, does not of itself fully answer the contentions raised by Texas, and we pass on to other considerations.

B. The pregnant woman cannot be isolated in her privacy. She carries an embryo and, later, a fetus, if one accepts the medical definitions of the developing young in the human uterus. See Dorland's Illustrated Medical Dictionary, 478-479, 547 (24th ed. 1965). The situation therefore is inherently different from marital intimacy, or bedroom possession of obscene material, or marriage, or procreation, or education, with which *Eisenstadt, Giswold, Stanley, Loving, Skinner, Pierce,* and *Meyer* were respectively concerned. As we have intimated above, it is reasonable and appropriate for a State to decide that at some point in time another interest, that of health of the mother or that of potential human life, becomes significantly involved. The woman's privacy is no longer sole and any right of privacy she possesses must be measured accordingly.

Texas urges that, apart from the Fourteenth Amendment, life begins at conception and is present throughout pregnancy, and that, therefore, the State has a compelling interest in protecting that life from and after conception. We need not resolve the difficult question of when life begins. When those trained in the respective disciplines of medicine, philosophy, and theology are unable to arrive at any consensus, the judiciary, at this point in the development of man's knowledge, is not in a position to speculate as to the answer.

It should be sufficient to note briefly the wide divergence of thinking on this most sensitive and difficult question. There has always been strong support for the view that life does not begin until live birth. This was the belief of the Stoics.[56] It appears to be the predominant, though not the unanimous, attitude of the Jewish faith.[57] It may be taken to represent also the position of a large segment of the Protestant community, insofar as that can be ascertained; organized groups that have taken a formal position on the abortion issue have generally regarded abortion as a matter for the conscience of the individual and her family.[58] As we have noted, the common law found greater significance in quickening. Physicians and their scientific colleagues have regarded that event with less interest and have tended to focus either upon conception or upon live birth or upon the interim point at which the fetus becomes "viable," that is, potentially able to live outside the mother's womb, albeit with artificial aid.[59] Viability is usually placed at about seven months (28 weeks) but may occur earlier, even at 24 weeks.[60] The Aristotelian theory of "mediate animation," that held sway throughout the Middle Ages and the Renaissance in Europe, continued to be official Roman Catholic dogma until the 19th century, despite opposition to this "ensoulment" theory from those in the Church who would recognize the existence of life from the moment of conception.[61] The latter is now, of course, the official belief of the Catholic Church. As one of the briefs *amicus* discloses, this is a view strongly held by many non-Catholics as well, and by many physicians. Substantial problems for precise definition of this view are posed, however, by new embryological data that purport to indicate that conception is a "process" over time, rather than an event, and by new medical techniques such as menstrual extraction, the "morning-after" pill, implantation of embryos, artificial insemination, and even artificial wombs.[62]

In areas other than criminal abortion the law has been reluctant to endorse any theory that life, as we recognize it, begins before live birth or to accord legal rights to the unborn except in narrowly defined situations and except when the rights are contingent upon live birth. For example, the traditional rule of tort law had denied recovery for prenatal injuries even though the child was born alive.[63] That rule has been changed in almost every jurisdiction. In most States recovery is said to be permitted only if the fetus was viable, or at least quick, when the injuries were sustained, though few courts have squarely so held.[64] In a recent development, generally opposed by the commentators, some States permit the parents of a stillborn child to maintain an action for wrongful death because of prenatal injuries.[65] Such an action, however, would appear to be one to vindicate the parents' interest and is thus consistent with the view that the fetus, at most, represents only the potentiality of life. Similarly, unborn children have been recognized as acquiring rights or interests by way of inheritance or other devolution of property, and have been represented by guardians *ad litem*.[66] Perfection of the interests involved, again, has generally been contingent upon live birth. In short, the unborn have, never been recognized in the law as persons in the whole sense.

X

In view of all this, we do not agree that, by adopting one theory of life, Texas may override the rights of the pregnant woman that are at stake. We repeat, however, that the State does have an important and legitimate interest in preserving and protecting the health of the pregnant woman, whether she be a resident of the State or a nonresident who seeks medical consultation and treatment there, and that it has still *another* important and legitimate interest in protecting the potentiality of human life. These interests are separate and distinct. Each grows in substantiality as the woman approaches term and, at a point during pregnancy, each becomes "compelling."

With respect to the State's important and legitimate interest in the health of the mother, the "compelling" point, in the light of present medical knowledge, is at approximately the end of the first trimester. This is so because of the now established medical fact, referred to above at p. 34, that until the end of the first trimester mortality in abortion is less than mortality in normal childbirth. It follows that, from and after this point, a State may regulate the abortion procedure to the extent that the regulation reasonably relates to the preservation and protection of maternal health. Examples of permissible state regulation in this area are requirements as to the qualifications of the person who is to perform the abortion; as to the licensure of that person; as to the facility in which the procedure is to be performed, that is, whether it must be a hospital or may be a clinic or some other place of less-than-hospital status; as to the licensing of the facility; and the like.

This means, on the other hand, that, for the period of pregnancy prior to this "compelling" point, the attending physician, in consultation with his patient, is free to determine, without regulation by the State, that in his medical judgment the patient's pregnancy should be terminated. If that decision is reached, the judgment may be effectuated by an abortion free of interference by the State.

With respect to the State's important and legitimate interest in potential life, the "compelling" point is at viability. This is so because the fetus then presumably has the capability of meaningful life outside the mother's womb. State regulation protective of fetal life after viability thus has both logical and biological justifications. If the State is interested in protecting fetal life after viability, it may go so far as to proscribe abortion during that period except when it is necessary to preserve the life or health of the mother.

Measured against these standards, Art. 1196 of the Texas Penal Code, in restricting legal abortions to those "procured or attempted by medical advice for the purpose of saving the life of the mother," sweeps too broadly. The statute makes no distinction between abortions performed early in pregnancy and those performed later, and it limits to a single reason, "saving" the mother's life, the legal justification for the procedure. The statute, therefore, cannot survive the constitutional attack made upon it here.

This conclusion makes it unnecessary for us to consider the additional challenge to the Texas statute asserted on the grounds of vagueness. See *United States* v. *Vuitch*, 402 U. S. 62, 67-72 (1971).

XI

To summarize and to repeat:

1. A state criminal abortion statute of the current Texas type, that excepts from criminality only a *life saving* procedure on behalf of the mother, without regard to pregnancy stage and without recognition of the other interests involved, is violative of the Due Process Clause of the Fourteenth Amendment.

(a) For the stage prior to approximately the end of the first trimester, the abortion decision and its effectuation must be left to the medical judgment of the pregnant woman's attending physician.

(b) For the stage subsequent to approximately the end of the first trimester, the State, in promoting its interest in the health of the mother, may, if it chooses, regulate the abortion procedure in ways that are reasonably related to maternal health.

(c) For the stage subsequent to viability the State, in promoting its interest in the potentiality of human life, may, if it chooses, regulate, and even proscribe, abortion except where it is necessary, in appropriate medical judgment, for the preservation of the life or health of the mother.

2. The State may define the term "physician," as it has been employed in the preceding numbered paragraphs of this Part XI of this opinion, to mean only a physician currently licensed by the State, and may proscribe any abortion by a person who is not a physician as so defined.

In *Doe* v. *Bolton, post,* procedural requirements contained in one of the modern abortion statutes are considered. That opinion and this one, of course, are to be read together.[67]

This holding, we feel, is consistent with the relative weights of the respective interests involved, with the lessons and example of medical and legal history, with the lenity of the common law, and with the demands of the profound problems of the present day. The decision leaves the State free to place increasing restrictions on abortion as the period of pregnancy lengthens, so long as those restrictions are tailored to the recognized state interests. The decision vindicates the right of the physician to administer medical treatment according to his professional judgment up to the points where important state interests provide compelling justifications for intervention. Up to those points the abortion decision in all its aspects is inherently, and primarily, a medical decision, and basic responsibility for it must rest with the physician. If an individual practitioner abuses the privilege of exercising proper medical judgment, the usual remedies, judicial and intra-professional, are available.

XII

Our conclusion that Art. 1196 is unconstitutional means, of course, that the Texas abortion statutes, as a unit, must fall. The exception of Art. 1196 cannot be stricken separately, for then the State is left with a statute proscribing all abortion procedures no matter how medically urgent the case.

Although the District Court granted plaintiff Roe declaratory relief, it stopped short of issuing an injunction against enforcement of the Texas statutes. The Court has recognized that different considerations enter into a federal court's decision as to declaratory relief, on the one hand, and injunctive relief, on the other. *Zwickler* v. *Koota,* 389 U. S. 241, 252-255 (1967); *Dombrowski* v. *Pfister,* 380 U. S. 479 (1965). We are not dealing with a statute that, on its face, appears to abridge free expression, an area of particular concern under *Dombrowski* and refined in *Younger* v. *Harris,* 401 U. S., at 50.

We find it unnecessary to decide whether the District Court erred in withholding injunctive relief, for we assume the Texas prosecutorial authorities will give full credence to this decision that the present criminal abortion statutes of that State are unconstitutional.

The judgment of the District Court as to intervenor Hallford is reversed, and Dr. Hallford's complaint in intervention is dismissed. In all other respects the judgment of the District Court is affirmed. Costs are allowed to the appellee.

It is so ordered.

NOTES

NOTE· Where it is deemed desirable, a syllabus (headnote) will be released, as is being done in connection with this case, at the time the opinion is issued. The syllabus constitutes no part of the opinion of the Court but has been prepared by the Reporter of Decisions for the convenience of the reader. See *United States* v. *Detroit Lumber Co.,* 200 U.S. 321, 337.

[42]See, for example, *YWCA* v. *Kugler,* 342 F. Supp. 1048, 1074 (N.J. 1972); *Abele* v. *Markle,* 342 F. Supp. 800, 805-806 (Conn. 1972) (Newman, J., concurring), appeal pending; *Walsingham* v. *Florida,* 250 So. 2d 857, 863 (Ervin, J., concurring) (Fla. Supp. 1972); *State* v. *Gedicke,* 43 N.J.L. 86, 80 (Sup. St. 1881); Means II, at 381-382.

[43]See C. Haagensen & W. Lloyd, A Hundred Years of Medicine 19 (1943).

[44]Potts, Postconception Control of Fertility, 8 Int'l J. of G. & O. 957, 967 (1970) (England and Wales); Abortion Mortality, 20 Morbidity and Morality, 208, 209 (July 12, 1971) (U.S. Dept. of HEW, Public Health Service (New York City); Tietze, United States: Therapeutic Abortions, 1963-1968, 59 Studies in Family Planning 5, 7 (1970); Tietze, Mortality with Contraception and Induced Abortion, 45 Studies in Family Planning 6 (1969) (Japan, Czechoslovakia, Hungary); Tietze & Lehfeldt, Legal Abortion in Eastern Europe, 175 J.A.M.A. 1149, 1152 (April 1961). Other sources are discussed in Lader 17-23.

[45]See Brief of Amicus National Right to Life Foundation; R. Drinan, The Inviolability of the Right to Be Born, in Abortion and the Law 107 (D. Smith, editor, 1967); Louisell, Abortion, The Practice of Medicine, and the Due Process of Law, 16 UCLA L. Rev. 233 (1969); Noonan 1.

[46]See, *e.g., Abele* v. *Markle,* 342 F. Supp. 800 (Conn. 1972), appeal pending.

[47]See discussions in Means I and Means II.

[48]See, *e.g., State* v *Murphy,* 27 N.J.L. 112, 114 (1858).

[49]*Watson* v. *State,* 9 Tex. App. 237, 244-245 (1880); *Moore* v. *State,* 37 Tex. Crim. R. 552, 561, 40 S W. 287, 290 (1897); *Shaw* v. *State,* 73 Tex. Crim. R. 337, 339, 165 S.W. 930, 931 (1914); *Fondren* v. *State,* 74 Tex. Crim. R. 552, 557, 169 S.W. 411, 414 (1914); *Gray* v. *State,* 77 Tex. Crim. R. 221, 229, 178 S.W. 337, 341 (1915). There is no immunity in Texas for the father who is not married to the mother. *Hammett* v. *State,* 84 Tex. Crim. R. 635, 209 S. W. 661 (1919); *Thompson* v. *State,* —— Tex. Crim. R. —— (1971), appeal pending.

[50]See *Smith* v *State,* 33 Me. 48, 55 (1851); *In re Vince,* 2 N.J. 443, 450, 67 A. 2d 141, 144 (1949). A short discussion of the modern law on this issue is contained in the Comment to the ALI's Model Penal Code § 207.11, at 158 and nn. 35-37 (Tent. Draft No. 9, 1959).

[51] Tr. of Rearg. 20-21.

[52] Tr. of Rearg. 24.

[53] We are not aware that in the taking of any census under this clause, a fetus has ever been counted.

[54] When Texas urges that a fetus is entitled to Fourteenth Amendment protection as a person, it faces a dilemma. Neither in Texas nor in any other State are all abortions prohibited. Despite broad proscription, an exception always exists. The exception contained in Art. 1196, for an abortion procured or attempted by medical advice for the purpose of saving the life of the mother, is typical. But if the fetus is a person who is not to be deprived of life without due process of law, and if the mother's condition is the sole determinant, does not the Texas exception appear to be out of line with the Amendment's command?

There are other inconsistencies between Fourteenth Amendment status and the typical abortion statute. It has already been pointed out, n. 49, *supra,* that in Texas the woman is not a principal or an accomplice with respect to an abortion upon her. If the fetus is a person, why is the woman not a principal or an accomplice? Further, the penalty for criminal abortion specified by Art. 1195 is significantly less than the maximum penalty for murder prescribed by Art. 1257 of the Texas Penal Code. If the fetus is a person, may the penalties be different?

[55] Cf. the Wisconsin abortion statute, defining "unborn child" to mean "a human being from the time of conception until it is born alive," Wis. Stat. § 940.04 (6) (1969), and the new Connecticut statute, Public Act No. 1, May 1972 Special Session, declaring it to be the public policy of the State and the legislative intent "to protect and preserve human life from the moment of conception."

[56] Edelstein 16.

[57] Lader 97-99; D. Feldman, Birth Control in Jewish Law 251-294 (1968). For a stricter view, see I. Jakobovits, Jewish Views on Abortion, in Abortion and the Law 124 (D. Smith ed. 1967).

[58] Amicus Brief for the American Ethical Union et al. For the position of the National Council of Churches and of other denominations, see Lader 99-101.

[59] L. Hellman & J. Pritchard, Williams Obstetrics 493 (14th ed. 1971); Dorland's Illustrated Medical Dictionary 1689 (24th ed. 1965).

[60] Hellman & Pritchard, *supra,* n. 58, at 493.

[61] For discussions of the development of the Roman Catholic position, see D. Callahan, Abortion: Law, Choice and Morality 409-447 (1970); Noonan 1.

[62] See D. Brodie, The New Biology and the Prenatal Child, 9 J. Fam. L. 391, 397 (1970); R. Gorney, The New Biology and the Future of Man, 15 UCLA L. Rev. 273 (1968); Note, Criminal Law—Abortion—The "Morning-After" Pill and Other Pre-Implantation Birth-Control Methods and the Law, 46 Ore. L. Rev. 211 (1967); G. Taylor, The Biological Time Bomb 32 (1968); A. Rosenfeld, The Second Genesis 138-139 (1969); G. Smith, Through a Test Tube Darkly: Artificial Insemination and the Law, 67 Mich. L. Rev. 127 (1968); Note, Artificial Insemination and the Law, U. Ill. L. F. 203 (1968).

[63] Prosser, Handbook of the Law of Torts 335-338 (1971); 2 Harper & James, The Law of Torts 1028-1031 (1956); Note, 63 Harv. L. Rev. 173

(1949).

[64] See cases cited in Prosser, *supra,* n. 62, at 336-338; Annotation, Action for Death of Unborn Child, 15 A.L.R. 3rd 992 (1967).

[65] Prosser, *supra,* n. 62, at 338; Note, The Law and the Unborn Child, 46 Notre Dame Law. 349, 354-360 (1971).

[66] D. Louisell, Abortion, The Practice of Medicine, and the Due Process of Law, 16 UCLA L. Rev. 233, 235-238 (1969); Note, 56 Iowa L. Rev. 994, 999-1000 (1971); Note, The Law and the Unborn Child, 46 Notre Dame Law. 349, 351-354 (1971).

[67] Neither in this opinion nor in *Doe* v. *Bolton, post,* do we discuss the father's rights, if any exist in the constitutional context, in the abortion decison. No paternal right has been asserted in either of the cases, and the Texas and the Georgia statutes on their face take no cognizance of the father. We are aware that some statutes recognize the father under certain circumstances. North Carolina, for example, 1B N.C. Gen. Stat. § 14-45.1 (Supp. 1971), requires written permission for the abortion from the husband when the woman is a married minor, that is, when she is less than 18 years of age, 41 N.C.A.G. 489 (1971); if the woman is an unmarried minor, written permission from the parents is required. We need not now decide whether provisions of this kind are constitutional.

H. J. RES. 427
IN THE HOUSE OF REPRESENTATIVES
March 13, 1973
JOINT RESOLUTION

Proposing an amendment to the Constitution of the United States. *Resolved by the Senate and House of Representatives of the United States of America in Congress assembled (two-thirds of each House concurring therein),* That the following article is proposed as an amendment to the Constitution of the United States, to be valid only if ratified by the legislatures of three-fourths of the several States within seven years after the date of final passage of this joint resolution:

"ARTICLE—

"Section 1. Nothing in this Constitution shall bar any State or territory or the District of Columbia, with regard to any area over which it has jurisdiction, from allowing, regulating, or prohibiting the practice of abortion."

S. J. RES. 119
IN THE SENATE OF THE UNITED STATES
May 31, 1973
JOINT RESOLUTION

Proposing an amendment to the Constitution of the United States for the protection of unborn children and other persons.

Resolved by the Senate and House of Representatives of the United States of America in Congress assembled (two-thirds of each House concurring therein), That the following article is proposed as an amendment to the Constitution of the United States, which shall be valid to all intents and purposes as part of the Constitution when ratified by the legislatures of three-fourths of the several States within seven years from the date of its submission by the Congress:

"ARTICLE—

Section 1. With respect to the right to life, the word 'person' as used in this article and in the fifth and fourteenth articles of amendment to the Constitution of the United States, applies to all human beings, including their unborn offspring at every stage of their biological development, irrespective of age, health, function, or condition of dependency.

"Sec. 2. This article shall not apply in an emergency when a reasonable medical certainty exists that continuation of the pregnancy will cause the death of the mother.

"Sec. 3. Congress and the several States shall have power to enforce this article by appropriate legislation within their respective jurisdictions."

BIBLIOGRAPHY

This brief bibliography is somewhat broader than most in philosophy books, for important material relative to abortion from the standpoints of law, medicine, theology, psychology, and sociology has been added. Supplementary references to material in all of these areas can be found in two bibliographies:

Dollen, Charles, *Abortion in Context: A Select Bibliography*. Metuchen: Scarecrow Press, 1970. 150 pp.

Pinson, William M., *Resource Guide to Current Social Issues*. Waco: Word Books, 1968.

I. BOOKS

Callahan, Daniel, *Abortion: Law, Choice, and Morality*. New York, Macmillan and Company, 1970. 524 pp.

Chartier, Michel, *Avortement et respect de la vie humaine*. Paris: Editions du Sueil, 1972.

Committee on Psychiatry and Law of the Group for the Advancement of Psychiatry, *The Right to Abortion: A Psychiatric View*. New York: Charles Scribners

Cooke, Robert E., *The Terrible Choice: The Abortion Dilemma*. Fwd. by Pearl S. Buck. New York: Bantam Books, 1968. 110 pp.

Curran, Charles E., *Contraception: Authority and Dissent*. New York: Herder and Herder, 1969.

Cutler, Donald R., *Updating Life and Death: Essays in Ethics and Medicine*. Boston: Beacon Press, 1969.

Ebon, Martin, *Every Woman's Guide to Abortion*. New York: Universe Books, 1971. 256 pp.
Feldman, David M., *Birth Control in Jewish Law*. New York: N.Y. University Press, 1968. 322 pp.
Fletcher, Joseph, *Morals and Medicine*. Boston: Beacon Press, 1960.
Frazier, Claude A., *Should Doctors Play God*. Nashville: Broadman Press, 176 pp.
Galbally, R. T. J., *The Right to be Born*. Melbourne: A.C.T.S. Publications, 1970. 31 pp.
Granfield, David. *The Abortion Decision*. New York: Doubleday, 1969. 240 pp.
Grisez, Germain Gabriel, *Abortion: The Myths, the Realities and Arguments*. New York: Corpus Books, 1970. 559 pp.
Guttmacher, Alan Frank, *The Case for Legalized Abortion Now*. Berkeley, California: Diablo Press, 1967. 154 pp.
Hall, Robert E., *Abortion in a Changing World* (two volumes). New York: Columbia University Press, 1970.
Horden, Anthony, *Legal Abortion, the English Experience*. Oxford: Pergamon Press, 1971.
Joyce, Robert E., and Mary Rosera, *Let Us Be Born; The Inhumanity of Abortion*. Chicago: Franciscan Herald Press, 1970. 98 pp.
Kummer, Jerome M., *Abortion: Legal and Illegal: A Dialogue between Attorneys and Psychiatrists* (second ed.). Santa Monica: J. M. Kummer, 1969. 63 pp.
Labby, Daniel H., *Life or Death, Ethics and Options*. Seattle: U. of Washington Press, 1968.
Lader, Lawrence, *Abortion*. Indianapolis: Bobbs-Merril, 1966. 212 pp.
Lader, Lawrence, *Abortion II: Revolution in the Making*. Boston: Beacon Press, 1973. 242 pp.
Lee, Nancy Howell, *The Search for an Abortionist*. Chicago: University of Chicago Press, 1969. 207 pp.
Lowe, David, *Abortion and the Law*. Pocket Books, 1966.
McFadden, C. J., *Medical Ethics*. London, 1962.
Mondrone, Domenico, *Mamma, Why Did You Kill Us?* Tr. by Dino Soria. Baltimore, 1970. 47 pp.
Monsma, John Clover, *Religion and Birth Control*. New York: Doubleday, 1963.
Noonan, John T., Jr., *The Morality of Abortion; Legal and Historical*

232   *Bibliography*

Perspectives. Cambridge: Harvard University Press, 1970. 276 pp.
Rachels, James, *Moral Problems,* New York: Harper and Row, 1971. 390 pp.
Ransil, Bernard Jerome, *Abortion.* Paramus, N. J.: Paulist Press, 1969. 121 pp.
Rosen, Harold, *Abortion in America* (originally published as *Therapeutic Abortion*). Boston: Beacon Press, 1967. 368 pp.
Schulder, Diane and Florynce Kennedy, *Abortion Rap—Shirley Chisholm, Member of Congress.* New York: McGraw-Hill, 1971. 238 pp.
Schur, Edwin M., *Crimes without Victims: Deviant Behavior and Public Policy: Abortion, Homosexuality, Drug Addiction.* Englewood Cliffs, N. J.: Prentice-Hall, 1965. 180 pp.
Shaw, Russel B., *Abortion on Trial.* London: Hale, 1969. 176 pp.
Smith, David T., *Abortion and the Law.* Cleveland: Western Reserve University, 1967. 237 pp.
Spitzer, Walter A. and Carlyle Saylor, *Symposium on the Control of Human Reproduction.* Wheaton, Ill.: Tyndale House, 1969. 590 pp.
St. John-Stevas, N., *The Right to Life.* London: Hodder and Soughton, 1963. 128 pp.
Tarnesby, Herman Peter, *Abortion Explained.* London: Sphere Books, 1969. 110 pp.
Williams, Glanville, *The Sanctity of Life and Criminal Law.* New York: Knopf, 1968.
Wittgenstein, Ludwig, *Philosophical Investigations.* Tr. by G. E. M. Anscombe. New York, 1953.

II. ARTICLES

Beinaert, Louis, "L'avortement est-il infanticide," *Etudes,* 337 (1970), 547-561.
Bennett, J., Whatever the Consequences," *Analysis,* 26 (1966), 83-102.
Bennett, John C., et al., *Christianity and Crisis,* 32 (1973), 287-298. Special issue devoted to abortion (four articles by Bennett, Margaret Mead, Howard Mood, Daniel Callahan).
Blake, Judith, "Abortion and Public Opinion: the 1960-1970 Decade," *Science,* 171 (1971), 540-549.
Bok, Sissela, "Ethical Problems of Abortion" in *Raising Children in Modern Urban America,* ed. Nathan Talbot, M D New York.

Little, Brown and Co. Forthcoming.
Bok, Sissela, "The Leading Edge of the Wedge," *The Hastings Center Report*, 3 (1971), 9-11.
Brandt, Richard B., "The Morality of Abortion," *The Monist*, 56 (1972), 504-526.
Brady, B. A., "Abortion and the Law," *Philosophy Journal*, 68 (1971), 357-369.
Brady, B. A., "Abortion and the Sanctity of Human Life," *American Philosophical Quarterly*, 10 (1973), 133-140.
Brody, Baruch A., "Thomson on Abortion," *Philosophy and Public Affairs*, 1 (1972), 335-340.
Buss, M. J., "Beginnings of Human Life as an Ethical Problem," *Journal of Religion*, 17 (1967), 244-255.
Callahan, Daniel, "The Sanctity of Life," *Updating Life and Death: Essays in Ethics and Medicine*, ed. by Donald R. Cutler. Boston: Beacon Press, 1969.
Callahan, Daniel, "Contraception and Abortion: American Catholic Response," *Annals of the American Academy of Political and Social Science*, 387 (1970), 109-117.
Coffey, Patrick J., "Toward a Sound Moral Policy on Abortion," *"The New Scholasticism*, 47 (1973), 105-112.
Curran, Charles E., "Abortion: Law and Morality in Recent Roman Catholic Thought," *The Jurist*, 33 (1973).
Donceel, Joseph, "Abortion: Mediate and Immediate Animation," *Continuum*, 5 (1969), 167-171.
Dyck, Henry P., "Perplexities of the Would-be Liberal in Abortion," *Journal of Reproductive Medicine*, 8 (1972), 351-354.
Finnis, John M., "Three Schemes of Regulation," in *The Morality of Abortion*, ed. by John T. Noonan, Jr. Cambridge: Harvard University Press, 1970.
Foot, Philippa, "The Problem of Abortion and the Doctrine of the Double Effect," *Oxford Review*, 5 (1967).
Friedmann, Theodore, "Prenatal Diagnosis of Genetic Disease," *Scientific American*, Nov. (1971), 34-42.
Gerber, D., "Abortion: The Uptake Argument," *Ethics*, 83 (1972), 80-83.
Gerber, Rudof J., "Abortion: Parameters for Decision," *International Phiosophical Quarterly*, 11 (1971), 561-584.
Gerber, R. J., "Abortion: Parameters for Decision," *Ethics*, 82

(1972), 137-154.

Grisez, Germain G., "Toward a Consistent Natural Law Ethics of Killing," *American Journal of Jurisprudence*, 15 (1970), 64-96.

Gustafson, James M., "A Protestant Ethical Approach," in *The Morality of Abortion*, ed. by John T. Noonan. Cambridge: Harvard University Press, 1970.

Guttmacher, A. F., and H. F. Pilpee, "Abortion and the Unwanted Child," *Family Planning Perspectives*, 2 (1970), 16-24.

Hardin, G., "Abortion or Compulsory Pregnancy," *Marriage and the Family*, 30 (1968), 246-251.

Haring, Bernard, "A Theological Evaluation," *The Morality of Abortion*, ed. by John T. Noonan. Cambridge: Harvard University Press, 1970. pp. 123-145.

Heer, D. M., "Abortion, Contraception, and Population Policy in the Soviet Union," *Soviet Studies*, 17 (1965), 76-83.

Ingram, I. M., "Abortion Games: An Inquiry into the Working of the Act," *The Lancet*, Oct. 30 (1971), 969-970.

Kohl, Marvin, "Abortion and the Argument from Innocence," *Inquiry*, 14; 147-151.

Leavy, Z. and J. Kummer, "Criminal Abortion: Human Hardship and Unyielding Laws," *Southern California Law Review*, 35 (1962), 123-128.

Leebensohn, Zigmond M., "Abortion, Psychiatry and the Quality of Life," *American Journal of Psychiatry*, 128; 946-954.

Lincoln, C. Eric, "Why I Reversed My Stand on Laissez-Faire Abortion," *Christian Century*, Apr. 25 (1973), 477-479.

Louisell, David W., and John T. Noonan, Jr., "Constitutional Balance," in *The Morality of Abortion*, ed. by John T. Noonan. Cambrdige: Harvard University Press, 1970. pp. 220-260.

McCormick, Richard A., S. J., "Past Church Teaching on Abortion," *Proceedings of the Catholic Theological Society of America*, Yonkers, New York. 23 (1968), 131-151.

McCormick, Richard A., "Notes on Moral Theology," *Theological Studies*, 33 (1972), 68-78.

Mileti, D. S., and L. D. Barnett, "Nine Demographic Factors and Their Relationship toward Abortion Legalization," *Social Biology*, 19 (1972), 43-50.

Milhaven, Giles, "The Abortion Debate: An Epistemological Interpretation," *Theological Studies*, 31 (1970).

Noonan, John T., Jr., "An Almost Absolute Value in History," *The Morality of Abortion*. Cambridge: Harvard University Press, 1970.

Noonan, John T., Jr., "Abortion and the Catholic Church: A Summary History," *National Law Forum*, 12 (1967), 85-131.

Novak, Michael, "Abortion is Not Enough," *Christian Century*, 84 (1967), 430-431.

O'Conner, John, "On Humanity and Abortion," *National Law Forum*, 13 (1968), 127-133.

Potter, Ralph, "The Abortion Debate," *Updating Life and Death: Essays in Ethics and Medicine*, ed. by Donald R. Cutler. Boston: Beacon Press, 1969.

Quay, Eugene, "Justifiable Abortion," *Georgetown Law Journal*, 49 (1961).

Ramsey, Paul, "The Sanctity of Life," *Dublin Review*, 241 (1967), 3-21.

Ramsey, Paul, "Feticide/Infanticide upon Request," *Religion in Life*, 39 (1970), 170-186.

Ramsey, Paul, "Reference Points in Deciding about Abortion," *The Morality of Abortion*, ed. by John T. Noonan. Cambridge: Harvard University Press, 1970.

Ramsey, Paul, "The Morality of Abortion," *Moral Problems*. New York: Harper and Row, 1971. 390 pp.

Ramsey, Paul, "Abortion: A Review Article," *The Thomist*, 37 (1973), 174-226.

Rosner, Fred, "The Jewish Attitude Toward Abortion," *Tradition*, 10 (1968), 48-71.

Schuller, Bruno, "Typen ethischer Argumentution in der katholischen Moraltheologie," *Theologie und Philosophie*, 45 (1970), 526-550.

Shainess, Natalie, "Abortion: Inalienable Right," *New York State Journal of Medicine*, July (1972), 1772-1775.

Shils, Edward, "The Sanctity of Life," *Life and Death: Ethics and Options*. Seattle: University of Washington Press, 1968. pp. 2-38.

Simms, M., "Abortion Act after Three Years," *Political Quarterly*, 42 (1971), 269-286.

Smith, Harmon L., "Abortion, Death, and the Sanctity of Life," *Social Science and Medicine*, 5 (1971), 211-218.

Smith, Harmon L., "Life as Relationship: Insight on Abortion," *Christian Advocate*, 14 (1970), 7-8.

Smith, Harmon L., "Religious and Moral Aspects of Population Control," *Religion in Life,* 34 (1970), 193-204.

Smith, Harmon L., "Abortion and the Right to Life," *Ethics and the New Medicine.* Nashville: Abingdon Press, 1970. pp. 17-54.

Smith, Harmon L. (with Louis W. Hodges), "The Human Shape of Life," *The Christian and His Decisions.* Nashville: Abingdon Press, 1969. pp. 233-252.

Stone, Alan A., "Abortion and the Supreme Court: What Now?" *Modern Medicine,* April (1973), 30-37.

Thomson, Judith Jarvis, "A Defense of Abortion," *Philosophy and Public Affairs,* Princeton University Press, 1 (1971) 47-66.

Tooley, Michael, "Abortion and Infanticide," *Philosophy and Public Affairs,* 2 (1972), 37-65.

Tooley, Michael, "A Defense of Abortion and Infanticide," *The Problem of Abortion,* ed. by Joel Feinberg. Belmont, California, 1973.

Tooley, Michael, "Michael Tooley Replies," *Philosophy and Public Affairs,* 2 (1973).

Van der Poel, Cornelius, "The Principle of Double Effect," *Absolutes in Moral Theology?,* ed. by Charles E. Curran. Washington: Corpus Books, 1968. pp. 186-210.

Wahlberg, Rachel Conrad, "The Woman and the Fetus," *New Theology No. 10,* ed. by Martin E. Marty and Dean G. Peerman. New York: Macmillan, 1973.

Wertheimer, Roger, "Understanding the Abortion Argument," *Philosophy and Public Affairs,* 1 (1971), 67-95.

Williams, G. H., "The Sacred Condominium," *The Morality of Abortion,* ed. by John T. Noonan, Jr. Cambridge: Harvard University Press, 1970. pp. 146-171.

Williams, G. H., "Religious Residues and Presuppositions in the American Debate on Abortion," *Theological Studies,* 31 (1970), 10-75.